Event Studies for Financial Research

Event Studies for Financial Research

A Comprehensive Guide

Doron Kliger and Gregory Gurevich

palgrave
macmillan

EVENT STUDIES FOR FINANCIAL RESEARCH

Softcover reprint of the hardcover 1st edition 2014 978-1-137-43538-5

First published in 2014 by
PALGRAVE MACMILLAN®
in the United States—a division of St. Martin's Press LLC,
175 Fifth Avenue, New York, NY 10010.

Where this book is distributed in the UK, Europe and the rest of the world, this is by Palgrave Macmillan, a division of Macmillan Publishers Limited, registered in England, company number 785998, of Houndmills, Basingstoke, Hampshire RG21 6XS.

Palgrave Macmillan is the global academic imprint of the above companies and has companies and representatives throughout the world.

Palgrave® and Macmillan® are registered trademarks in the United States, the United Kingdom, Europe and other countries.

ISBN 978-1-349-49318-0 ISBN 978-1-137-36879-9 (eBook)
DOI 10.1057/9781137368799

Library of Congress Cataloging-in-Publication Data

Kliger, Doron.
Event studies for financial research : a comprehensive guide / by Doron Kliger and Gregory Gurevich.
pages cm
Includes bibliographical references and index.
1. Efficient market theory. 2. Capital market. 3. Finance—Research. I. Gurevich, Gregory. II. Title.

HG4061.K475 2014
332′.0415072—dc23 2014021967

A catalogue record of the book is available from the British Library.

Design by Newgen Knowledge Works (P) Ltd., Chennai, India.

First edition: November 2014

10 9 8 7 6 5 4 3 2 1

Transferred to Digital Printing in 2015

To my father, with endless longing...
—Doron

To my family and friends, near and far.
—Gregory

Contents

Figures

Tables

Acknowledgments

We wish to thank Noa Josef, Andrey Kudryavtsev, Mahmod Qadan, Tiran Rothman, Smadar Siev, Valentin Vancak, and Or Zorea for helpful proofing; Yarden Kliger for helping with bringing the cover design to life.

Chapter 1

Introduction

Event studies are overwhelmingly widespread in financial research. They encompass tools that are well suited for assessing the impact of numerous types of finance-related episodes on security prices and trading activity of publicly traded firms. Furthermore, they are capable of capturing the flow of information into security prices, shedding light, by doing so, on the efficiency of capital markets.

The event study approach (ESA) is considered one of the major instruments of modern corporate finance research. Its importance and wide usage are evident from the vast and still growing research literature. The scope of activities amenable to this analysis is very broad. It includes, naming just a few, such events as earnings announcements; releases of quarterly and annual financial reports; announcements of dividends, stock splits, and mergers; as well as initial public offerings.

Mastering the ESA is essential to researchers and practitioners. The goal of this book is to serve as a guide to event studies and help readers to become familiar with the capacities and facets of ESA. The book enables the readers to acquire hands-on experience with conducting event studies and gain the required technical skills for devising their own comprehensive event studies. It is accompanied by an online library of exercises and solutions, in the shape of spreadsheet templates, facilitating down-to-practice experimentation of the introduced empirical tools. The links for accessing chapter-specific data sets for practice are contained throughout this volume.

The sophistication of state-of-the-art statistical methods often renders the research literature that is dealing with event studies virtually inaccessible for many potential users. Our aim is to help the readers to overcome this obstacle by providing a concise summary and detailed application of the approach. We hope our target audience of researchers (including graduates and senior undergraduates) and practitioners (including financial analysts, fund managers, and institutional and private investors) would benefit from gaining access to this multipurpose tool through this focused guide.

The chapters of this book are organized in a way that permits gradual acquaintance with the subject, starting from theoretical background and introduction of ESA down to practical applications accompanied by spreadsheet templates, walkthrough instructions, and complete solutions.

Chapter 2 provides the background of ESA, focusing on the celebrated efficient market hypothesis (EMH). Specifically, the chapter outlines the theoretical foundations of EMH and its three (weak, semistrong, and strong) versions and presents some well-known empirical studies of EMH and the diversity of their results. In particular, the chapter delves into the aspects of EMH that are most pertinent for ESA and discusses their implications for conducting event studies.

Chapter 3 is the core theoretical chapter. It introduces the basic logic behind ESA, proceeds with technical specifications that are essential for the implementation of the approach, and concludes by presenting the nature of the results, their interpretation, and possible implications for market efficiency and information content of the analyzed events.

Chapter 4 presents a simplified ESA example, which is aimed at facilitating the more technical discussion presented in chapters 5 and 6 and the hands-on exercises in chapters 7 and 8. Specifically, we investigate the impact of air crashes on stock prices of involved airline companies. We construct the example on a very small data specimen to make the analysis as transparent as possible and concentrate on the core features of data processing, leaving various potentially complicating caveats for the sequel.

Chapter 5 introduces a basic, yet complete, ESA design. Specifically, it describes the main stages of data manipulation, hypothesis testing, construction of test statistics, and corresponding statistical analysis. Toward the end of the chapter, we devise a couple of hypothetical ESA cases and illustrate how they may be used to (1) quantify share price reactions to the studied events and (2) shed light on the question of market efficiency.

Chapter 6 draws a map of a smorgasbord of issues in ESA design that are likely to be encountered in practice and shows how they could be addressed. In particular, we discuss the issues of event clustering, nonparametric ESA design, bidirectional hypotheses, bond and whole-firm reactions, long-run reactions, and return frequency.

Chapter 7 is the core practical chapter. It provides readers with basic hands-on experience in the form of a complete ESA exercise. The chapter is accompanied by a spreadsheet template (one from the online library of templates and solutions), which is predesigned to accommodate the event study solution steps. Guiding instructions are presented, which would take the readers hand-in-hand through the solution process. For solving the exercise, the readers may either choose to follow the guiding instructions and fill the provided template or download a copy of the dataset and work independently. The chapter concludes with a detailed explanation of the exercise results.

Chapter 8 offers further hands-on exercises, based on the data provided in the previous chapter. In particular, it addresses several of the event study-related issues raised in previous chapters. The chapter is enforced by spreadsheet templates, for all of which complete solutions are provided. Specifically, templates and solutions (downloadable from the online library) are included for the following issues: conducting a clustering-adjusted event study procedure, applying nonparametric testing tools, applying the single-factor model of returns as an alternative benchmark of normal returns (the naïve model is applied in the basic exercise in chapter 7; both models are introduced in chapter 3), analyzing the effect of the magnitude of the surprise embedded in the disseminated information, and dissecting the sample to discover differential effects by the companies' sectors. As in the previous chapter, the readers may either solve the exercises by following the guiding instructions and filling the provided templates or download a copy of the dataset and work independently.

Chapter 9 provides concluding remarks and the book's summary.

Chapter 2

Infrastructure: The Efficient Market Hypothesis

During the past several decades, the efficient market hypothesis (EMH) has been recognized as one of the basic building blocks of modern financial economics. Due to the profound effect of EMH on financial thought, researchers and practitioners nowadays perceive the rationale behind it as intuitive. In a nutshell, it asserts the following: as investors strive to earn profit from market trading, they exploit every useful piece of data, thereby causing market prices to reflect all of the relevant information at any given moment.

Apparently, the origins of this idea of "wisdom of the crowds" are quite old. As Robert Shiller points out (1992, 438), attempts to provide a formal representation of the concept may be traced as far back as 1889, when George Gibson wrote in his book on major stock exchanges: "When shares become publicly known in an open market, the value which they acquire there may be regarded as the judgment of the best intelligence concerning them."

Following this logic, news arriving at the market must bring about an immediate and appropriate market reaction, and because news, by definition, relates to the unexpected component of the information, the future conduct of market prices is unpredictable. Consequently, traders' inability to consistently "beat" the market, that is, generate systematic excess gains by trading, is a sign of market efficiency.[1]

Such theoretical considerations led Louis Bachelier, in 1900, to the first formulation of what we know today as *random walk theory*, an immediate consequence of EMH. Random walk theory states that prices in efficient markets move randomly, thus precluding any possibility of using available information for generating sustained extra trading profits.

In some instances, the alleged ability of exceptionally talented investors to beat the market turns out to be a plain fraud. One blatant example is the story of Bernard Lawrence Madoff. Started in 1960 as a small over-the-counter trading firm, Madoff's empire eventually spread from Hollywood to Abu Dhabi, acquiring clients among prominent individual investors and solid institutions.

In retrospect, Madoff's early actions in the 1970s proved successful as his revolutionary and cash-backed belief in electronic trade has definitely paid off. Somewhat more questionable was his custom of paying fees to get brokerage orders, which attracted clients but also accusations of bribery. Madoff's reaction was nonapologetic, as he claimed this practice enhanced competition and reduced brokerage costs. That way or another, according to de la Merced (2008), by the end of the 1980s, Madoff was running up to 5 percent of the total New York Stock Exchange trading volume and, at some point in 2000, he was the largest market maker on the NASDAQ electronic market. The returns of Madoff's hedge fund seemed exceptionally steady and consistently beating the market, while none of the rival funds were able to perform similarly.

Interestingly, quite a few years before the scandal erupted, the secrecy surrounding Madoff's trading strategies began raising the suspicion of several professionals such as financial analyst Harry Markopolos, hedge fund industry reporter Michael Ocrant, and financial journalist Erin Arvedlund. However, the public buzz was not followed by any preventive action by the Securities and Exchange Commission, and the fund proceeded with its undisclosed activities (see Arvedlund, 2009, and Markopolos et al., 2010, for more details). During these prosperous years of Madoff's hedge fund, entrance into this exclusive "money club" was apparently impossible for a layperson, as new investors could hope to join only via informal recommendations and close friends' circles. The business was going and growing remarkably smoothly as long as a lengthy queue of investors was struggling to get their money in, and it all came tumbling down as investors started asking to opt out, primarily due to the 2008 financial crisis.

In 2008, Madoff confessed that the miraculous performance of his hedge fund was nothing but a giant Ponzi scheme—a financial pyramid based on new investors' money being paid to cover upcoming dues. Neither beating the market nor any legitimate financial investment at all was involved. The scale of the revealed fraud was enormous, not the least of which was due to the world markets' globalization. Charity organizations, university endowments, and pension funds, among other clients, totaling more than 4,000 accounts, had fallen prey to this unprecedented hoax. According to Madoff's own statement, as much as $50 billion of institutional and individual investors' money was lost in the quest for high returns, which eventually earned its designer 150 years in prison for 11 criminal counts.

Figure 2.1 Apropos: "Beating the market?—The case of Bernard L. Madoff."

A comprehensive historical account of EMH may be found in Sewell (2011).[2] As elaborated there, the theoretical roots of EMH date back to the work of sixteeenth-century Italian mathematician Girolamo Cardano (c. 1564), who analyzed the principles of games of chance and their implications for gamblers. Further developments and contributions derive from the work of nineteenth-century Scottish botanist Robert Brown (1828) and French mathematician Louis Bachelier (1964). Albert Einstein (1905), Benoit Mandelbrot (1966), Milton Friedman (1953), and several other eminent scientists have contributed rigorous mathematical and economic foundations to EMH. Henceforth, we focus on the modern definition of EMH, its implications, and relation to the ESA. The extensive literature dealing with methodical issues pertaining to ESA (e.g., the classical work of Brown and Warner in the 1980s) is addressed by subsequent chapters, wherein we discuss its practical implementation.

Although the concept of random walk may seem rather convincing, its empirical testing might be complicated. For instance, one must clarify the kind of information that investors employ to devise their trading strategies and how extra profits are to be measured. Many world-renowned financial economists, most notably Eugene Fama, have contributed to the precise theoretical definitions of EMH and the appropriate empirical tools for testing it.[3] As we elaborate in the sequel, ESA has gained prominence as an empirical approach designed to deal with the question of market efficiency.

The next section elaborates on the exact formulation of EMH and the way ESA is employed for its empirical testing. The section following it reviews some specific event studies, discusses their results, and explains the benefits of further exploring this area of research.

2.1 EMH: Theory

The primary definition of EMH, as endorsed by Fama et al. (1969) and Fama (1970), refers to security price conduct. In particular, it is asserted that in efficient markets security prices are rapidly adjusted upon the arrival of new information. Subsequently, the definition has been somewhat revised, referring to a market as efficient when the security prices reflect all available information at any given moment (Fama 1991).

Although considerably self-explanatory, the contemporaneous definition of EMH invites some clarification. In particular, the notion of

In 2013, Eugene Francis Fama was awarded, jointly with Lars Peter Hansen and Robert James Shiller, the Sveriges Riksbank Prize in Economic Sciences in Memory of Alfred Nobel, commonly known as the Nobel Prize in Economics. According to the Royal Swedish Academy of Sciences, the 2013 prize laureates "have laid the foundation for the current understanding of asset prices."

Widely recognized today as "one of the fathers of modern finance" (*Chicago Booth Magazine*, Fall 2013), Eugene Fama began his research on financial markets in the 1960s by looking at historical trading data and trying to come up with predictions of future price movements. He argues that past price patterns cannot effectively forecast future prices. The conclusion drawn by Fama was that, in the short run, market prices are driven by continuously arriving news, which is random, and thus the resulting price movements are random as well. The market efficiently incorporates all new information, thus rendering price movement predictions ineffective—a perhaps surprising but inescapable insight formalized by Fama in a series of papers leading to implications that shaped financial research for decades ahead.

Far beyond the academic arena, "field" investment practices have been taking a new form due to the works published by Fama, his collaborators, and followers. If investors are unable to foresee upcoming changes and thereby "beat the market," then passive investment in a diversified market portfolio should be superior to active, trend-seeking, stock-picking investment management. Having carefully analyzed the actual performance of active fund managers, Fama and his long-time colleague, Kenneth R. French, have corroborated this prediction (Fama and French 2010), showing that the great majority of actively managed mutual funds consistently underperform their market benchmarks, and even if there are some truly skilled active fund managers who are able to cover the costs of their strategies, they are far outnumbered by those who are not. The conclusion is in line with previous studies that found no real support either for the superiority of active investment management or for the existence of skilled or informed mutual fund portfolio managers (Carhart 1997).

The data-driven research undertaken by Fama and colleagues over the years has made a profound impact on the financial services industry and academic research community. Thus, index funds, which emerged in the 1970s as a rather controversial enterprise (see Figure 2.4), gained impetus and reached their current multitrillion-dollar volume not in the least due to the empirical work of Fama and his collaborators. The contribution of Fama to academic research in economics and finance includes popularizing the Center for Research in Securities Prices as the source of historical stock market data, examining market efficiency by advancing the event study approach, as well as developing a multifactor asset pricing model that takes into account the observed pricing anomalies. Besides the 2013 Nobel Prize in Economics and numerous other awards, Fama was the first to receive three major prizes for research in finance: the Deutsche Bank Prize in Financial Economics, 2005; the Morgan Stanley American Finance Association Award for Excellence in Finance, 2007; and the Onassis Prize in Finance, 2009.

Figure 2.2 Apropos: "Father of modern finance—Eugene F. Fama."

"available information" should be elaborated. To that end, three versions, or forms, of EMH have been proposed:

1. *The weak form* states that security prices reflect the information embedded in past prices.
2. *The semistrong form* states that security prices reflect all publicly available information, including the information embedded in past prices.
3. *The strong form* states that security prices reflect all information, regardless of whether that information is publicly available or merely private.

The EMH versions are successively inclusive; that is, strong form efficiency implies semistrong form efficiency, which implies weak form efficiency. Fama (1970) suggests the following classification of market efficiency testing:[4] first, weak efficiency tests attempt to predict future prices from past records, refuting this version of efficiency in case they succeed doing so; second, semistrong efficiency tests measure the speed of price reaction to the dissemination of public information, disproving this efficiency version in case of discovering postdissemination price reactions; and third, strong efficiency tests try to detect whether market prices reflect *confidential* information.[5] Fama's 1970 article reviews early work in this area, discusses the methods employed for each type of tests, and summarizes the accumulated empirical results. Fama (1991) reiterates, relying on a more recent body of research, and Sewell (2011) discusses a further list of studies.

Any discussion of market efficiency would be incomplete without mentioning *technical analysis*, a popular trading approach hinging on forecasting the direction of prices through the study of past market data. Clearly, the existence of profitable technical analysis tools contradicts market efficiency, even in its weak form.

The foundations of technical analysis in its modern form are viewed to be laid by Charles Dow (1851–1902), cofounder of Dow Jones & Company, with Edward Jones and Charles Bergstresser, and founder and first editor of the *Wall Street Journal*, who created *Dow Theory*, a series of principles for understanding and analyzing market behavior.

Interestingly, Alfred Cowles has shown as early as in 1932 that forecasting the market according to the Dow Theory failed to beat the market.[6] Moreover, according to the same report, the selection of securities for investment advised by 16 financial services, 25 insurance companies, and 24 financial publications during the years 1928 to 1932 failed to produce results better than those attributable to pure chance. Similar results were

Is the market random and unpredictable? This possibility was out of the question for Jesse Lauriston Livermore, dubbed "the Boy Plunger" in a 1940 *TIME* Magazine article describing him as the "most fabulous living U.S. stock trader." Livermore, who had studied market behavior and price patterns for decades, summarized his insights in a book titled *How to Trade in Stocks* (Livermore 1940)—alas, at the end of his career, when, following his ultimate bankruptcy, he committed suicide, leaving a note deeming himself "a failure" (Smitten 2001).

Earning and losing several multimillion-dollar fortunes during his career as a stock exchange speculator, Livermore became a truly legendary figure whose biography inspired a semidocumentary bestseller novel by Edwin Lefévre, first published in 1923 and reedited numerous times since, culminating in an annotated version published in 2010.

Jesse Livermore started his career at a bucket shop, a place that was "more like a horse-betting parlor than a true broker's office" (Smitten 2001, 28). Soon enough, he was banned from all bucket shops in Boston for winning too much money and moved on to legitimate markets. After all, this was the place where the stocks he was betting on were actually traded, so he figured the same principles must apply there as well. And it was there that he made $3 million and $100 million at the times of 1907 and 1929 market crashes, respectively—that is, when nearly everyone else was losing immense amounts of money.[a] In fact, Livermore's great success at the dawn of the Great Depression was so blatant that he was personally blamed for the 1929 "Black Tuesday" market crash; an angry article in *The New York Times* was followed by life-threatening calls, letters, and telegrams. Not long after, in 1934, he had managed to lose nearly all of his money under some undisclosed circumstances and, after filing for bankruptcy (for the fourth time in his life), was suspended from the Chicago Board of Trade, never again to return to the top. Jesse Livermore shot himself in the head at the age of 63, on November 28, 1940, in a cloakroom of the Sherry Netherland Hotel in Manhattan. It is better left for psychologists to decide whether turbulent personal life, clinical depression, bankruptcy, or any combination of these factors had the fatal impact on this remarkable market speculator.

Livermore's trading rules were considered controversial at the time of their first exposition and remain so today. Interestingly, some of the instructions brought forth in his book (e.g., Livermore 1940, 83) seem similar to today's technical analysis recipes that are known to be unsupported by empirical evidence (see Malkiel 2005). Other rules such as the importance of market timing, money management, and emotional control leave much room for different interpretations (Smitten 2001, 302).

Interestingly, the words that open the first chapter of Jesse Livermore's book, "The game of speculation is the most uniformly fascinating game in the world," seem, in retrospect, to describe not just the riddle of technical analysis but also the author's enigmatic life experience.

[a] In current dollars, the amounts correspond to almost $80 million and $1.4 billion, respectively.

Figure 2.3 Apropos: "Plunger Boy Jesse Lauriston Livermore."

obtained by Fama (1965) who, after having studied the performance of 39 mutual funds from 1950 to 1960, concluded that "so far the sophisticated analyst has escaped detection" (92).

Evidently, although the research by Cowles, Fama, and others suggests that there is no free (technical) lunch, the technical analysis industry seems to be alive and kicking. It should be noted that judging whether technical analysis works or not is beyond the scope of our discussion. Nevertheless, we comment that "beating" the market in that way might be difficult, if not impossible, for the common investor.[7]

Having debated the weak form of EMH, we turn now to elaborate on the other pole of the efficiency spectrum, namely its strong form. As Jensen (1978) points out, the strong form of EMH is hardly ever taken seriously by anyone. Rather, this form serves mainly as an extreme condition that completes the set of theoretical possibilities. In the same vein, Fama (1970) views strong efficiency not as an empirical possibility but rather as "a benchmark against which deviations from market efficiency (interpreted in its strictest sense) can be judged" (415).

Grossman and Stiglitz (1980) demonstrated that in real markets in which data collecting is not necessarily free, security prices reflect only the information whose benefits do not fall below the costs of obtaining it, corroborating the conclusion that the strong form of EMH is unlikely. Fama (1991) discusses a range of studies showing that insider trading permits generating extra profits, thereby empirically refuting the strong form efficiency. Therefore, the semistrong form of EMH has received the most attention from both theoreticians and empiricists. ESA is primarily designed to deal with this version of EMH. Henceforth, thus, in discussing efficiency, we refer to the semistrong form, unless we explicitly state otherwise.

The semistrong form of EMH postulates that investors take advantage of every piece of useful and publicly available information, and market prices, therefore, reflect everything relevant at any given moment. As a consequence, news arrival must bring about an immediate market reaction, and because news, by definition, is always unexpected, the conduct of market prices is unpredictable.

Importantly, for the market reaction to be detected and assessed, a norm for security returns has to be devised and employed. Putting it in other words, for *abnormal* trading profits to be detected, *normal* trading profits have to be defined first, which amounts to defining a model of market price conduct. This observation brings forth the *joint hypothesis* problem, because any empirical study of EMH must employ a pricing model as a benchmark for assessing normal returns, and testing market efficiency is thus dependent on the chosen model. One can establish a practical remedy to this problem by employing several benchmark models of normal returns and testing the consistency of the results inferred from each. In this context, the robustness of general conclusions would be corroborated if the results obtained under the various models portray similar pictures. In the sequel, we get back to this point, define various specifications of normal-return benchmark models, and discuss how to employ them to arrive at reliable empirical conclusions when practicing ESA.

Existing methods of examining EMH may be crudely divided into direct and indirect tests of market efficiency. Direct tests focus on the reaction of prices to arriving news, whereas indirect tests concentrate on the basic implications of the efficiency hypothesis, namely, the impossibility of predicting market prices on the basis of, and therefore making abnormal profits from, publicly available information.

Regarding indirect tests of market efficiency, Samuelson (1965) demonstrated that in a market that rapidly adjusts to new information, prices should fluctuate randomly. Hence critics of EMH try to identify some observable quantities or conditions that would permit the prediction of market prices, which then would indicate that the market is not exclusively driven by news and, therefore, is not efficient. Some of the most prominent phenomena used to criticize market efficiency by appealing to the non-randomness of asset prices are short-term momentum, long-run reversals, and seasonal and day-of-the-week patterns; moreover, further criticism engages securities' and firms' characteristics, such as dividend yields and price-earnings multiples, which are claimed to predict prices. A concise survey of market efficiency tests making use of these phenomena may be found in Malkiel (2003), who also reviews possible causes of unexplained market conduct, including ostensibly irrational investor behavior that resulted in the market crash of 1987 and the Internet bubble of the 1990s (as well as, perhaps, the housing bubble that peaked in 2006 and the 2008 financial crisis, both of which took place after Malkiel published his essay). As Malkiel notes, although markets are not expected to be invariably efficient, the inefficiencies mentioned above seem to be an exception rather than the rule. Moreover, the well-

Burton Gordon Malkiel's bestseller, *A Random Walk down Wall Street*, was first published in 1973. The book's title corresponds with random walk theory, the underlying foundation of market efficiency, which states that market prices are affected only by random news, making security returns unpredictable. Mutual funds, which practice actively traded investment strategies, represent the opposite view, asserting that professional skills have the ability to detect "winner" investment opportunities, thereby raising the million-dollar question in this context: Who is right?

Malkiel, one of the most ardent proponents of EMH, argues that active investment management is essentially futile. Accordingly, the fact that some funds have managed to yield high returns may not be considered a proof of fund managers' superior abilities because, statistically, some funds are always bound to win just by chance. Moreover, as Malkiel points out, even if some "anomaly" arises that makes beating the market possible, it is likely to evaporate soon after being discovered by ever-profit-seeking investors. By contrast, simple passive strategies, such as buying and holding a broad market index, are inexpensive to perform and thus often provide higher net-of-fees returns than those of the actively managed funds.

Malkiel endorsed investing in a well-diversified portfolio, such as the security mixture represented by the broad market index, as the most sensible investment strategy already in the early 1970s. Nevertheless, this investment approach was not easy to implement, because there was no straightforward way to invest directly in the index.

In 1976, Vanguard mutual fund, founded in 1975 by John C. Bogle, introduced the first individual investors' index fund, called Vanguard 500, tracing the S&P 500 Index. Malkiel joined the Vanguard Group's board of directors in 1977 and held this position until his retirement in 2005 (while remaining a member of the European Vanguard board, which imposed no age limit; see Mason 2005). Vanguard Group has been active ever since, making it possible to invest in a broad range of indices, including market-wide, industrial, market-cap, country-specific, and others. Today, Vanguard is a multitrillion-dollar enterprise, spreading hundreds of funds worldwide.

The scale of today's index fund industry is impressive, especially given that money managers have objected to the ideas endorsed by Malkiel and Vanguard Group since their introduction. Today, the exchange-traded products (ETPs) market is growing rapidly, encompassing, beside standard equity indices, customized equity bundles, bonds, commodities, and various financial products. The low transaction costs make ETPs an especially attractive investment vehicle that provides exposure to any noticeable slice of the market. According to Morningstar Direct's Asset Flows report (see Davidson 2012), worldwide ETP assets have shown an explosive growth since the beginning of the twenty-first century, totaling many trillions of dollars.

Figure 2.4 Apropos: "A Random Walk down Wall Street—Burton G. Malkiel."

documented inability of fund managers to consistently exploit any of these alleged means of prediction serves as a testimony of the overall market efficiency, at least as follows from these indirect tests of EMH (cf. Malkiel 2005). In other words, attempts to disprove randomness and thereby *indirectly* refute EMH seem to result in mixed, sporadic, and ineffectual evidence.[8]

Perhaps, the state-of-the-art wisdom in the research of market behavior is expressed in the scientific background for the Sveriges Riksbank Prize in Economic Sciences in Memory of Alfred Nobel 2013, which has been awarded to Professors Fama, Hansen, and Shiller, for "their empirical analysis of asset prices." As the Prize Committee has declared, "there is no way to predict whether the price of stocks and bonds will go up or down over the next few days or weeks. But it is quite possible to foresee the broad course of the prices of these assets over longer time periods, such as, the next three to five years. These findings, which may seem both surprising and contradictory, were made and analyzed by this year's Laureates, Eugene Fama, Lars Peter Hansen and Robert Shiller." The Prize Committee has further emphasized that "although we do not yet fully understand how asset prices are determined, the research of the Laureates has revealed a number of important regularities that are helping us to arrive at better explanations."[9]

Direct tests of EMH address efficiency in a more straightforward fashion. ESA enters the scene here, because market efficiency is primarily about the reaction to new information. As Fama (1991, 1607) explains, "Event studies can give a clear picture of the speed of adjustment of prices to information." Recall that the semistrong form of EMH refers to the release of public information. Therefore, analyzing the security prices around the event dates may shed light on the properties of market reaction to the news and, as a result, on the market efficiency. The simplicity of ESA makes it an appealing way to test market efficiency, as well as provide a means of conveniently assessing financial issues of broad interest, as explained by Fama (1991, 1607):

> There is a large event-study literature on issues in corporate finance. The results indicate that on average stock prices adjust quickly to information about investment decisions, dividend changes, changes in capital structure, and corporate-control transactions. This evidence tilts me toward the conclusion that prices adjust efficiently to firm-specific information. More important, the research uncovers empirical regularities, many surprising,

that enrich our understanding of investment, financing, and corporate-control events, and give rise to interesting theoretical work.

Technicalities of ESA may differ depending on the specific information it is applied to and the nature of the available data. However, the basic idea is always the same: price behavior is tracked along a chronological period from a point in time before to a point in time after the information release. In such a way, any irregular price adjustment reflecting the market reaction may be detected, timed, and measured. Most importantly, to support EMH, the market reaction has to be quick and full; more specifically, any irregular price adjustment has to commence without delay as the information is released, or earlier in cases of information "leakage" prior to the public announcement, but not after the release, and it must not take too long, so that no useful predictions can be made once the reaction is detected. A more precise technical description of the method is left for the sequel.

2.2 EMH: Empirical Testing

Testing market efficiency comprises an area of research that has generated an enormous amount of studies, many of them having ESA as their designated tool; long prior to this writing, event studies have become a "research industry" (Fama 1991, 1599). Our purpose in the current section is to illustrate the approach by referring to some select event studies, emphasizing the diversity of obtained results, and making clear the importance of further research of market efficiency.

Fama et al. (1969) introduced one of the earliest event studies, an investigation that dealt with market reaction to stock splits.[10] Although one among the pioneering research in the area, the study employed all of the prominent features of modern ESA.[11] The study made use of the fact that past stock splits were often followed by generous dividend increases, so there was a substantial reason to believe that stock splits may serve as a signal of upcoming good news. In such a case, an efficient market should react immediately by adjusting the stock prices upward as the expected cash flows are reevaluated based on the signal. Therefore, Fama designed the study to detect any irregularity in stock prices in the months surrounding the stock split; technically, he tested the behavior of stock returns for a period of 24 to 60 months around the split. Consistent with the considerations mentioned above, to detect abnormal returns, the study made use of a market model that allowed for "adjusting security returns for general market conditions" (Fama et al. 1969, 3). The abnormal return was then defined as a deviation of the return from that predicted by the model. Finally, to reduce the influence of possibly idiosyncratic behavior of specific stocks, the study concentrated on the average price behavior of a large data set, consisting of 940 individual splits. Fama et al. (1969, 20) concluded thus:

> On the average the market's judgments concerning the information implications of a split are fully reflected in the price of a share at least by the end of the split month but most probably almost immediately after the announcement date. Thus the results of the study lend considerable support to the conclusion that the stock market is "efficient" in the sense that stock prices adjust very rapidly to new information.

Another study was conducted by Aharony and Swary (1980). They employed ESA to distinguish between reactions to information conveyed by dividend announcements and quarterly earnings announcements. Beside demonstrating that dividend announcements were indeed perceived as a valuable signal on its own merits, the study provided a general support for market efficiency by showing that the prices adjusted quickly to the new information inherent in the companies' quarterly announcements. Keown and Pinkerton (1981) provided further support for market efficiency, by analyzing market reaction to merger announcements. They showed that a price reaction commenced in advance of the public statement, probably due to leakage of inside information, and has been manifested to its full extent on the day of the official release, after which no irregular price adjustments were detected, consistently with market efficiency implications.

The evidence accumulated over the years includes also rejections of EMH. Rendleman, Jones, and Latané (1982) sketched out a noteworthy list of studies showing that the market does not seem to react immediately to announcements of unexpected earnings (i.e., deviations of actual earnings from prior expectations), even though such "surprises" should provide an important basis for stock price reevaluations. As discussed above, an efficient market fully absorbs the information as soon as it has been released; however, a range of studies showed that this immediate absorption does not necessarily occur in practice. Rendleman, Jones, and Latané documented the exact pattern of price responses to the earnings' positive and negative surprises. According to their report, as much as 51% of the total reaction to the most significant positive surprises and 45% of the reaction to the most significant negative surprises were observed in a delayed manner, over the 90 days after the official announcement.

Evidently, in efficient markets full price adjustment to commonly known information is not expected to take as long as three months to complete; the results of this study are clearly at odds with the basic EMH. Moreover, as the authors mentioned, a range of other studies of market reaction to earnings announcements has reported similar results. Fama (1991, 1602) addressed the issue of "post-announcement drift in abnormal returns" and referred to studies that attempted to resolve the matter either by refining the techniques of abnormal-returns measurement or, alternatively, by suggesting that the apparent market inefficiency is genuine and stems from market participants' poor understanding of the disseminated information.

Obviously, the diversity of the obtained results emphasizes the importance of further work; the controversy pertaining to the market efficiency research area as a whole makes ESA an indispensable tool because, according to Fama (1991, 1602), "event studies are the cleanest evidence we have on efficiency." As even the rather fragmentary survey above suggests, the conclusions are occasionally mixed; many additional examples of "attacks on EMH" may be found, for example, in the historical survey of market efficiency studies by Sewell (2011). However, as noted by Fama (1991), it is generally admitted that most of the evidence supports EMH, as confirmed by a range of event studies that comprise a primary research tool in this controversial field of research.

Beyond the topic of market efficiency, but relevant to the subject of this book, the broad spectrum of areas where event studies may be useful is worth emphasizing. The following excerpt from MacKinlay (1997, 13) gives a general outline of some directly related disciplines:

> In accounting and finance research, event studies have been applied to a variety of firm specific and economy wide events. Some examples include mergers and acquisitions, earnings announcements, issues of new debt or equity,

> and announcements of macroeconomic variables such as the trade deficit. However, applications in other fields are also abundant. For example, event studies are used in the field of law and economics to measure the impact on the value of a firm of a change in the regulatory environment... and in legal liability cases event studies are used to assess damages.

To conclude, as an advanced yet very accessible tool of financial analysis, ESA bears high potential for researchers and practitioners, both within and outside the area of market efficiency research. In the next chapter, we turn to a detailed description of ESA and refer to the issue of market efficiency and the information content of the studied events.

Chapter 3

The Event Study Approach

As explained in the previous chapter, ESA comprises an effective tool for assessing the information content of events, as perceived by market participants, as well as for shedding light on the issue of market efficiency. The underlying idea in common event studies is to track the market prices of securities whose issuing firms were involved in the studied event, in order to detect market-related reactions. The prices are tracked over a period that is potentially relevant for evaluating the effect of the event on the prices of the traded securities; this period is termed the *event window*.[1]

Commonly, the market reaction to the studied events has a predictable direction. That is, in events consisting of good news, the market participants are expected to react positively, raising thereby the security prices of the firms undergoing the studied event, and, conversely, in bad-news events, the market participants are expected to react negatively, and the security prices are expected to fall. For instance, mergers are usually perceived as good news for the equity holders of the acquired companies (e.g., Keown and Pinkerton 1981), so a positive reaction is expected for the stocks of these firms around their merger announcements.

In cases of events for which there is no unidirectional expectation for security returns, aggregating the price reactions across the pooled sample would miss the point as opposite directions would tend to cancel each other out. For instance, in the event of earnings announcements, there may be cases of positive- and negative-earnings surprises, as well as announcements that are not surprising at all. In the study of such cases, the sample should be partitioned into positive, negative, and possibly also no-surprise subsamples, each of which should be separately analyzed.

Occasionally, there may be events for which it may be hard or even impossible to hypothesize the direction of market reaction. In such cases, it may still be possible to extract information on the relevance of the event to market participants, by considering other aspects of reaction, such as the magnitude of returns (irrespective of their direction) or the trading volume around the event.[2]

Given a legitimate sample in the sense just explained, we may proceed with its analysis, concentrating on the average reaction over the sample of events. According to EMH, the price reaction to news in efficient markets is instantaneous and complete, that is, the price adjustment should happen, without any delay, at the time of information release, or even earlier in cases of information "leakage" prior to the announcement date. Furthermore, the price adjustment should be quick enough so that no profit-generating predictions could be made upon the news release. Having established this basic logic underlying ESA, we henceforth elaborate on the technical aspects of the approach. Specifically, we describe, stage by stage, the basic ESA application to the analysis of the announcing firms' stock-price behavior.[3]

3.1 Abnormal Return (AR)

The main premise behind ESA is that in efficient markets stock prices are updated immediately upon the arrival of pricing-relevant information. The updates in stock prices automatically translate into stock returns, which are the percentage changes of the prices:

> Definition: The *arithmetic return* of stock *i*, $R(a)_t^i$ is defined as the percentage change of its price.

$$R(a)_t^i \equiv (P_t^i - P_{t-1}^i)/P_{t-1}^i,^4 \qquad (3.1)$$

where

$R(a)_t^i$ is stock *i*'s return at period *t* (from time $t-1$ to time *t*);[5]

P^i_t is stock i's price at time t; and
P^i_{t-1} is stock i's price at time $t-1$.

Alternatively, financial studies may employ *logarithmic returns*. Among other things, logarithmic returns provide a mathematically convenient compounding basis for calculations and prevent modeled stock prices from turning negative.[6]

Definition: The *logarithmic return* of stock i, $R(l)^i_t$ is defined as the natural logarithm of the current to previous price ratio; equivalently, it is the natural logarithm of the *gross* arithmetic return.

$$R(l)^i_t \equiv ln\frac{P^i_t}{P^i_{t-1}} = ln(R(a)^i_t + 1), \qquad (3.2)$$

where

$R(l)^i_t$ is stock i's period t logarithmic return;
P^i_t is stock i's price at time t;
P^i_{t-1} is stock i's price at time $t-1$;
$R(a)^i_t$ is stock i's period t arithmetic return; and
ln is the natural (base e) logarithm.

As the event studied using ESA must be, by construction, unusual by daily routine standards, our goal is to detect an event-related stock return beyond the return in other "normal" days. The latter return is called *normal return* (NR), and the former *abnormal return* (AR). In effect, AR comprises the first and foremost indicator of market reaction to the news and serves as the basis for all subsequent ESA calculations.

Practically, there are various ways of assessing NR, each of which relies on a predefined model of stock returns, that is, a framework within which conditional expected stock returns may be determined on the basis of their individual characteristics and prevailing economic conditions. We introduce specific benchmark models of stock returns in the following subsections.

Definition: NR is the return that is expected to occur conditional on the employed model of returns. It, therefore, comprises a benchmark against which actual returns may be evaluated.

Note that it is customary in ESA studies to employ more than one benchmark model for NR, as it helps assessing the robustness of the results to model specification. The rationale behind employing alternative benchmarks is straightforward: if using different models leads to qualitatively different results, one should cast doubt on the validity of these results. Such differences suggest that the models used for analysis might spuriously influence and distort the picture regarding market efficiency and information content of the event.[7]

Using the above description, AR, to wit, the deviation of the stock return from its NR is defined as follows:

Definition: Stock *i*'s AR, AR^i, is defined as the deviation of its return from the NR.

$$AR_t^i \equiv R_t^i - NR_t^i, \tag{3.3}$$

where

AR_t^i is stock *i*'s period *t* AR;
R_t^i is stock *i*'s period *t* return; and
NR_t^i is stock *i*'s period *t* NR.

Henceforth we present several useful benchmark models of NR, the first, and most basic of which is the *naïve benchmark*, a basic model assuming the NR for all stocks to be the market return as represented by a broad stock market index, such as the Standard & Poor's 500 Stock Price Index (S&P 500) or the Center for Research in Security Prices (CRSP) composite value-weighted or equal-weighted indices in the United States, the FTSE 100 in Britain, or the Nikkei 225 in Japan.[8] Several commonly used equity indices are listed in figure 3.1.[9]

Other useful benchmark models of NR include the *single-factor benchmark*, assuming linear relations between stocks' and market-index returns, and two related *multifactor benchmarks* of NR, which extend the number of factors affecting the stocks' returns beyond the market-index returns. Each of the two multifactor benchmarks takes into account a set of variables that have been empirically found to explain observed stock returns; the underlying models of stock returns are primarily driven by the data and so are *statistical* by their nature. Another brand comprises *economic*

Equity indices are virtual bundles composed of stocks in such a way that the final product may be used to assess and track average performance of certain sectors of financial markets or of the economy as a whole. This is usually accomplished by computing an average market price of representative stocks. Equity indices serve as tracking devices giving investors the opportunity to measure the aggregate performance of the market and its sectors, make investment decisions, and assess the performance of existing investments. Mutual and exchange-traded funds employ market indices both as performance benchmarks and passive investment management devices. The following plaque lists some commonly used equity indices.

Equity index	**Brief description**
Dow Jones Industrial Average	Thirty "blue-chip" US industrial companies; (historically) price-weighted
NYSE Composite Index	Over 2000 US and non-US stocks; designed to measure performance of all NYSE common stocks, including ADRs, REITs and tracking stocks; free-float market cap-weighted
S&P 100	Hundred leading US stocks with exchange-listed options; selected for sector balance, tend to be the largest companies in S&P 500
S&P 500 Composite Stock Price Index	Stocks of 500 large companies listed on NYSE or NASDAQ; market capitalization-weighted
Russell 1000 Index	~1,000 large-cap segment of US equity universe; based on a combination of their market cap and current index membership
Russell 2000 Index	~2,000 small-cap segment of the US equity universe; based on a combination of their market cap and current index membership
Russell 3000 Index	Largest 3,000 US companies representing approximately 98% of the investable US equity market
NASDAQ 100 Index	Stocks issued by 100 of the largest nonfinancial companies listed on the NASDAQ; (modified) market capitalization-weighted
NASDAQ Composite Index	Broad-based index of stocks in all three NASDAQ tiers: Global Select, Global Market, and Capital Market; capitalization-weighted
FTSE 100	Stocks of 100 most highly capitalized companies listed on the London Stock Exchange; capitalization-weighted
Nikkei 225	Two hundred twenty-five top-rated Japanese companies listed in the First Section of the Tokyo Stock Exchange; price-weighted

Figure 3.1 Apropos: "Equity indices".

models developed as theoretical frameworks; these include the capital asset pricing model (CAPM), for which we provide a brief background description in the Appendix to this chapter.

3.1.1 The Naïve Benchmark of Returns

The *naïve benchmark* is based on possibly the simplest of all models of stock returns. It ignores even the most basic individual characteristics of stocks, such as differences in their degree of riskiness, and assumes instead that the NR for all stocks is the market return as represented by a broad stock market index. Putting it simply, in this framework the return of the market index serves as the norm for returns of all traded stocks.

The naïve modeling approach of stock returns assumes a constant conditional expected stock return, which is identical for all stocks and equals market return. This relation is described by the following equation:

$$R_t^i = R_t^m + \varepsilon_t^i, \tag{3.4}$$

where

R_t^i is stock i's return at period t;
R_t^m is the market return at period t; and
ε_t^i is the model's error term.

Hence the formula for estimating NR according to the naïve benchmark is simply:

$$\widehat{NR}_t^i \equiv R_t^m, \tag{3.5}$$

where

$\widehat{NR}_t^i$ is stock i's estimated NR at period t, and
R_t^m is the market return at period t.

Accordingly, the estimated AR, derived by inserting this specific $\widehat{NR}$ into equation (3.3), is:

$$\widehat{AR}_t^i \equiv R_t^i - \widehat{NR}_t^i = R_t^i - R_t^m, \tag{3.6}$$

where

$\widehat{AR}_t^i$ is stock i's estimated AR at period t;
R_t^i is stock i's return at period t;
$\widehat{NR}_t^i$ is stock i's estimated NR at period t; and
R_t^m is the market return at period t.

In effect, the naïve benchmark regards anything different from the average market behavior as abnormal. It is termed *naïve* because it ignores basic economic presumptions, such as allowing riskier stocks to command higher expected returns due to investors' risk aversion.[10]

3.1.2. The Single-Factor Benchmark of Returns

The *single-factor benchmark* is based on the single-factor model of returns devised by Sharpe (1963), who addressed the celebrated theory of portfolio selection due to Markowitz (1952).[11] It employs a more advanced modeling approach to stock returns as compared to the naïve approach, by assuming linear relations between stocks' and market contemporaneous returns. The relation is described by the following equation:

$$R_t^i = \alpha_i + \beta_i R_t^m + \varepsilon_t^i, \tag{3.7}$$

where

R_t^i is stock i's return at period t;
R_t^m is the market return at period t;
α_i and β_i are the model's parameters; and
ε_t^i is the model's error term.

The parameters α_i and β_i are usually estimated by a linear regression with the stock return as the dependent (explained) variable and the market return as independent (explanatory) variable. To obtain estimates that are not affected by the studied event, the data range for the regression must be chosen in a way that minimizes possible influence of the event, that is, the range should not belong to the event window. The rationale for this is to estimate parameters that are representative of the stock but unaffected by the event, so they enable estimation of the "regular" or "normal" stock return, which in turn would enable detecting irregularities or "abnormal"

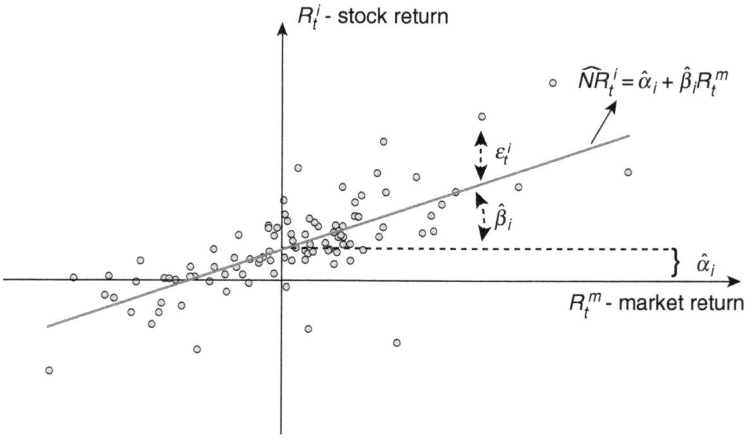

Figure 3.2 Graphical representation of stock *i*'s characteristic line.

The graph depicts stock *i*'s estimated normal return ($\widehat{NR}_t^i$) conditional on the contemporaneous market return; the estimated stock's *Alpha* is the intercept, and the estimated stock's *Beta is* the slope of the line of best fit (regression line) between the market returns (horizontal axis) and the stock's returns (vertical axis).

returns. The resulting estimates are denoted by $\hat{\alpha}_i$ and $\hat{\beta}_i$ (spelled "alpha hat" and "beta hat"), to distinguish between sample estimates and unobservable "true" population parameters. The expression $\widehat{NR}_t^i = \hat{\alpha}_i + \hat{\beta}_i R_t^m$ is called the stock's *characteristic line*, as explained below and illustrated by Figure 3.2.

Note that the parameters α_i and β_i are specific to each stock and reflect its behavior relative to the market. In particular, β_i, the stock's *Beta*, captures the stock's systematic risk, reflecting the comovement of the stock and market returns. Thus, a change of 1 percent in market return, on average, corresponds to a contemporaneous change of β_i percent in stock *i*'s return. Stock Betas may vary significantly across different stocks. By construction, the average Beta in the market is 1; stocks with Betas in excess of unity are considered relatively risky, and stocks with lower Betas are considered more solid. The stock's *Alpha* may be interpreted as the return expected from the stock in case the market return is zero. Given the estimates for Alpha and Beta, the expression $\hat{\alpha}_i + \hat{\beta}_i R_t^m$ is stock *i*'s estimated *conditional return*, that is, its return expected when market return is R_t^m.

In effect, this conditional return is NR according to the single-factor benchmark.

The NR estimated according to the single-factor benchmark is:

$$\widehat{NR}_t^i \equiv \hat{\alpha}_i + \hat{\beta}_i R_t^m, \tag{3.8}$$

where

$\widehat{NR}_t^i$ is stock i's estimated NR at period t;
R_t^m is the market return at period t; and
$\hat{\alpha}_i$ and $\hat{\beta}_i$ are the estimated model's parameters.

Accordingly, AR is estimated by plugging this $\widehat{NR}$ into equation (3.3):

$$\widehat{AR}_t^i \equiv R_t^i - \widehat{NR}_t^i = R_t^i - \left(\hat{\alpha}_i + \hat{\beta}_i R_t^m\right), \tag{3.9}$$

where

$\widehat{AR}_t^i$ is stock i's estimated AR at period t;
R_t^i is stock i's return at period t;
$\widehat{NR}_t^i$ is stock i's estimated NR at period t;
R_t^m is the market return at period t; and
$\hat{\alpha}_i$ and $\hat{\beta}_i$ are the estimated model's parameters.

Figure 3.2 depicts a sample of market return and stock return dyads and the estimated characteristic line, which demonstrates how stock returns are explained by market returns according to the single-factor model of returns.

The deviation of the realized return from the characteristic line at any given period ($\hat{\varepsilon}_t^i$ in equation (3.7)) is captured in the figure by the vertical distance from the realized return to the line of best fit (estimated conditional return). That deviation, which is in fact $\widehat{AR}_t^i$, reflects the fact that the characteristic line is supposed to hold on average, while at any given moment some deviation from it may occur. The expected deviation is zero, as, by construction, the characteristic line captures the expected part of the stock return conditional on the contemporaneous market return. In the present context, any systematic deviation of the realized return from the characteristic line across the employed sample is attributed to the studied event.

To sum up, the single-factor benchmark acknowledges the existence of individual differences in stock returns and captures them with the systematic risk coefficients, the stocks' Betas. Importantly, the estimated model parameters are used to estimate stock *i*'s expected return, conditioned on the market return, that is, assess the stock's "normal" conditional behavior. In the context of ESA, it means that these parameters are to be estimated on the basis of data outside the event window, to avoid possible bias due to the stock's reaction to the event.[12]

3.1.3. The Three-Factor Return Benchmark

Multifactor benchmarks are aimed at analyzing stock returns in a more detailed manner than the naïve and single-factor benchmarks, by referring to additional possible sources of systematic stocks returns. Presumably, multiple factors allow accounting for higher proportions of return variability; at the same time, it is worth noting that the more advanced benchmarks entail more complicated structures and so might be prone to more estimation error. Thus, notwithstanding their simplified nature, the naïve and single-factor benchmarks have their own merits.

Different factors have been proposed to enhance the explanatory power of return models.[13] In this and next subsections, we present two related multifactor models based on variables that have been found by empirical research as possessing substantial explanatory power.

In a series of papers, Fama and French identify and employ three common risk factors in stock returns, the first of which is an overall market factor (employed also by the single-factor model), the second is related to the firm size (equity market capitalization), and the third to the ratio of its book and market equity values.[14] Accordingly, stock *i*'s conditional return is represented by Fama and French's three-factor model as follows:

$$R_t^i - R_t^f = \alpha_i + \beta_i (R_t^m - R_t^f) + s_i SMB_t + h_i HML_t + \varepsilon_t^i, \qquad (3.10)$$

where

R_t^i is stock *i*'s return at period *t*;
R_t^f is the risk-free return at period *t*;

R_t^m is the market return at period t;
SMB_t and HML_t are the "size" and book-to-market equity factors;
α_i, β_i, s_i, h_i are the model's firm-specific parameters; and
ε_t^i is the model's error term.

The NR estimated according to the three-factor benchmark is:

$$\widehat{NR}_t^i = R_t^f + \hat{\alpha}_i + \hat{\beta}_i(R_t^m - R_t^f) + \hat{s}_i SMB_t + \hat{h}_i HML_t, \tag{3.11}$$

where

$\widehat{NR}_t^i$ is stock i's estimated NR at period t;
R_t^f is the risk-free return at period t;
R_t^m is the market return at period t;
SMB_t and HML_t are the "size" and book-to-market equity factors; and
$\hat{\alpha}_i, \hat{\beta}_i, \hat{s}_i, \hat{h}_i$ are the estimated model's parameters.

The AR is estimated by plugging the NR estimate into equation (3.3):

$$\widehat{AR}_t^i \equiv R_t^i - \widehat{NR}_t^i = R_t^i - (R_t^f + \hat{\alpha}_i + \hat{\beta}_i(R_t^m - R_t^f) + \hat{s}_i SMB_t + \hat{h}_i HML_t), \tag{3.12}$$

where

$\widehat{AR}_t^i$ is stock i's estimated AR at period t;
R_t^i is stock i's return at period t;
$\widehat{NR}_t^i$ is stock i's estimated NR at period t;
R_t^f is the risk-free return at period t;
R_t^m is the market return at period t;
SMB_t and HML_t are the "size" and book-to-market equity factors; and
$\hat{\alpha}_i, \hat{\beta}_i, \hat{s}_i, \hat{h}_i$ are the estimated model's parameters.

The size and book-to-market equity factors are constructed as follows.[15] The firms are sorted into two size (equity market capitalization) groups, denoted by S (small) and B (big); another sorting of the firms is into three groups of book-to-market equity. The sorting into S and B groups is performed according to the median size, and the book-to-market equity groups are formed based on the breakpoints for the bottom 30 percent (L, for "low"), middle 40 percent (M, for "medium"), and top 30 percent (H, for "high") of the ranked book-to-market equity values. *SMB* is the difference between the average of the returns on the three small-stock portfolios (S/L, S/M, and S/H) and the average of the returns on the three big-stock portfolios (B/L, B/M, and B/H); *HML* is the difference between the average of the returns on the two high book-to-market equity portfolios (S/H and B/H) and the two low book-to-market equity portfolios (S/L and B/L).

3.1.4. The Four-Factor Benchmark of Returns

Carhart (1997) indicates yet another variable of substantial importance for stock returns in addition to the three factors advocated by Fama and French, namely, the momentum factor. Including this variable in the model allows taking into account the commonly observed tendency of rising stock prices to continue to rise and of declining stock prices to continue to decline. Thus, stock *i*'s return is represented by Carhart's four-factor model as follows:

$$R_t^i - R_t^f = \alpha_i + \beta_i(R_t^m - R_t^f) + s_i SMB_t + h_i HML_t + p_i PR1YR_t + \varepsilon_t^i, \quad (3.13)$$

where

R_t^i is stock *i*'s return at period *t*;
R_t^f is the risk-free return at period *t*;
R_t^m is the market return at period *t*;
SMB_t and HML_t are the "size" and book-to-market equity factors;
$\alpha_i, \beta_i, s_i, h_i$ are the model's firm-specific parameters;
$PR1YR_t$ is the momentum factor;
p_i is the model's firm-specific parameter related to the momentum factor; and
ε_t^i is the model's error term.

The NR estimated according to the four-factor benchmark is:

$$\widehat{NR}_t^i = R_t^f + \hat{\alpha}_i + \hat{\beta}_i(R_t^m - R_t^f) + \hat{s}_i SMB_t + \hat{h}_i HML_t + \hat{p}_i PR1YR_t, \quad (3.14)$$

where

$\widehat{NR}_t^i$ is stock *i*'s estimated NR at period *t*;
R_t^f is the risk-free return at period *t*;

R_t^m is the market return at period t;
SMB_t, HML_t, $PR1YR_t$ are the "size," book-to-market equity, and momentum factors; and
$\hat{\alpha}_i, \hat{\beta}_i, \hat{s}_i, \hat{h}_i, \hat{p}_i$ are the estimated model's parameters.

The AR is estimated by plugging the NR estimate into equation (3.3):

$$\widehat{AR}_t^i \equiv R_t^i - \widehat{NR}_t^i = R_t^i - \begin{pmatrix} R_t^f + \hat{\alpha}_i + \hat{\beta}_i(R_t^m - R_t^f) + \hat{s}_i SMB_t \\ + \hat{h}_i HML_t + \hat{p}_i PR1YR_t \end{pmatrix}, \tag{3.15}$$

where

$\widehat{AR}_t^i$ is stock i's estimated AR at period t;
R_t^i is stock i's return at period t;
$\widehat{NR}_t^i$ is stock i's estimated NR at period t;
R_t^f is the risk-free return at period t;
R_t^m is the market return at period t;
SMB_t, HML_t, $PR1YR_t$ are the "size," book-to-market equity, and momentum factors; and
$\hat{\alpha}_i$, $\hat{\beta}_i$, $\hat{s}_i$, $\hat{h}_i$, $\hat{p}_i$ are the estimated model's parameters.

The momentum factor, $PR1YR_t$, is constructed as the difference in the average returns of firms with the highest 30 percent 11-month returns and firms with the lowest 30 percent 11-month returns, both lagged one month.[16]

According to Carhart, the four-factor benchmark provides improved fit due to the empirical importance of the one-year momentum factor.[17] In the context of event studies, this may allow for more precise measurement of NRs and, consequently, more accurate estimation of market reaction to the studied event.

3.2. Average AR (AAR)

Using ARs, rather than raw returns, for measuring the reaction to events is important in order to control for contemporaneous market-wide movements. There is, however, a need to control for another source of return fluctuations, which are not related to the studied event, to wit, firm-specific fluctuations. Such idiosyncratic movements may result from other events that take place simultaneously, may they be reported by the media or not. For example, consider an event study aimed at detecting reactions to financial report announcements. It could be the case that around the announcements there would be rumors that some holders of a company in the studied sample are considering replacing its chief executive officer. Another company may be involved in a merger process, and a third one may be just about having developed a new, path-breaking drug. In fact, most of the stocks are routinely affected by events that may not be pinpointed by inspecting the media sources: generally, stock prices continuously change, while only rarely these changes may be linked to specific information releases. Thus, observed return fluctuations are likely to contain "noise" due to a smorgasbord of factors that are unrelated to the studied event. The means taken in ESA for reducing this noise rely on the "law of big numbers," to wit, on the observation that averages eliminate noise. Statistically speaking, concentrating on the average AR (AAR) would help raising the *signal-to-noise ratio* of the measured security price reaction to the studied event. Below we explain how AARs are estimated. Note that for reasons explained at the beginning of this chapter, care should be taken when averaging the ARs to arrive at AAR. In particular, the average should be calculated across observations whose returns are hypothesized to move in the same direction.

Definition: AAR is the arithmetic average of ARs across the subsample of observations having the same hypothesized AR sign, for a specific time relative to the event.

According to this definition, AAR is estimated as follows:

$$\widehat{AAR}_t = \frac{\sum_{i=1}^{n} \widehat{AR}_t^i}{n}, \tag{3.16}$$

where

$\widehat{AAR}_t$ is the estimated AAR at period t;
$\widehat{AR}_t^i$ is stock i's estimated AR at period t; and
n is the number of observations in the subsample of observations having the same hypothesized AR sign.

3.3. Cumulative AAR(CAAR)

Estimating cumulative AAR (CAAR) constitutes the last stage of the basic ESA application. By this stage, we have already estimated AAR, date by date, along the event window. For any irregularity in the estimated AAR to be revealed, the estimated CAAR is calculated as the sum of all $\widehat{AAR}s$ over time.[18]

Definition: CAAR for a period is the sum of all AARs over that period.

The cumulative sum of $\widehat{AAR}s$, that is, $\widehat{CAAR}$, is expected to manifest the accumulated price reaction. In case of good news, the $\widehat{AAR}s$ are more likely to be positive, so $\widehat{CAAR}$ should reveal an upward irregularity. Conversely, for bad news, the $\widehat{AAR}s$ are more likely to be negative and then a downward irregularity in $\widehat{CAAR}$ should prevail.

According to this definition, CAAR from period s to t is estimated as follows:

$$\widehat{CAAR}_{s,t} \equiv \sum_{\tau=s}^{t} \widehat{AAR}_{\tau}, \tag{3.17}$$

where

$\widehat{CAAR}_{s,t}$ is the estimated CAAR from period s to t, and
$\widehat{AAR}_{\tau}$ is the estimated AAR at period τ.

Alternatively, $\widehat{CAAR}$ may also be computed recursively as follows:

$$\widehat{CAAR}_{s,s} \equiv \widehat{AAR}_{s}, \tag{3.18}$$

$$\widehat{CAAR}_{s,t} \equiv \widehat{CAAR}_{s,t-1} + \widehat{AAR}_{t}\,;\, for\ t \geq s+1, \tag{3.19}$$

where

$\widehat{CAAR}_{s,t}$ is the estimated CAAR from period s to t, and
$\widehat{AAR}_{t}$ is the estimated AAR at period t.

This recursive calculation manifests the idea behind $\widehat{CAAR}s$ as accumulators of the price reaction over selected trading periods.

To sum up, $\widehat{CAARs}$ provide a nice, lucid representation of trends in stock estimated ARs around the date of the analyzed event. Statistical analysis is required to judge whether the detected irregularities are real or spurious. In a nutshell, $\widehat{CAAR}$ irregularities that are detected before the event indicate information leakage, and irregularities observed after the event date may reflect market inefficiency.

3.4. From AR to CAAR via CAR

As explained in section 3.3, there are two ways of arriving at the $\widehat{CAAR}$ series. To wit, $\widehat{ARs}$ may be first averaged across stocks and then accumulated through time, according to equations (3.16) and (3.17), or, alternatively, first accumulated through time and then averaged across stocks. The latter way, elaborated henceforth, is advantageous when the event windows of the sample securities are not overlapping, such that the ARs of different stocks are independent. When this is not the case, as we explain in more detail in chapter 6, the former way of arriving at the $\widehat{CAAR}$ series is more to the point.

> Definition: Stock *i*'s CAR for a period is the sum of its ARs over that period.

According to this definition, CAR from period s to t is estimated as follows:

$$\widehat{CAR}^i_{s,t} \equiv \sum_{\tau=s}^{t} \widehat{AR}^i_{\tau}, \tag{3.20}$$

where

$\widehat{CAR}^i_{s,t}$ is stock *i*'s estimated CAR from period s to t, and
$\widehat{AR}^i_{\tau}$ is stock *i*'s estimated AR at period τ.

Note that, alternatively, $\widehat{CAR}^i_{s,t}$ may be calculated recursively as follows:

$$\widehat{CAR}^i_{s,s} \equiv \widehat{AR}_s, \tag{3.21}$$

$$\widehat{CAR}^i_{s,t} \equiv \widehat{CAR}^i_{s,t-1} + \widehat{AR}^i_t;\ for\ t \geq s+1, \tag{3.22}$$

where

$\widehat{CAR}^i_{s,t}$ is stock i's estimated CAR from period s to t, and
$\widehat{AR}^i_t$ is stock i's estimated AR at period t.

To arrive at the estimated CAARs, the $\widehat{CARs}$ are averaged across observations whose returns are hypothesized to move in the same direction. Thus, having denoted n as the number of observations in the subsample of observations having the same hypothesized AR sign, $\widehat{CAAR}_{s,t}$, to wit, the estimated CAAR from period s to t is computed as follows, yielding the same result as equation (3.17):

$$\widehat{CAAR}_{s,t} \equiv \frac{1}{n}\sum_{i=1}^{n}\widehat{CAR}^i_{s,t}, \tag{3.23}$$

where

$\widehat{CAR}^i_{s,t}$ is stock i's estimated cumulative abnormal return from period s to t, and
$\widehat{CAAR}_{s,t}$ is the estimated CAAR from period s to t.

3.5. Market Efficiency and Information Content of the Event

As noted above, concentrating on $\widehat{CAARs}$ over different parts of the event window may lead to important conclusions regarding different aspects of market reaction. In particular, irregular $\widehat{CAAR}$ behavior (i.e., substantial nonzero estimated CAARs) around the event date indicates investors' reaction to the studied event. In the case of market reaction, the exact characteristics of the estimated CAAR behavior may suggest possible interpretations and more detailed conclusions. Thus, irregularities before the official news announcement may indicate information leakage prior to the information release. While ESA may not detect the specific actions taken by individuals, it still may raise suspicions of trading using inside information.[19] Unrelated to the legislation aspect, the mere detection of $\widehat{CAAR}$ irregularities around the event date indicates that market participants acknowledge the pricing relevance of the news for the stock value. In other words, the investors' reaction as embodied in stock return patterns serves as a testimony for the existence of information content in the analyzed event.

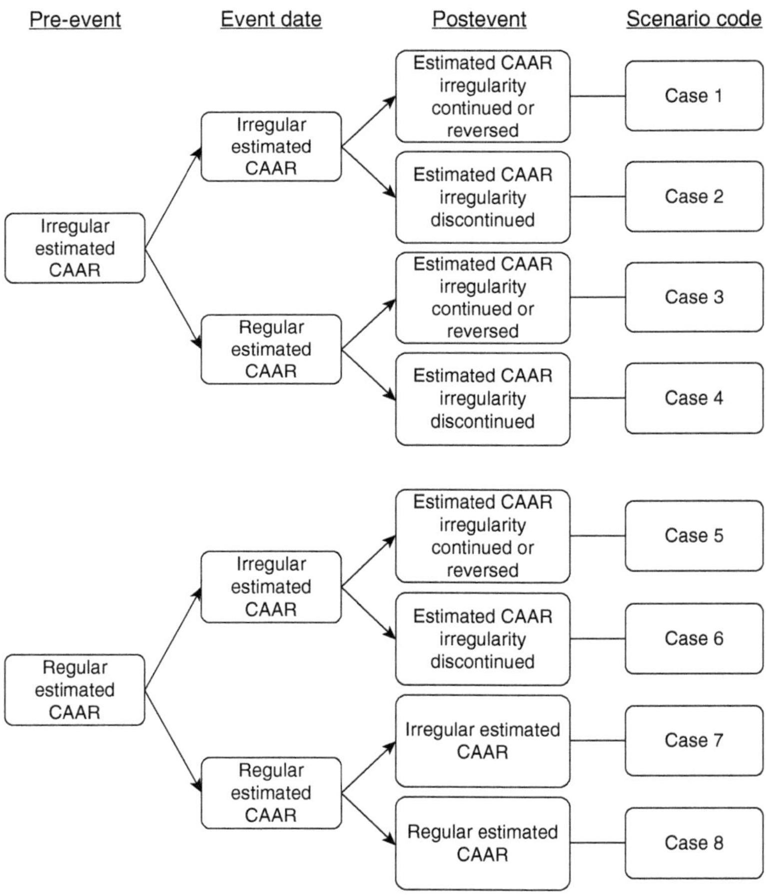

Figure 3.3 Possible behavior of the estimated CAAR series over different parts of the event window.

There may be a sharp upward or downward jump in $\widehat{CAAR}$ on the event date or immediately after it.[20] This would also indicate that there is information content in the event and, furthermore, may suggest that the news was genuinely surprising so that no information had a chance to leak out and be used until the event date. In contrast, the absence of

Table 3.1 Interpreting possible behavior of the estimated CAAR series over different parts of the event window (for the cases depicted in Figure 3.3)

Case no.	Information content	Market efficiency	Annotation (abbreviated)
1	Yes	No	Early reaction due to information leakage; overt reaction to public news arrival; delayed reaction or overreaction with correction, contrary to EMH
2	Yes	Yes	Early reaction due to information leakage; full timely reaction to public news arrival in accordance with EMH
3	Yes	No	Early reaction due to information leakage; no overt reaction to public news arrival; delayed reaction or overreaction with correction, contrary to EMH
4	Yes	Yes	Early reaction due to information leakage; no overt reaction to public news arrival; full reaction in accordance with EMH
5	Yes	No	No information leakage; overt timely reaction to public news arrival; delayed reaction or overreaction with correction, contrary to EMH
6	Yes	Yes	No information leakage; full timely reaction to public news arrival in accordance with EMH
7	Yes	No	No information leakage; no overt timely reaction to public news arrival; delayed reaction contrary to EMH
8	No	Irrelevant	No market reaction; market efficiency question may not be answered as there is no sign for information content being acknowledged by the market

irregularities in $\widehat{CAAR}$*s* around the event date may indicate the event is not perceived by the market as possessing information content. However, there is another possible interpretation for the absence of $\widehat{CAAR}$ irregularities, apart from the lack of importance, namely, that the market has already fully absorbed the news long before, as a result, for example, of gradual information outflow, preliminary reports release, or other information sources used by investors (see Clatworthy, 2005, for a discussion of information sources used in the analysis of corporate equity). In this case, no new information content is acknowledged by the market within the event window.

Finally, market efficiency is assessed by inspecting the $\widehat{CAAR}$*s* after the event, that is, from the date of the event, onward. Recall (chapter 2) that, according to EMH, the event-related irregular price adjustment (or estimated CAAR irregularity in current terms) has to occur not later than the information dissemination, and price adjustments must not take too long, so that no useful predictions can be made once the reaction is detected. In other words, if no irregularities are detected in the postevent part of the event window, one may infer that the information has been fully absorbed by the market. Note that in this case no profitable predictions can be made on the basis of publicly available information, which is the hallmark of market efficiency. In contrast, if $\widehat{CAAR}$ irregularity occurs after the event date, then it may be deduced that the information has not been fully absorbed until its dissemination, meaning the market did not react efficiently; in this case one may check further the possibility of taking advantage of the detected irregularity to "beat the market," contrary to the EMH assertion. Alternatively, the lack of efficiency may be revealed by a postevent $\widehat{CAAR}$ *reversal*, which may be interpreted as a price correction following an initial overreaction to the information dissemination.

To recap, analyzing $\widehat{CAAR}$*s* over different parts of the event window sheds light on different aspects of market participants' reaction to the news. These primarily consist of information content, that is, the effect of the event on the security values, and market efficiency, which is reflected by the timeliness of the reaction. Figure 3.3 presents a variety of conceivable results in a systematic way and summarizes the possible patterns of the estimated CAAR series around the event. In particular, the figure refers to three distinct stages within the event window—before, on, and after the event date—and considers possible $\widehat{CAAR}$ behavior at each stage. At each one of these three stages, two possible $\widehat{CAAR}$ patterns are possible (irregular or regular), totaling eight possible cases, numbered 1 to 8 in the rightmost column of the figure. Table 3.1 offers a brief annotation for each one of the cases, emphasizing the aspects of information content and market efficiency.

As Figure 3.3 and Table 3.1 purport to show, the two important issues dealt with by ESA, namely market efficiency and information content of the event, are addressed by concentrating on different parts of event window. In particular, lack of market efficiency is inferred by inspecting the postevent period, whereas information content is inferred by the presence of market reaction around the event, irrespectively of its timing. As shown by Table 3.1, in one out of the eight scenarios depicted in Figure 3.3, namely for case 8, no information content may be inferred; such conclusion is obtained only when no $\widehat{CAAR}$ irregular pattern, whatsoever, is detected either before, at the time of, or after the event. It is clear that in such a case the question of market efficiency may not be answered using the study results.[21] In contrast, under all other scenarios there is evidence that market participants acknowledge the information content, generating thereby irregular price adjustments before, at the time of, or after the event, and these are reflected by the corresponding irregularities in $\widehat{CAAR}$.

In cases where information content is acknowledged, the exact timing of market reaction sheds light on the question of market efficiency. In particular, EMH is violated if the reaction continues after the event, as in cases 1, 3, 5, and 7, since under all these scenarios there is some period when the price does not fully reflect all publicly available information (and in fact that is why the reaction continues beyond the news release). Finally, EMH is not rejected if the reaction cannot be traced beyond the point of the public news release, as in cases 2, 4, 6, and 8, since under all these scenarios there is no period when the price does not fully reflect all publicly available information.

To sum up, different $\widehat{CAAR}$ patterns within the event window may lead to specific conclusions regarding the two major issues dealt with by ESA, namely, information content of events and market efficiency. The next chapter presents a simplified example of event study aimed at substantiating the ideas presented here. The example is constructed using a very small data specimen to make the analysis as transparent as possible and concentrates on the most salient features of data processing.

3.6. Appendix: CAPM: An Economic Model of Returns

As noted in section 3.1, CAPM is one of the economic models of returns that may be employed to assess abnormal returns while taking account of differences in return characteristics among different securities. Economic models rest upon theoretical foundations and assumptions that are often subject to substantial critique. At the same time, an important advantage of using economic models is the intuition they provide, thus facilitating the understanding of fundamental phenomena that often appear unexplained by mere statistical models. We introduce CAPM here primarily in order to provide such an intuition. One must note at the outset that CAPM is a theory whose domain and implications extend much beyond event studies, and only some elements of it are employed by ESA. Below we sketch out only the most fundamental highlights of CAPM that are essential to ESA applications.

In a nutshell, CAPM is a theory that permits explaining security returns by referring to the compensation for the risk required by risk-averse investors (i.e., investors who prefer a certain return over an uncertain return with the same expected value). The model was independently developed by Sharpe (1964), Lintner (1965), and Mossin (1966), who have built on the seminal work on risk diversification by Markowitz (1952), a framework also known as modern portfolio theory (MPT).[22] According to MPT, investing in different securities permits reducing the overall portfolio risk as long as the involved securities are not perfectly correlated, that is, if random fluctuations in the prices of some securities are at least partially offset by also random but opposite fluctuations in the prices of other securities. Essentially, this appears to suggest the ancient wisdom of "not putting all eggs in one basket," a dictum well known to even minimally experienced investors and often used in everyday parlance with or without reference to financial markets. The advancement offered by MPT is in placing this old insight on solid mathematical foundations and providing grounds for a practical way of applying it to the construction of optimal portfolios. Armed with the optimization rules offered by MPT, investors may exploit the possibility of risk diversification. In turn, CAPM assumes (among other things) that the investors, by and large, engage in risk diversification, and the market on the whole is affected by the massive use of optimal investment strategy.

It is well known that CAPM refers to investment in all assets; however, common applications focus on stocks. Here we align our discussion accordingly and refer to stocks only. According to CAPM, the best possible financial position is achieved by holding a portfolio whose risky component is invested in the *market portfolio*, which is the package that contains all existing risky assets in amounts proportional to their market values (or *market capitalization*). The market variance of returns is minimal given its expected return—that is, changing the composition of the portfolio cannot further reduce its risk without lowering its expected return. The risk which cannot be eliminated, or diversified away, is called *market risk* (other terms used to identify market risk are *systematic*, *nondiversifiable*, or sometimes *Beta risk*). A portfolio containing only a small number of randomly chosen assets is likely to be more risky than the market portfolio, since in addition to the market risk it would be subject to the risk that may be effectively eliminated by diversification; this additional risk is called *nonsystematic*, *diversifiable*, or *specific risk*. The existence of systematic risk, in effect, reflects the fact that most assets are correlated to some extent. The reason for this correlation is not hard to point out: there is a range of factors affecting most of the market simultaneously (though different assets may be affected to different degrees). These factors may include housing and energy prices, interest and currency rates, employment and inflation levels, and many other economy-wide variables; moreover, specific occurrences such as financial crises, wars, natural disasters, and other global events are certainly also on the list. All of those are at the source of correlation among asset returns and, therefore, of systematic or market risk which cannot be eliminated by diversification.

According to CAPM, to obtain the best investing position, investors need only to decide how to allocate their investment between the market portfolio and government riskless bonds offering low but certain returns. The division of funds between these two investment channels is where individual risk attitudes may be expressed. Specifically, the more risk-averse the investor is, the higher proportion of the invested amount that investor has to allocate to the riskless bonds.

Beside suggesting how to invest, and directly relevant to ESA, CAPM explains how expected returns are determined by the market. In that sense, the theory offers a way of determining normal returns, providing a benchmark against which realized returns may be measured. According to CAPM, expected returns compensate investors for the systematic risk inherent in the investment. Assessing the stock's systematic risk involves measuring the extent of this stock's "synchronization" with the market, that is, the extent to which the stock and the market portfolio returns tend to comove.

One observation regarding CAPM that is relevant to our discussion is that the relation between stock and market returns may be described as a linear equation with the addition of an error component, as in equation (3.7) in subsection 3.1.2, rewritten here:

$$R_t^i = \alpha_i + \beta_i R_t^m + \varepsilon_t^i, \tag{3.24}$$

where

R_t^i is stock i's return at period t;
R_t^m is the market return at period t;
α_i and β_i are the model's parameters; and
ε_t^i is the model's error term.

Thus, similarly to the single-factor model of returns, CAPM implies linear relationship between assets' expected returns and Betas. However, recall, as we noted in the beginning of section 3.1, that while the single-factor model is statistical, CAPM is an economic framework based on theoretical arguments. As such, CAPM might, and in fact often does, become a subject of substantial critique, while the single-factor model is more immune to such attacks.[23]

Here we have primarily aimed at emphasizing the basic logic behind the theory and refrained from presenting a full axiomatic framework with definitions, proofs, and caveats. The interested reader should consult more comprehensive sources for a detailed presentation on CAPM and its applications. For instance, on the basics of the theory and its place in a wider financial economics perspective, see Elton, Gruber, Brown, and Goetzmann (2003) and references therein; another introductory and wide-ranging account is offered by Haugen (1997).

Chapter 4

A Simplified Example: The Effect of Air Crashes on Stock Prices

In this chapter, we present a simplified example of ESA to facilitate the more technical discussion presented in chapters 5 and 6 and the hands-on exercises in chapters 7 and 8. Here, we pick a handful of observations and treat this specimen as our "data sample" to illustrate the ESA in a succinct format. We concentrate on the most salient features of data processing, while leaving out complicated caveats. You may download the Excel file (http://dx.doi.org/10.6084/m9.figshare.1221810) with tables, calculations, and graph of this simplified example from the book's website.

Among the most noticeable events bearing potential importance for the value of the firm are those related to product safety. For instance, consider product recall announcements, such as in the automobile and healthcare industries. Obviously, this kind of news is bound to attract particular attention due to the relevance to the public in general and, consequently, may give rise to substantial market reactions. For instance, Chen and Nguyen (2013) examine the impact of recall announcements on stock prices and earnings forecasts of analysts and report negative effect of the recalls on both analyzed measures. Perhaps even more dramatic are the possible consequences of noticeable product or service failures such as aircraft accidents. As demonstrated by Bosch, Eckard, and Singal (1998), who studied incidents of air crashes, not only were the stock prices of the airline involved affected, but the stock prices of other airlines were affected as well.

For the sake of demonstrating the ESA in a concise, elementary setup, we have picked up four air crashes and processed their data according to the steps described in the previous chapter.[1]

Table 4.1 depicts the specimen of four commercial airline crashes picked for the current exercise. For each crash, the table reports its calendar date, "day zero" date, general location, airline operator involved, and its exchange ticker. "Crash date" is the actual calendar date of the crash, and "day zero date" denotes the date of first closing price after the crash. These dates differ from each other when the crash occurred after the trading hours.

We start by retrieving the stock prices of the airlines involved around the event day. Table 4.2 reports the closing stock prices of the four airlines, for the event window starting six days before day zero and ending six days after it.[2]

The next step is to calculate the stock returns (R) along the event window. Recall the two possible return definitions, arithmetic return $R(a)$, and logarithmic return $R(l)$, introduced in the previous chapter. Throughout the simplified example, we employ arithmetic returns. We use the prices from Table 4.2 and equation (3.1) from section 3.1, which in this case becomes:[3]

$$R_t^i \equiv (P_t^i - P_{t-1}^i) / P_{t-1}^i;\ t = -5,\ldots,6. \tag{4.1}$$

Table 4.1 Specimen of airline crashes

Case no.	Crash date	Day zero date	Crash location	Airline	Ticker
1	Jan. 31, 2000	Feb. 1, 2000	California	Alaska Airlines	ALK
2	Nov. 12, 2001	Nov. 12, 2001	New York City	American Airlines	AAMRQ
3	Apr. 1, 2011	Apr. 2, 2011	Arizona	Southwest Airlines	LUV
4	Aug. 14, 2013	Aug. 14, 2013	Alabama	UPS Airlines	UPS

Table 4.2 Airlines' stock prices around the event dates

Case\Day	−6	−5	−4	−3	−2	−1	0	1	2	3	4	5	6
1	14.97	15.16	16.03	15.84	16.22	15.84	15.78	15.81	15.47	15.25	15.10	14.94	14.70
2	18.74	18.90	18.36	18.55	18.28	18.13	16.49	17.01	17.94	18.75	20.06	20.77	19.86
3	12.53	12.43	12.36	12.66	12.48	12.52	12.31	12.05	12.01	11.66	11.54	11.64	11.70
4	86.79	86.72	86.96	86.65	86.61	86.55	86.30	85.43	85.52	85.55	85.77	85.56	86.43

Table 4.3 Airlines' stock returns around the event dates (in %)

Case\Day	−5	−4	−3	−2	−1	0	1	2	3	4	5	6
1	1.27	5.74	−1.19	2.40	−2.34	−0.38	0.19	−2.15	−1.42	−0.98	−1.06	−1.61
2	0.85	−2.86	1.03	−1.46	−0.82	−9.05	3.15	5.47	4.52	6.99	3.54	−4.38
3	−0.80	−0.56	2.43	−1.42	0.32	−1.68	−2.11	−0.33	−2.91	−1.03	0.87	0.52
4	−0.08	0.28	−0.36	−0.05	−0.07	−0.29	−1.01	0.11	0.04	0.26	−0.24	1.02

The results are reported in Table 4.3. Note that returns are calculated starting from day (–5), that is, from one day after the beginning of the event window.

Next we will calculate the stocks' ARs, as explained in section 3.1. For this purpose, we retrieve S&P 500 Index-level data for the same calendar dates for which we collected the stock prices reported in Table 4.2 (see Table 4.4).

The S&P 500 Index-level data are converted to returns using equation (4.1), with i referring to the S&P 500 Index. The results are reported in Table 4.5.

Now we are ready to estimate ARs according to the naïve benchmark of returns, introduced in subsection 3.1.1.[4] According to that model, AR is the difference between the corresponding stock and index returns, which are reported in Tables 4.3 and 4.5, respectively. The calculation is represented by equation (3.6) from subsection 3.1.1 whose special case for this example appears henceforth. The estimated ARs are reported in Table 4.6.

$$\widehat{AR}_t^i \equiv R_t^i - \widehat{NR}_t^i = R_t^i - R_t^m;\ i = 1,\ldots,4;\ t = -5,\ldots,6, \tag{4.2}$$

where

$\widehat{AR}_t^i$ is stock i's estimated AR at period t;

R_t^i is stock i's return at period t;

$\widehat{NR}_t^i$ is stock i's estimated NR at period t; and

R_t^m is the market return at period t, here proxied by the S&P 500 Index return.

Table 4.4 S&P 500 Index levels around the event dates

Case\ Day	–6	–5	–4	–3	–2	–1	0	1	2	3	4	5	6
1	1401.91	1410.03	1404.09	1398.56	1360.16	1394.46	1409.28	1409.12	1424.97	1424.37	1423.00	1441.75	1411.71
2	1087.20	1102.84	1118.86	1115.80	1118.54	1120.31	1118.33	1139.09	1141.21	1142.24	1138.65	1151.06	1142.66
3	1313.80	1310.19	1319.44	1328.26	1325.83	1332.41	1332.87	1332.63	1335.54	1333.51	1328.17	1324.46	1314.16
4	1697.37	1690.91	1697.48	1691.42	1689.47	1694.16	1685.39	1661.32	1655.83	1646.06	1652.35	1642.80	1656.96

Table 4.5 S&P 500 Index returns around the event dates (in %)

Case\Day	–5	–4	–3	–2	–1	0	1	2	3	4	5	6
1	0.58	–0.42	–0.39	–2.75	2.52	1.06	–0.01	1.12	–0.04	–0.10	1.32	–2.08
2	1.44	1.45	–0.27	0.25	0.16	–0.18	1.86	0.19	0.09	–0.31	1.09	–0.73
3	–0.27	0.71	0.67	–0.18	0.50	0.03	–0.02	0.22	–0.15	–0.40	–0.28	–0.78
4	–0.38	0.39	–0.36	–0.12	0.28	–0.52	–1.43	–0.33	–0.59	0.38	–0.58	0.86

Table 4.6 Estimated ARs around the event dates (in %)

Case\Day	–5	–4	–3	–2	–1	0	1	2	3	4	5	6
1	0.69	6.16	–0.79	5.14	–4.86	–1.44	0.20	–3.28	–1.38	–0.89	–2.38	0.48
2	–0.58	–4.31	1.31	–1.70	–0.98	–8.87	1.30	5.28	4.42	7.30	2.45	-3.65
3	–0.52	–1.27	1.76	–1.24	–0.18	–1.71	–2.09	–0.55	–2.76	-0.63	1.15	1.29
4	0.30	–0.11	0.00	0.07	–0.35	0.23	0.42	0.44	0.63	–0.12	0.33	0.15

The next step is to compute the estimated AARs ($\widehat{AARs}$) as explained in section 3.2. We do this using the $\widehat{ARs}$ from Table 4.6 and equation (3.16) from section 3.2, which now becomes:

$$\widehat{AAR}_t = \frac{\sum_{i=1}^{4} \widehat{AR}_t^i}{4}; \; i = 1, \ldots, 4; \; t = -5, \ldots, 6. \tag{4.3}$$

The results are reported in Table 4.7.

The final step is to calculate the estimated CAAR using the $\widehat{AARs}$ from Table 4.7 and Equation (3.17) from section 3.3. The results are reported in Table 4.8.

$$\widehat{CAAR}_{-5,t} \equiv \sum_{\tau=-5}^{t} \widehat{AAR}_\tau; \; t = -5, \ldots, 6. \tag{4.4}$$

Note that $\widehat{CAARs}$ may also be computed recursively, according to equations (3.18) and (3.19), as follows:

$$\widehat{CAAR}_{-5,-5} \equiv \widehat{AAR}_{-5}, \tag{4.5}$$

$$\widehat{CAAR}_{-5,t} \equiv \widehat{CAAR}_{-5,t-1} + \widehat{AAR}_t; \; t = -4, \ldots, 6. \tag{4.6}$$

Figure 4.1 plots the $\widehat{CAARs}$ reported in Table 4.8, providing the estimated cumulative market reaction to air crashes in the analyzed data specimen.

Table 4.7 Estimated AARs around the event dates (in %)

Day	**–5**	**–4**	**–3**	**–2**	**–1**	**0**	**1**	**2**	**3**	**4**	**5**	**6**
AAR	–0.03	0.12	0.57	0.57	–1.59	–2.95	–0.04	0.47	0.23	1.41	0.39	–0.43

Table 4.8 Estimated CAARs around the event dates (in %)

Day	**–5**	**–4**	**–3**	**–2**	**–1**	**0**	**1**	**2**	**3**	**4**	**5**	**6**
CAAR	–0.03	0.09	0.66	1.23	–0.37	–3.31	–3.36	–2.89	–2.66	–1.24	–0.86	–1.29

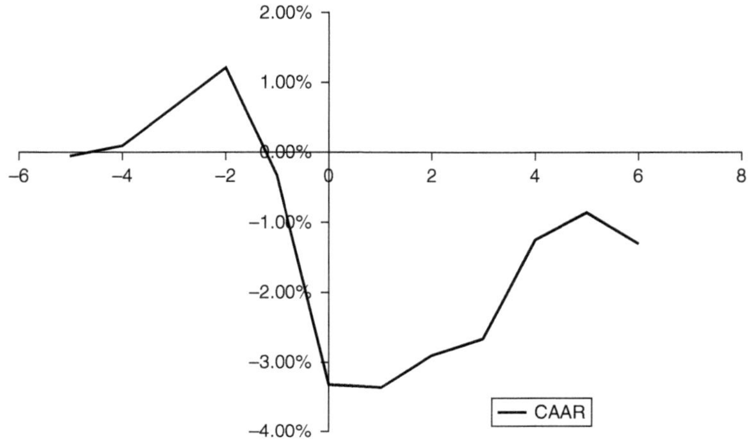

Figure 4.1 Estimated CAAR around the event date (in percent).

As Figure 4.1 indicates, there is a noticeable plunge in $\widehat{CAAR}$ on the event day (day 0), from near zero to below –3 percent.[5] Another thing to note is the partial reversal over the following few days. Overall, the picture seems to fit case 5, which was defined in chapter 3 (see Figure 3.3 and Table 3.1), that is, a pattern of overreaction with correction.

To summarize, using a specimen of data we demonstrated here the application of ESA in the most elementary setup. In chapter 5 we will outline the basic design of ESA in a thorough form, introducing hypothesis testing and corresponding statistical analysis. Further, a range of complicating issues and caveats that may arise in specific cases depending on the nature of analyzed events and various properties of the data is dealt with in chapter 6.

Chapter 5

The Basic ESA Design

In chapter 3 we introduced the basic logic behind ESA, proceeded with technical specifications for its practical implementation, and concluded by describing the result interpretation regarding market efficiency and information content of the analyzed event. In chapter 4 we illustrated these ideas by using a simplified example. Hereafter, we recapitulate and elaborate on the main stages of ESA. While there is no unique structure encompassing all event studies, the flow of analysis we bring here may be of relevance to many cases. In particular, we introduce hypothesis testing and corresponding basic statistical analysis, for the case where there is no *clustering* among the observations, to wit, the event windows of the sampled securities are not overlapping.[1] We refer here to the analysis of stock returns with daily frequency. Some of the definitions and equations introduced in chapter 3 are replicated here for convenience.

5.1. Basic ESA Data Manipulation

Having decided to employ ESA for studying a specific event, the relevant data have to be sampled. To that end, selection criteria such as time span of the study and characteristics of the firms undergoing the event are to be determined. At the same time, it is worthwhile to delineate the distribution of these sample characteristics. It is also worthwhile to consider any potential biases that might have been introduced by the sample selection process.

The first step of the procedure is to estimate ARs, which comprise the key indicator of market reaction to the studied event and serve as a basis for all subsequent ESA calculations. Estimating ARs necessitates first defining NRs, which serve as a benchmark against which *actual* (or *realized*) returns can be assessed to evaluate the effect of the event on the prices of related securities. The NRs are estimated according to a benchmark model of returns; generic examples of relevant models, presented in chapter 3, include the naïve and single-factor benchmarks, as well as the more advanced multifactor models of returns. In using factor models, it is conventional practice to estimate the NRs by ordinary least squares (OLS) over a time period preceding the event window, which is assumed to be representative of the return process and unaffected by the event. This period is often referred to as the *estimation window* (Figure 5.1). Under general conditions and the assumption that the returns are jointly multivariate normal and independently and identically distributed over time, OLS provides consistent estimates for the resulting NRs.[2]

Recall that $\widehat{AR}$ is calculated as the deviation of realized return from the estimated norm, prescribed by the selected benchmark model.[3]

Formally, $\widehat{AR}$ is defined as follows (according to equation (3.3)):

$$\widehat{AR}_t^i \equiv R_t^i - \widehat{NR}_t^i, \tag{5.1}$$

where

$\widehat{AR}_t^i$ is stock i's period t estimated AR;
R_t^i is stock i's period t return; and
$\widehat{NR}_t^i$ is stock i's period t estimated NR.

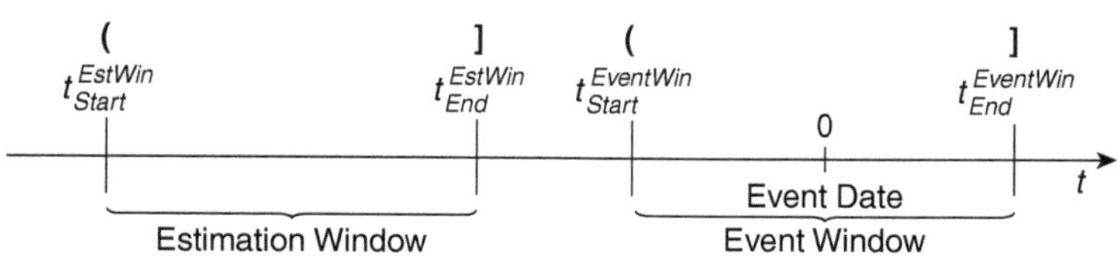

Figure 5.1 ESA timeline: event window, event date, and estimation window.

The second step of the procedure is to estimate CARs, with the aim of detecting the market reaction to the studied event around news dissemination.

The formal definition of $\widehat{CAR}$ is as follows:

$$\widehat{CAR}^{i}_{s,t} \equiv \sum\nolimits_{\tau=s}^{t} \widehat{AR}^{i}_{\tau}, \tag{5.2}$$

where

$\widehat{CAR}^{i}_{s,t}$ is stock i's estimated cumulative abnormal return from a specific starting point s within the event window, up to a subsequent date t taking place till the end of the event window, and
$\widehat{AR}^{i}_{\tau}$ is stock i's estimated AR at period τ.

The third and final step of the procedure is to estimate CAARs. The CAARs are estimated for each time point as the average of all estimated CARs of the stocks having the same hypothesized direction of reaction to the news according to the proposed underlying story. Concentrating on average return fluctuations in a sample of stocks that underwent the event in question essentially lowers the risk of error inherent in analyzing returns of a single stock, as explained in the sequel.

$$\widehat{CAAR}_{s,t} \equiv \frac{1}{n}\sum_{i=1}^{n} \widehat{CAR}^{i}_{s,t}, \tag{5.3}$$

where

$\widehat{CAAR}_{s,t}$ is the estimated CAAR from a specific starting point within the event window, up to subsequent dates till the end of the event window;
$\widehat{CAR}^{i}_{s,t}$ is the estimated CAR from a specific starting point within the event window, up to subsequent dates till the end of the event window; and
n is the number of observations in the subsample of observations having the same hypothesized AR sign.

The CAARs are the carriers of ESA final results, and the interpretation of their estimated values, in the shape of the $\widehat{CAAR}$ series, facilitates arriving at the conclusions with respect to the market reaction to the studied event, as well as regarding market efficiency. As explained in chapter 3, an irregularity in $\widehat{CAAR}$ before the event date suggests that the market information aggregation process may have captured, at least partially, the value of information before its release. Inter alia, the irregularity may be indicative of information leakage prior to the official news release. An irregularity in $\widehat{CAAR}$ on the event date reflects immediate market reaction to the news dissemination. Lastly, the occurrence of further $\widehat{CAAR}$ irregularity after the event date, either in the same initial direction or reverse, suggests market inefficiency.

CAARs are random variables and thus their investigation requires statistical analysis. Henceforth, we demonstrate how to do so by employing hypothesis testing and relevant statistical tools. The procedure introduced here is basic and relies, among other things, on the assumption that the ARs are independent across stocks. We assume here that there is no clustering among the observations, that is, the event windows of the stocks in the sample are not overlapping.

According to the above assumptions and statistical approach, the following properties hold for AR under the null hypothesis that the event has no impact on return distribution:[4]

$$E(AR_t^i) = 0, \tag{5.4}$$

where

$E(AR_t^i)$ is the expected value of stock i's AR at period t,

and

$$Var(AR_t^i) = \sigma_i^2, \tag{5.5}$$

where

$Var(AR_t^i)$ is the variance of stock i's AR at period t.

That is to say, σ_i^2 is the variance of AR_t^i in the absence of an effect by the event under study, henceforth referred to as "regular" variance. Further, it is conventional to approximate the distribution of AR under the null hypothesis by normal distribution, that is to say,

$$AR_t^i \sim N(0,\sigma_i^2), \tag{5.6}$$

where

AR_t^i is stock i's AR at period t.

The conditional variance of $\widehat{AR}$, $\sigma_i^2(\widehat{AR}_t^i)$ is comprised of two components. The first is disturbance variance of stock return, σ_i^2, and the second is additional variance due to sampling error in the parameter estimates of $\widehat{NR}$. The latter, which is common to all the observations over the event window, introduces also serial correlation of AR estimates (even though the "true" ARs are time-wise independent). As the estimation window becomes longer, however, this term approaches zero, due to the diminishing of sampling error. Thus, the conditional variance of $\widehat{AR}_t^i$ approaches σ_i^2 and the estimated ARs become time-wise independent.[5] In practice, a large enough estimation window may often be chosen, so as to practically satisfy these asymptotical properties.[6]

We concentrate now on the analysis from the point where NRs have already been estimated for all the securities and analyze a subsample consisting of n observations with the same hypothesized market reaction according to the proposed underlying story.[7]

- For each security i, we generate a series of estimated ARs over the estimation and event windows (see Figure 5.1 for timeline notation):

$$\widehat{AR}_t^i \equiv R_t^i - \widehat{NR}_t^i;\ i = 1,\ldots,n;\begin{cases} t=t_{Start}^{EstWin}+1,\ldots,t_{End}^{EstWin} \\ t=t_{Start}^{EventWin}+1,\ldots,t_{End}^{EventWin} \end{cases}. \tag{5.7}$$

  The distributional properties of $\widehat{ARs}$ under the null hypothesis may be inferred from the estimation window calculations. They serve to draw inferences regarding the effect of the studied event over any subperiod within the event window. Under the null hypothesis, conditional on the event window market realizations, these $\widehat{ARs}$ are jointly normally distributed, with a zero conditional mean and conditional variance $\sigma_i^2\left(\widehat{AR}_t^i\right)$.

- We aggregate $\widehat{AR}$s from s to t within the event window to yield cumulative estimates. We denote this series, for each security i, as:

$$\widehat{CAR}^i_{s,t} \equiv \sum_{\tau=s}^{t} \widehat{AR}^i_{\tau}. \tag{5.8}$$

Asymptotically, for a long estimation window, the variance of $\widehat{CAR}^i_{s,t}$ becomes:[8]

$$Var\left(\widehat{CAR}^i_{s,t}\right) = (t-s+1)\sigma_i^2. \tag{5.9}$$

For tractability of hands-on analyses presented in this book, we assume that this is the case throughout and employ this relation in our calculations.

Having $\widehat{ARs}$ aggregated over time into $\widehat{CARs}$, we analyze the return fluctuations within a sample of stocks that underwent the event in question. The inspection of a group of observations essentially raises the signal-to-noise ratio and lowers the risk of error inherent in analyzing returns of a single stock, which might be nonrepresentative. To that end, $\widehat{CARs}$ are averaged to yield $\widehat{CAARs}$ within each group of observations having the same hypothesized direction of reaction according to the proposed underlying story (i.e., positive, negative, or neutral):

$$\widehat{CAAR}_{s,t} \equiv \frac{1}{n}\sum_{i=1}^{n} \widehat{CAR}^i_{s,t}, \tag{5.10}$$

where n denotes the number of observations within the group.

The $\widehat{CAARs}$ have the following variance estimators:

$$\hat{\sigma}^{CAAR}_{s,t} = \frac{(t-s+1)}{n^2}\sum_{i=1}^{n} \hat{\sigma}_i^2, \tag{5.11}$$

or standard deviation estimators:

$$\hat{\sigma}^{CAAR}_{s,t} = \left(\frac{(t-s+1)}{n^2}\sum_{i=1}^{n} \hat{\sigma}_i^2\right)^{1/2}. \tag{5.12}$$

These variance estimators are constructed under the assumption that there is no clustering among the observations, so the covariance terms are zero.

Next, we draw inferences about market reaction to the studied event. Practically, the unknown disturbance variance of stock return may usually be replaced by the sample variance measure from the benchmark model of stock returns. Thus, the null hypothesis of no reaction to the studied event may be tested for each $\widehat{CAAR}_{s,t}$, with the following test statistic (TS), which has approximately a standard normal distribution, for a large number of observations and a long estimation window:[9]

$$TS_{s,t} \equiv \widehat{CAAR}_{s,t} / \hat{\sigma}_{s,t}^{CAAR} \stackrel{\cdot}{\sim} N(0,1), \tag{5.13}$$

which, after plugging the standard deviation (5.12) and expressing in daily terms according to equation (5.9), yields:

$$TS_{s,t} = \frac{\widehat{CAAR}_{s,t}}{\frac{1}{n}\sqrt{(t-s+1)\sum_{i=1}^{n}\hat{\sigma}_i^2}}. \tag{5.14}$$

The TS thus calculated enables to infer p-values and calculate confidence intervals. Note that asymptotically (sample size wise) and for a long enough estimation window, the p-values may be approximated by the standard normal distribution. $\widehat{CAARs}$ and their confidence intervals along the event window shed light on the information content of the event. In terms of hypothesis testing in this context, the null hypothesis, presuming the absence of reaction to the studied event, is tested against a specified alternative hypothesis:[10]

H_0: no stock-price reaction to the studied event;
H_1: stock-price reaction in a specific direction according to the proposed underlying story.

The general idea is to confront the null hypothesis with $\widehat{CAARs}$. If they are too "irregular" and point to the proposed underlying story, the null hypothesis is to be rejected. Technically speaking, the distributional properties of $\widehat{CAARs}$ provide the probability that they exceed any specific value at any point within the event window, under the null hypothesis of no effect of the studied event on stock prices. If this probability is found to be rather low, say less than 5 percent or some other predefined threshold, then the null hypothesis is rejected.

5.2. Two Hypothetical ESA Cases

We henceforth illustrate the analysis of the following two questions: (1) have the stock prices reacted to the studied event? and (2) what may be inferred regarding market efficiency? To do so, we introduce a couple of hypothetical cases, case I and case II, and their resulting $\widehat{CAAR}$ series, denoted by $\widehat{CAAR}(I)$ and $\widehat{CAAR}(II)$, respectively. For both cases, we assume that the null hypothesis of no reaction to the studied event is tested against the alternative of positive reaction (i.e., the underlying story conveyed by disseminated information is "good news").

We start with the exploration of case I and the first question regarding stock-price reaction to the studied event. Recall that a reaction to the event may start even before public dissemination of the information. Thus, our first inspection should employ a $\widehat{CAAR}$ series that begins before the event date. Conceivably, often a starting date within a few weeks before the event date is selected. Henceforth, we denote the starting date by s, keeping in mind that, practically, the $\widehat{CAAR}$ series starts at the beginning of the event window. Figure 5.2 depicts $\widehat{CAAR}_{s,t}(I)$, that is, $\widehat{CAAR}(I)$ from the beginning of the event window (vertical axis is placed at $t = 0$). In addition to $\widehat{CAAR}_{s,t}(I)$, two confidence thresholds are plotted, for testing the null hypothesis of no stock-price reaction against the alternative of positive price reaction, with confidence levels of 95 percent and 99 percent, to wit, respective significance levels of 5 percent and 1 percent (light and dark grey curves). Evidently, $\widehat{CAAR}_{s,t}(I)$ never crosses either one of the confidence thresholds, so that the null hypothesis of "no reaction" cannot be rejected at the significance levels determined above, when tested on $\widehat{CAAR}_{s,t}(I)$, from the beginning of the event window.

Having detected no pattern rejecting the null hypothesis with tests on periods starting from s, we turn to look at the $\widehat{CAAR}$ series from the event date. In Figure 5.3, $\widehat{CAAR}_{s,t}(I)$ is offset vertically, such that the resulting

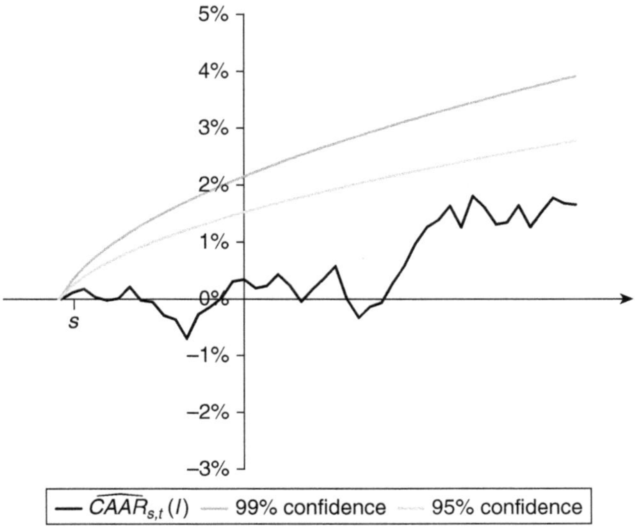

Figure 5.2 $\widehat{CAAR}_{s,t}(I)$ and confidence thresholds from time *s*.

Evidently, $\widehat{CAAR}_{s,t}(I)$ (black curves) does not exceed the confidence thresholds of 95 and 99 percent (light and dark grey curves, respectively), leading to the conclusion that no market reaction was detected by tests inspecting the $\widehat{CAAR}$ pattern from the beginning of the event window.

graph crosses the horizontal axis just before the event date. We refer to the resulting series as $\widehat{CAAR}_{0,t}(I)$ and depict it in a dashed manner till the event date, and in a continuous graph from that date on, to stress the fact that only the latter part is inspected now. Evidently, $\widehat{CAAR}_{0,t}(I)$ also never crosses either one of the confidence thresholds, so that the null hypothesis of "no reaction" cannot be rejected at these significance levels also when the $\widehat{CAAR}$ pattern is inspected from the event date.

Thus far, case I illustrated how to deal with the first question of stock-price reaction to the studied event and showed that the null hypothesis of no market reaction cannot be rejected in this case. We would have turned now to the second question, to wit, the issue of market efficiency. However, in the absence of any irregular pattern in $\widehat{CAAR}(I)$, quantifying the characteristics of the reaction toward shedding light on market efficiency is impossible. Thus, we turn to the second hypothetical case,

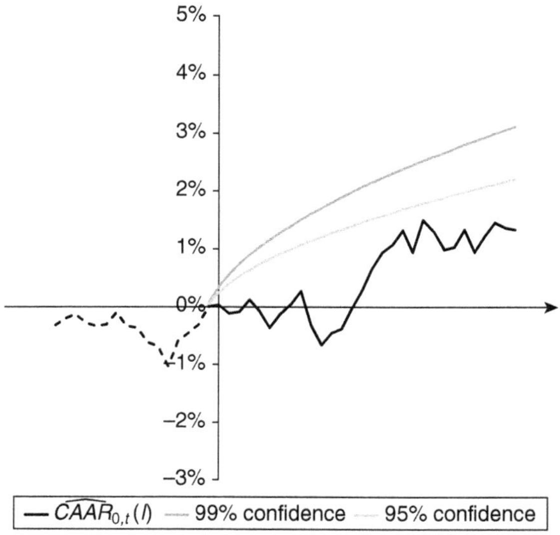

Figure 5.3 $\widehat{CAAR}_{0,t}(I)$ and confidence thresholds from the event date.

Evidently, $\widehat{CAAR}_{0,t}(I)$ (black curve) does not exceed either one of the confidence thresholds of 95 and 99 percent (light and dark grey curves, respectively), leading to the conclusion that no reaction was detected when the $\widehat{CAAR}$ pattern is inspected from the event date.

case II, for which we reiterate the steps for dealing with the question of stock-price reaction to the studied event and pursue also the issue of market efficiency.

Figure 5.4 provides estimated CAAR series for case II, namely, $\widehat{CAAR}_{s,t}(II)$ (black curve). The figure also depicts the 95 percent and 99 percent confidence thresholds emanating from the starting point of the event window (light and dark grey curves). In this case, $\widehat{CAAR}_{s,t}(II)$ appears to cross the 95 percent confidence threshold (light grey curve), while not crossing the 99 percent confidence threshold (dark grey curve). Thus, the null hypothesis of "no reaction" is rejected in favor of the alternative hypothesis of positive stock-price reaction to the studied event at the 95 percent confidence level, but not at the 99 percent confidence level.

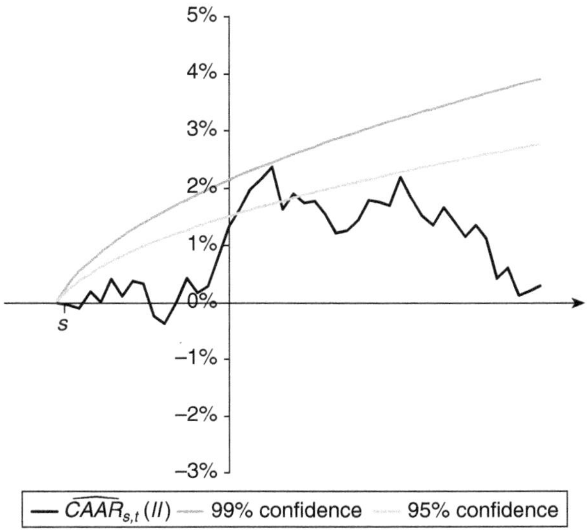

Figure 5.4 $\widehat{CAAR}_{s,t}(II)$ and confidence thresholds from time s.

$\widehat{CAAR}_{s,t}(II)$ (black curve) exceeds the confidence threshold of 95 percent (light grey curve), while not exceeding the 99 percent threshold (dark grey curve), leading to the conclusion that reaction to the studied event is detected at the 95 percent confidence level, but not at the 99 percent confidence level.

To further evaluate the effect of the studied event on stock prices, we concentrate on the ARs from the event day on by vertically offsetting $\widehat{CAAR}_{s,t}(II)$ to obtain a graph that crosses the horizontal axis just before the event day. We denote this series by $\widehat{CAAR}_{0,t}(II)$.

Figure 5.5 depicts $\widehat{CAAR}_{0,t}(II)$ along with its corresponding 95 percent (light grey) and 99 percent (dark grey) confidence thresholds. As seen in the figure, $\widehat{CAAR}_{0,t}(II)$ crosses both thresholds, rejecting thereby the null hypothesis of "no reaction" in favor of the alternative hypothesis of positive stock-price reaction at both (95 and 99 percent) confidence levels. Numerically, a reaction to the studied event is estimated at about 0.5 percent on the event date and accumulates to about 1.5 percent within the subsequent four days.

Having established that the studied event has an effect on stock prices, we turn to the issue of market efficiency. For doing so, the stock-price

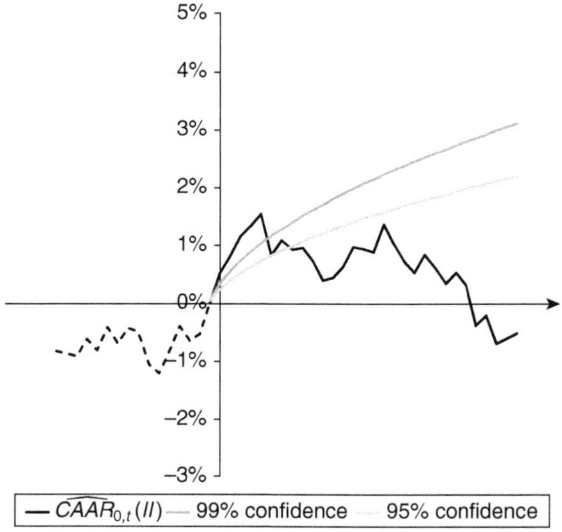

Figure 5.5 $\widehat{CAAR}_{0,t}(II)$ and confidence thresholds from the event date.

Evidently, $\widehat{CAAR}_{0,t}(II)$ (black curve) exceeds the confidence thresholds of 95 and 99 percent (light and dark grey curves, respectively) and accumulates to about 1.5 percent within four days from the event date.

reaction on the event day requires special attention. Its interpretation depends on the exact timing of events within the day. For the sake of this example, we assume the news release took place within the daily trading period, such that the closing prices on day 0 were recorded afterwards. Due to this sequence and the daily frequency nature of the return data, some of the day-0 AR may have taken place before the public release of the information. Thus, in the absence of intraday data, testing for market efficiency has to be performed by looking at returns from $t = 1$, that is, excluding day-0 returns.

To concentrate on ARs after the event day, we vertically offset $\widehat{CAAR}(II)$ to obtain a graph that crosses the horizontal axis on day $t = 0$ (again, the part of the graph before intersection with the horizontal axis is dashed). We denote this series by $\widehat{CAAR}_{1,t}(II)$. Figure 5.6 depicts $\widehat{CAAR}_{1,t}(II)$ along with its corresponding 95 percent (light grey) and 99 percent (dark grey) confidence thresholds. As seen in the figure, $\widehat{CAAR}_{1,t}(II)$ crosses both

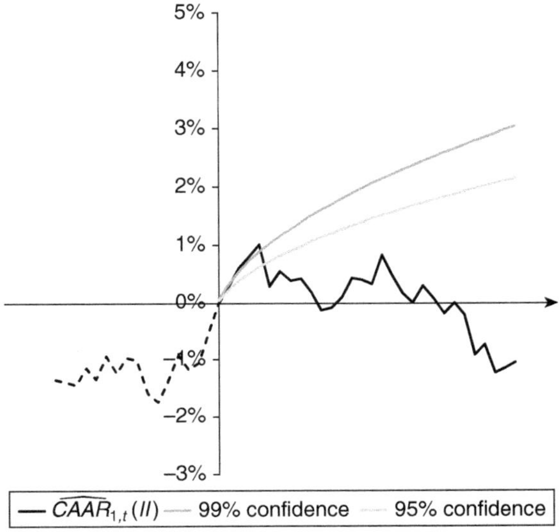

Figure 5.6 $\widehat{CAAR}_{1,t}(II)$ and corresponding confidence thresholds.

Evidently, $\widehat{CAAR}_{1,t}(II)$ (black curve) exceeds the confidence thresholds of 95 and 99 percent (light and dark grey curves, respectively), rejecting, therefore, market efficiency.

thresholds, rejecting thereby the null hypothesis of (semistrong) market efficiency with 99 percent confidence. According to this analysis, a CAAR of about 1 percent may be attributed to trading activity after information release, that is, may be tagged as inefficient reaction to the studied event.

To summarize, we employed two hypothetical cases for discussing the basic ESA design and analyzed the results with respect to reaction to the studied event, as well as regarding the issue of market efficiency. While these examples have shed light on the approach, note that each event study has its own specific properties and may require, therefore, specific adjustments. Chapter 6 elaborates on some frequently encountered issues, such as clustering of event dates, reaction with unspecified direction under the tested story, bond (as opposed to stock) price reaction, effect of the event on whole-firm value, long-run market reaction, and nonparametric event study designs.

Chapter 6

Issues in ESA Design

Chapter 3 outlined the fundamental stages of ESA, the essence of which we employed in the simplified example introduced in chapter 4, and chapter 5 presented a detailed recap of the basic ESA technique and demonstrated statistical analysis and hypothesis testing. The present chapter elaborates on frequently encountered technical issues and corresponding event study designs. In doing so, we do not purport to offer an exhaustive catalog embracing all existing caveats. Rather, our goal is to discuss common issues in a readily accessible manner, addressing the needs of academic researchers and practitioners who are interested in getting acquainted with ESA. Elaborate discussions on these and related topics are offered by a number of available ESA methodological reviews. For instance, Peterson (1989) and MacKinlay (1997) are two such relevant surveys. Another broad review by Kothari and Warner (2007) offers a thorough discussion on related issues with multiple references to classical, as well as more recent, event studies. We begin with the issue of *clustering* among the sample observations, to wit, with situations where event windows of the sampled securities are overlapping.

6.1. Clustering

The basic statistical analysis outlined in the previous chapter assumed that there was no clustering among the observations and hence returns of different securities comprising the sample were assumed to be independent.

The independence assumption was fundamental to the analysis, for in its absence the outlined procedure would result in inaccurate inferences (Brown and Warner 1980, 1985). In particular, the TS calculated by equation (5.14) in chapter 5 would have been biased upward (Kothari and Warner 2007).

In practice, the independence assumption is not always appropriate. For instance, if the event windows of some or even all sample securities overlap, that is, in case some stocks' ARs belong to the same calendar dates, it is conceivable that they would be somewhat correlated. This issue may be relevant in various empirical events, such as periodical releases of accounting information, or certain "big" events possibly affecting the entire market simultaneously (the former has been discussed by Bernard, 1987, and the latter by Kliger and Sarig, 2000, who examined market reaction to the refinement of Moody's credit rating system, an event that took place simultaneously for all of the rated bonds).[1]

The issue of clustering may be addressed by forming a portfolio of ARs and subsequently using its estimated variability for hypothesis testing. In this way, insofar as the time series of portfolio returns accounts for cross-sectional correlations of its constituents, the issue of clustering is resolved. Hence, the adjusted statistical procedure suitable for the analysis of clustered data is as follows.[2]

As in chapter 5, we start from the point where NRs have already been estimated for all the securities. In contrast to chapter 5, however, the following procedure does not assume cross-sectional independence among observations.

- For each security i, we generate a series of estimated ARs over the estimation and event windows (see Figure 5.1 for timeline notation):

$$\widehat{AR}_t^i \equiv R_t^i - \widehat{NR}_t^i;\ i{=}1,\ldots,n;\begin{cases} t=t_{Start}^{EstWin}+1,\ldots,t_{End}^{EstWin} \\ t=t_{Start}^{EventWin}+1,\ldots,t_{End}^{EventWin}. \end{cases} \tag{6.1}$$

- For each subsample consisting of observations with the same hypothesized market reaction according to the proposed underlying story, we calculate a series of estimated AARs over the event and estimation windows:

$$\widehat{AAR}_t = \frac{\sum_{i=1}^{n} \widehat{AR}_t^i}{n}; \quad i = 1,\ldots,n; \begin{cases} t = t_{Start}^{EstWin} + 1,\ldots,t_{End}^{EstWin} \\ t = t_{Start}^{EventWin} + 1,\ldots,t_{End}^{EventWin} \end{cases} \tag{6.2}$$

Note that these estimated AARs account for cross-sectional interdependencies among the observations. The basic statistical approach assumes, therefore, that they are approximately normal and independent and identically distributed random variables, to wit:

$$\widehat{AAR}_t \overset{\cdot}{\sim} N\left(0, \sigma^2\left(\widehat{AAR}_t\right)\right), \tag{6.3}$$

where $\sigma^2\left(\widehat{AAR}_t\right)$ is the conditional variance of $\widehat{AAR}_t$ under the null hypothesis of absence of any effect by the event under study.

- We estimate $\sigma^2\left(\widehat{AAR}_t\right)$ as follows:

$$\sigma^2\left(\widehat{AAR}_t\right) = \frac{1}{t_{End}^{EstWin} - t_{Start}^{EstWin}} \sum_{t=t_{Start}^{EstWin}}^{t_{End}^{EstWin}} \left[\widehat{AAR}_t - \overline{AAR}\right]^2, \tag{6.4}$$

where

$$\overline{AAR} \equiv \sum_{t=t_{Start}^{EstWin}}^{t_{End}^{EstWin}} \widehat{AAR}_t \,/\, (t_{End}^{EstWin} - t_{Start}^{EstWin}) \tag{6.5}$$

is the average of $\widehat{AARs}$.[3]

- We aggregate $\widehat{AARs}$ from a specific starting point s within the event window up to a subsequent date t taking place till the end of the event window, to yield cumulative estimates:

$$\widehat{CAAR}_{s,t} \equiv \sum_{\tau=s}^{t} \widehat{AAR}_\tau. \tag{6.6}$$

- We estimate the conditional variances of $\widehat{CAARs}$ from time s to t as follows:[4]

$$\sigma^2\left(\widehat{CAAR}_{s,t}\right) = (t-s+1)\ \sigma^2\left(\widehat{AAR}_t\right), \tag{6.7}$$

and their conditional standard deviations:

$$\hat{\sigma}^{CAAR}_{s,t} \equiv \sqrt{\sigma^2\left(\widehat{CAAR}_{s,t}\right)} = \sqrt{t-s+1}\ \sigma\left(\widehat{AAR}_t\right). \tag{6.8}$$

- Thus, the null hypothesis may be tested for each $\widehat{CAAR}_{s,t}$ with the following TS, which has approximately a standard normal distribution, for a large number of observations and long estimation window:

$$TS_{s,t} = \widehat{CAAR}_{s,t} / \hat{\sigma}^{CAAR}_{s,t} \mathrel{\dot\sim} N(0,1). \tag{6.9}$$

Plugging the standard deviation (6.7) and expressing in daily terms according to equation (6.4) yields the formula for the TS which may be directly applied to the data:

$$TS_{s,t} = \frac{\widehat{CAAR}_{s,t}}{\sqrt{(t-s+1)\left(\frac{1}{t^{EstWin}_{End} - t^{EstWin}_{Start}} \sum_{t=t^{EstWin}_{Start}}^{t^{EstWin}_{End}} [\widehat{AAR}_t - \overline{AAR}]^2\right)}}, \tag{6.10}$$

with $\overline{AAR}$ as in equation (6.5). From here, the process is similar to that described in chapter 5, to wit, TS enables performing the relevant hypothesis testing.

6.2. Nonparametric Design

The standard procedure of an event study outlined in chapter 5 requires, among other things, parametric estimation of AR distribution under the null hypothesis of no reaction to the studied event. Another way of approaching the analysis is by employing nonparametric testing. Some studies argue that nonparametric tests may be superior to parametric methods in event studies (Corrado 1989; Cowan 1992). However, other studies argue that under certain conditions the use of nonparametric, as compared to parametric, tests may be unwarranted (Berry, Gallinger, and Henderson, 1990). Thus, the choice of an appropriate test for any particular case deserves careful consideration. At any rate, as in the case with employing alternative return benchmarks, the robustness of results may also be assessed by using both parametric and nonparametric tests within the same study. Below we sketch two common nonparametric methods, namely, the sign and the rank tests.

The sign test (MacKinlay 1997) focuses on the signs of estimated ARs while presuming that under normal conditions these are equally likely to be positive or negative.[5] Thus, a TS for the sign test, denoted by TS_t^{sign}, which has asymptotically a standard normal distribution, may be employed:

$$TS_t^{sign} \equiv \left(\frac{n_t^+}{n} - 0.5\right)\frac{\sqrt{n}}{0.5} \mathrel{\dot\sim} N(0,1), \tag{6.11}$$

where

n_t^+ is the number of securities with positive $\widehat{AR}_t^i$, and n is the number of observations both counted in a subsample of observations having the same hypothesized AR sign.[6]

While a necessary condition for the appropriateness of the sign test is symmetry of the underlying distribution, this is not necessarily the case with actual AR distributions. Insofar as the skewness of daily ARs is consequential, the sign test is misspecified. The rank test (see Corrado 1989) was devised to overcome this problem. It inspects the ranks of the estimated ARs, thus allowing for unequal proportions of positive and negative returns under normal conditions, as is the case with skewed distributions.

To perform the rank test, the estimated ARs for each security within the event window are ranked from one to the number of days comprising the event window. The test presumes that under normal conditions the rank of $\widehat{AR}_t^i$ is expected to be $\left(t_{End}^{EventWin} - t_{Start}^{EventWin} + 1\right)/2$.[7] Accordingly, the statistic for the rank test for testing the hypothesis of no reaction to the studied event on day t, against its alternative, denoted by TS_t^{rank}, is defined as follows:

$$TS_t^{rank} = \frac{1}{n}\sum_{i=1}^{n}\left(K_t^i - \frac{t_{End}^{EventWin} - t_{Start}^{EventWin} + 1}{2}\right) / \, s(K) \stackrel{\cdot}{\sim} N(0,1), \qquad (6.12)$$

in that

$$s(K) = \sqrt{\frac{1}{t_{End}^{EventWin} - t_{Start}^{EventWin}} \sum_{\tau = t_{Start}^{EventWin}}^{t_{End}^{EventWin}} \left[\frac{1}{n}\sum_{i=1}^{n}\left(K_\tau^i - \frac{t_{End}^{EventWin} - t_{Start}^{EventWin} + 1}{2}\right)\right]^2}, \qquad (6.13)$$

where

n is the number of observations in the subsample of observations having the same hypothesized AR sign under the alternative hypothesis, and K_t^i is the rank of $\widehat{AR}_t^i$ within the event window.[8]

Under the null hypothesis of no reaction to the studied event, TS_0^{rank} is asymptotically normally distributed.[9]

6.3. Bidirectional Hypotheses

As noted in chapter 3, the reaction to the studied events often has a predictable direction. In the case of good news to security holders, they are expected to react positively to the event, raising the security prices, while in the case of bad news, they are expected to react negatively and, thus, security prices are expected to decline. Practically, to employ ESA, the data are to be partitioned into subsamples by the expected direction of reaction (positive, negative, and, possibly, no change); thus, the reaction within each of the subsamples should be separately portrayed. However, for some events it may be hard or even impossible to presume the direction of expected market reaction. In such cases, it may still be feasible to shed light on the relevance of the event to the market participants, by constructing bidirectional hypotheses. It is on this issue that we focus in the present section. Hereafter, we review a number of studies that dealt with the issue of unidentified hypothesized direction of security-price reaction.

The first situation to draw your attention to is where no specific direction may be hypothesized, but still it may be assumed that security prices will move in the *same* direction.[10] No particular assumption regarding the expected direction of price reaction would be appropriate when, for example, relevant theories suggest conceivable grounds for both directions. One such example is merger announcements' effect on stock prices of the acquiring firms, where synergy considerations suggest an upward movement of stock prices, while agency problems may suggest an opposite reaction.

Indeed, the picture emerging from the studies by Mandelker (1974), Langetieg (1978), and Dodd (1980) is mixed. The findings by Mandelker (1974) suggest that stockholders of acquiring firms earn NRs from mergers, consistent with the hypotheses that the market for acquisitions is perfectly competitive and information regarding mergers is efficiently incorporated into stock prices; Langetieg (1978) found negative stockholder gains from mergers; and Dodd (1980), who analyzed the returns of bidder firms' stock prices without assuming a specific direction of market reaction to the merger proposal announcements, leaving the data speak for themselves in that aspect, found a swift and large positive market reaction to the first public announcement of merger proposals, a subsequent positive reaction to the approval of completed proposals, and a negative reaction to cancelled proposals.

The second situation of unpredicted reaction direction is where the hypothesized direction of market reaction may vary among the sample securities. In this situation, the market reaction should be assessed by considering aspects other than unidirectional price changes. Such aspects include changes in trading volume, bid-ask spreads, and return volatility around the event. Henceforth, we elaborate on the first of these aspects, that is, assessing the market reaction by investigating the trading volume around the event.[11]

Campbell and Wasley (1996) studied methods of detecting abnormal trading volume by employing alternative benchmark models and parametric as well as nonparametric statistical testing. For illustrative purpose, we focus on one of the benchmarks employed by the authors and proceed to explain a parametric testing method.

To inspect the trading volume, Campbell and Wasley (1996) calculated the natural log of the percentage of firm *i*'s outstanding shares traded on day *t*, V_t^i, defined as follows:

$$V_t^i \equiv ln\left(\frac{n_t^i \times 100}{S_t^i}\right), \tag{6.14}$$

where

n_t^i is the number of firm *i*'s shares traded on day *t*, and
S_t^i is the total number of firm *i*'s outstanding shares on day *t*.

The estimated day *t* abnormal trading volume of firm *i*'s shares, $\widehat{AV}_t^i$, is defined as the deviation of V_t^i from the estimated normal trading volume of the firm's shares:

$$\widehat{AV}_t^i \equiv V_t^i - \widehat{NV}_t^i, \qquad (6.15)$$

where

V_t^i is firm *i*'s day *t* natural log of the percentage of outstanding shares traded, defined above, and

$\widehat{NV}_t^i$ is firm *i*'s day *t* normal estimated share trading volume.

The next step is to specify the normal trading volume. According to the *market model* benchmark, normal trading volume is determined according to the following equation:[12]

$$NV_t^i = \alpha_i + \beta_i V_t^m + \varepsilon_t^i, \qquad (6.16)$$

where

NV_t^i is stock *i*'s day *t* normal share trading volume;
V_t^m is the market trading volume measure;
α_i and β_i are stock *i*'s normal share-trading volume model parameters; and
ε_t^i is the model's error term.

Thus, firm *i*'s day *t* normal estimated share trading volume, $\widehat{NV}_t^i$, is:

$$\widehat{NV}_t^i = \hat{\alpha}_i + \hat{\beta}_i V_t^m, \qquad (6.17)$$

where

V_t^m is defined below, and

$\hat{\alpha}_i$ and $\hat{\beta}_i$ are stock i's estimated parameters obtained via OLS estimation over the estimation window.

The market index day t trading volume, V_t^m, is defined as follows:

$$V_t^m = \frac{1}{M}\sum_{j=1}^{M} V_t^j, \tag{6.18}$$

where

V_t^j is stock j's day t natural log of the percentage of outstanding shares traded, defined in equation (6.14), for each of the $j = 1,\ldots,M$ stocks comprising the market index.

The null hypothesis of the absence of any volume reaction to the studied event may be tested for any day t in the event window with the TS (TS_t^{volume}) defined below, which under conceivable assumptions has approximately a standard normal distribution, for a large number of observations and long estimation window:

$$TS_t^{volume} = \overline{AV}_t \,/\, s(\overline{AV}_t) \mathrel{\dot\sim} N(0,1), \tag{6.19}$$

where $\overline{AV}_t$ and $s(\overline{AV}_t)$ are the average and standard deviation of the estimated abnormal trading volume, respectively, calculated over n securities in the studied sample, to wit:

$$\overline{AV}_t \equiv \frac{1}{n}\sum_{i=1}^{n} \widehat{AV_t^i}; \tag{6.20}$$

$$s(\overline{AV}_t) = \sqrt{\frac{1}{t_{End}^{EstWin} - t_{Start}^{EstWin}} \sum_{\tau = t_{Start}^{EstWin}}^{t_{End}^{EstWin}} \left(\overline{AV}_\tau - \overline{AAV}\right)^2}; \tag{6.21}$$

and

$$\overline{AAV} \equiv \sum_{t = t_{Start}^{EstWin}}^{t_{End}^{EstWin}} \overline{AV}_t \,/\, (t_{End}^{EstWin} - t_{Start}^{EstWin}). \tag{6.22}$$

Plugging equation (6.22) in equation (6.19) yields the formula for the TS, which may be directly applied to the volume data:

$$TS_t^{volume} = \frac{\overline{AV}_t}{\sqrt{\frac{1}{t_{End}^{EstWin} - t_{Start}^{EstWin}} \sum_{\tau = t_{Start}^{EstWin}}^{t_{End}^{EstWin}} \left(\overline{AV}_\tau - \overline{AAV}\right)^2}}, \tag{6.23}$$

with $\overline{AAV}$ as in equation (6.22).[13]

6.4. Bond and Whole-Firm Reactions

While this book primarily focuses on employing ESA on common stock, the framework may be extended to study the effect of events on other securities, such as bonds, as well as on the whole-firm value. For instance, Weinstein (1977) studied the effect of bond rating changes on bond prices; Hite and Owers (1983) examined price reactions of stocks and bonds to corporate spin-offs; Handjinicolaou and Kalay (1984) evaluated the reactions of stock and bond prices to unexpected dividend changes; and Kliger and Sarig (2000) examined stock, bond, and whole-firm value reactions to the refinement of Moody's credit rating system.

Hereafter, we briefly discuss techniques employed for the analysis of other securities' reactions to events. Subsequently, we also discuss a multi-factor bond-return benchmark devised by Fama and French (1993). Note that our intention here is not to supply full instructions on the described methods, but rather to illustrate them and point to possible empirical approaches.

Similarly to the case with alternative benchmarks of stock returns discussed in chapter 3, different benchmarks of bond returns can be employed to assess bond-price reactions. Weinstein (1977) used bond rating portfolios to arrive at normal-return benchmarks. A bond's NR was defined as the return on a portfolio of bonds with the same rating, and its AR was estimated as follows:[14]

$$\widehat{AR}_t^i = R_t^i - R_t^B, \tag{6.24}$$

where

$\widehat{AR}_t^i$ is bond i's estimated AR at period t;
R_t^i is bond i's return at period t; and
R_t^B is the return on the portfolio of bonds with the same rating as that of bond i at period t.

The bond ARs thus estimated were accumulated along the event window to yield CAR estimates, which were then analyzed similarly as in stocks' event studies.

A different approach was taken by Hite and Owers (1983), who examined price reactions of various securities to corporate spin-off announcements. For the analyzed senior stakeholder securities, which included straight and convertible bonds and preferred stocks, the authors assumed that continuously compounded daily returns have a normal distribution with constant mean and variance, which were estimated from a period prior to the event window, that is:

$$R_t^i \sim N(\mu_i, \sigma_i^2), \tag{6.25}$$

where

R_t^i is security i's day t return;
μ_i is the mean of security i's daily return; and
σ_i^2 is the variance of security i's daily return.

Assuming serial independence, security i's cumulative daily return from a specific starting point s up to a subsequent date t, denoted by $CR_{s,t}^i$, has the following normal distribution:

$$CR_{s,t}^i \equiv \sum_{\tau=s}^{t} R_\tau^i \sim N\left((t-s+1)\mu_i, (t-s+1)\sigma_i^2\right), \tag{6.26}$$

where

R_τ^i is security i's day τ return;
μ_i is the mean of security i's daily return, and
σ_i^2 is the variance of security i's daily return.

Under these assumptions, security *i*'s CAR from *s* to *t*, denoted by $CAR^i_{s,t}$, is:

$$CAR^i_{s,t} \equiv CR^i_{s,t} - (t - s + 1)\mu_i, \tag{6.27}$$

where

$CR^i_{s,t}$ is security *i*'s cumulative return from *s* to *t*, and
μ_i is the mean of security *i*'s daily return.

Following the above, security *i*'s estimated CAR from *s* to *t*, denoted by $\widehat{CAR}^i_{s,t}$, is:

$$\widehat{CAR}^i_{s,t} \equiv CR^i_{s,t} - (t - s + 1)\hat{\mu}_i, \tag{6.28}$$

where

$CR^i_{s,t}$ is security *i*'s cumulative return from *s* to *t*, and
$\hat{\mu}_i$ is the estimated mean of security *i*'s daily return.

To arrive at TSs, the estimated variance, denoted by $\hat{\sigma}^2_i$, was used to standardize the estimated abnormal security returns, which were accumulated over the event window, similarly to the abnormal stock returns.

The third approach, to be briefly addressed here, was taken by Handjinicolaou and Kalay (1984), who evaluated the reactions of stock and bond prices to dividend surprises. Raw bond returns were adjusted by subtracting the returns on corresponding treasury bonds with closest coupon rate and maturity.

Finally, Kliger and Sarig (2000) examined stock, bond, and whole-firm value reaction to the refinement of Moody's credit rating system. Three different benchmarks were used to model investors' expectations before the event: a naïve benchmark, a benchmark based on S&P ratings, and a market-based benchmark. The bonds' reaction to Moody's credit rating system refinement was assessed in two alternative approaches: by estimating the bonds' ARs and by measuring changes in the bonds' yield spreads.

More specifically, in the first approach a bond's AR around the rating system refinement was defined as the difference between its return during the period of the event and preevent yield to maturity. The following regression equation specifies the AR as estimated under this approach:

$$AR_i = \beta_0 + \sum_R \beta_R \Delta TS_i Dur_i I_{R,i} + \beta_{good} I_{good,i} + \beta_{bad} I_{bad,i} + \varepsilon_i, \qquad (6.29)$$

where

AR_i is bond i's AR around the event;
β_0 is the regression intercept;
β_R are rating-specific coefficients measuring the impact of term structure changes on ARs;
ΔTS_i is the change in risk-free yield for bond i's duration;
Dur_i is bond i's preevent modified Macaulay duration;
$I_{R,i}$ is bond i's coarse rating indicator;
$I_{good,i}$ and $I_{bad,i}$ are bond i's fine-rating good and bad news indicators;
β_{good} and β_{bad} are good and bad news estimated impacts; and
ε_i is the model's error term.

This approach differentiates the bond's event-related AR from that which is due to possible simultaneous changes in the term structure of interest rates.

The second approach examines systematic changes in bond yield spreads around the event, according to the following equation:

$$\Delta YS_i = \gamma_0 + \sum_R \gamma_R \Delta TS_i I_{R,i} + \gamma_{good} I_{good,i} + \gamma_{bad} I_{bad,i} + \xi_i, \qquad (6.30)$$

where

ΔYS_i is bond i's change in yield spread around the event;
γ_0 is the regression intercept;
γ_R are rating-specific coefficients measuring the impact of term structure changes on yield spreads;
ΔTS_i is the change in risk-free yield for bond i's duration;
$I_{R,i}$ is bond i's coarse rating indicator;
$I_{good,i}$ and $I_{bad,i}$ are bond i's fine-rating good and bad news indicators;
γ_{good} and γ_{bad} are good and bad news estimated impacts; and
ξ_i is the model's error term.

Fama and French (1993) developed a multifactor bond-return benchmark, which may be viewed as an augmentation of the three-factor stock-return benchmark discussed in chapter 3 (subsection 3.1.3). The three factors in the stock-return benchmark consisted of an overall market factor, the firm's size (equity market capitalization), and its book-to-market equity ratio. For the case of bond returns, Fama and French identified two additional bond-market factors, related to bond maturity and default risks. The resulting five-factor benchmark may be used to assess bonds' NRs. The two bond-related factors were defined as follows.[15] The maturity risk factor, denoted *TERM*, is the difference between the monthly long-term government bond return and the one-month treasury bill rate. The default risk factor, denoted *DEF*, is the difference between the return on a proxy for the market portfolio of corporate bonds (a bond market index) and the monthly long-term government bond return. Accordingly, bond i's return is represented by Fama and French's five-factor benchmark as follows:

$$R_t^i - R_t^f = \alpha_i + \beta_i (R_t^m - R_t^f) + s_i SMB_t + h_i HML_t + m_i TERM_t + d_i DEF_t + \varepsilon_t^i, \tag{6.31}$$

where

R_t^i is bond i's return at period t;
R_t^f is the risk-free return at period t;
R_t^m is the market return at period t;
SMB_t and HML_t are the "size" and book-to-market equity stock market factors;
$TERM_t$ and DEF_t are the maturity and default risk bond market factors;
α_i, β_i, s_i, h_i, m_i, d_i are the model's bond-specific parameters; and
ε_t^i is the model's error term.

Using this model, normal bond returns may be estimated, and the rest of the procedure is similar to that employed for stocks (see subsection 3.1.3 in chapter 3).

To summarize, in chapter 3 we discussed alternative return benchmarks for assessing the reaction of stock prices to studied events. Here, we presented bond-return benchmarks, which may be employed in quantifying bond price reactions to events. Recall that employing different benchmark models within a specific study would help in assessing the robustness of the results to model specification. While advanced benchmarks may have the advantage of analyzing returns in a more detailed manner, for instance, by referring to additional sources of risk, one should keep in mind that the more advanced a benchmark is, the more complicated is the structure it entails, and so that benchmark might be prone to more estimation error, compared to relatively less sophisticated benchmarks. Thus, simple benchmarks have their own merits and should be considered as well for providing a comprehensive picture of the effect of the studied event on security prices.

6.5. Long-run Reactions

While many event studies are focused on short-horizon reactions, with days-long or at most weeks-long event windows, some may be interested in long-horizon analysis where multiple months and even multiple years are examined. These studies are typically concerned with prolonged price reactions whose existence may indicate market inefficiency, thus falling into the category of *anomalies*. Behavioral finance is a field of research that seeks to explain such anomalies by psychological biases affecting investors' decision making. A review of studies belonging to this rapidly growing research area may be found in Hirshleifer (2001). Evidently, behavioral finance makes extensive use of ESA. For instance, behavioral biases were shown to have persistent effects on prices of initial public offerings (IPOs). Anomalies in long-run IPO performance have been documented by Ritter (1991) and analyzed by several subsequent studies, a recent example of which may be found in Kliger, Gurevich, and Haim (2012). Further, seasoned equity offerings (SEOs) have been shown by Loughran and Ritter (1995) and Foerster and Karolyi (2000) to be followed by prolonged price reactions. Long-run anomalies were also identified in numerous studies of price reactions to corporate events other than IPOs and SEOs. Rendleman, Jones, and Latané (1982) documented anomalies associated with delayed reactions to unexpected earnings announcements; Lakonishok and Vermaelen (1990) reported anomalous long-run price behavior following repurchase tender offers;

other reported anomalies include reactions to analyst recommendations, corporate spin-offs, stock splits, dividend omissions, and an array of other events.[16]

As Kothari and Warner (2007) pointed out, long-run event studies have essentially the same basic issues as short-run studies, but the estimation problems often become more pronounced when longer time periods are considered. The most important issues include risk adjustment methods, abnormal performance measurement, and statistical significance testing. For the purpose of this book, we shall highlight some select issues.

While less acute in short-run studies, the issue of risk adjustment becomes critical in long-horizon analyses (see, e.g., Brown and Warner 1985). Furthermore, due to the accumulation of estimation errors over longer time periods, estimates of ARs become highly sensitive to the choice of return benchmarks, which complicates the interpretation of results and exacerbates the problem of joint hypothesis (see chapter 2). Moreover, corporate events may follow periods of unusual performance, as, for example, stock splits often follow periods of high returns; hence, to avoid bias inherent in estimates based on unusual performance periods, postevent window periods may be worthwhile to consider for benchmark estimation. The benchmark selection is still another question. Multifactor benchmarks of Fama and French (1993, 1995) and Carhart (1997) described in chapter 3 are among the models presumed to capture reasonably well the most important risk factors and thus to plausibly estimate the incremental impacts of studied events.

Beside the issue of risk adjustment, there is the specific question of practical quantification of abnormal performance. To that end, either the *Jensen's Alpha portfolio approach* or the *matched-firm buy-and-hold abnormal return (BHAR) approach* may be employed.

Under Jensen's Alpha portfolio approach, a portfolio of securities undergoing the studied event is formed over the calendar time period within which the securities underwent the studied event. As the calendar event times are security-specific, the portfolio is rebalanced over the sample period. The resulting portfolio returns are then assessed using a model of returns, such as the multifactor benchmark of Fama and French (1993) or Carhart (1997). The AR, which may be seen as a variant of Jensen's Alpha, is estimated as the OLS intercept in a regression of the portfolio excess returns on the market (value-weighted index) excess returns. In effect, Jensen's Alpha is the constant (over the event window) portion of the portfolio return, which is unrelated to the risk factors captured by the employed benchmark.

The BHAR approach is based on investing, for a time period specified in advance, in the securities that underwent the event and comparing the investment return to the return of a portfolio consisting of similar, event-unrelated securities over the same time period. The comparison is based on the difference in the two portfolios' buy-and-hold (geometric) returns over the chosen period. Obviously, to determine matching securities, one must consider risk factor models, so the issue of an appropriate benchmark is still relevant, albeit indirectly, and all questions related to the choice of the model, joint hypothesis, etc., remain in place.

Lastly, an essential task posing a considerable challenge to long-horizon studies is the proper way of testing the statistical significance of results. In this respect, it is important to note that long-run return distributions may defy the assumption of normality required by many testing methods; exhibit cross-sectional correlation due to clustering of events, or serial correlation due to overlapping event windows; and be subject to event-related changes in volatility. While the issue of deviations from normality is generally less severe when sample size is large, the problem of cross-sectional correlation due to clustering of events is more challenging and may substantially bias the results of statistical testing in the absence of appropriate adjustment for clustering.[17] Even if event dates of sample securities do not exactly coincide but are close in calendar time, the estimation windows of sample securities might partially overlap, leading to serial correlation. In such cases, explicitly taking account of the serial correlation present in the data, rather than assuming independence, may to some extent provide remedy to this problem.

6.6. Return Frequency

In discussing possible statistical procedures, we focused mainly on daily stock returns. In practice, other data frequencies may be employed. To address the issue of return frequency, we henceforth elaborate on the aforementioned issues and summarize select empirical findings reported in Brown and Warner (1980, 1985). Brown and Warner used simulations to compare the advantages of employing monthly and daily data in event studies and to compare various ESA methods.[18] Specifically, they examined *type I error* probability, that is, the probability of rejecting the null hypothesis of no ARs when it is true, and *power of test*, that is, the probability of detecting existing ARs under different setups.

It turns out that, while possibly allowing for more powerful empirical tests and enabling to pinpoint the timing of events more precisely, daily data also suffer from some major drawbacks. For instance, daily returns might be characterized by more severe deviations from normality as compared to monthly returns. In particular, empirical daily stock return distributions are often *leptokurtic*, having more observations in their central part and extreme tails than expected under normal distribution. Brown and Warner showed that similar deviations from normality are also manifested by daily firm-specific ARs. Deviations from normality in daily returns may be accounted for by investigating cross-sections of mean returns, which converge to be normally distributed as the number of securities in the sample is increased. The question in the context of ESA is the extent to which this asymptotic distribution is arrived at in cross-sections of AARs. Indeed, Brown and Warner demonstrated that departures from normality are less severe for AARs than for firm-specific ARs. However, they emphasized that the assumption of normality is well justified primarily for relatively large samples. The sensitivity of daily data-based event studies to sample size is, therefore, an important caveat deserving attention. The same conclusion applies to the TSs whose distribution was found to be, by and large, close to normal, but possibly slightly skewed and leptokurtic. The authors concluded that for most examined benchmark models the TSs are well specified and reliable, but significance levels obtained from smaller samples should be taken with caution. Overall, the empirical deviations of daily returns from normality do not seem to pose a substantial difficulty for ESA.

Another potentially problematic aspect of daily data stems from nonsynchronous trading of stocks and market index, as shown by Scholes and Williams (1977). The effect was found to generate biased and inconsistent OLS parameter estimates of the single-factor benchmark of returns, which are based on daily data. For instance, it has been shown that for relatively infrequently traded stocks, OLS Betas are biased downward, while for relatively frequently traded stocks, OLS Betas have an upward bias. The problem led to the development of alternative methods of parameter estimation. To clarify possible consequences of this issue for ESA, comparisons of different estimation procedures, including OLS and Scholes-Williams technique, were performed by Brown and Warner. The authors detected no advantage with the alternative techniques as compared to OLS parameter estimation. While reducing the bias in estimates, the alternative procedures conferred no clear improvement upon either model specification or the power of tests. Overall, the bias introduced into parameter estimates of the single-factor benchmark of returns by nonsynchronous trading seemed to be of no serious consequences to ESA.

Yet another complicating feature of daily data is the possibility of serial dependence in ARs. Indeed, empirical findings reported in Brown and Warner (1985) indicate statistically significant, although not especially large in magnitude, autocorrelations in ARs, which are not eliminated even by employing correctional procedures such as the technique proposed in Scholes and Williams (1977). One way to handle this problem is to explicitly account for serial correlation in statistical analysis. However, as Brown and Warner noted, doing so in most instances had no serious consequences. Only occasionally, adjustments for autocorrelation had a noticeable effect on TSs. Overall, the issue of autocorrelation does not seem to impede the use of daily data.

The general conclusion of the study by Brown and Warner (1985) was that the advantages of daily data, in particular the higher power of tests and the better time resolution as compared to monthly data, beat their drawbacks.

Chapter 7

Hands-on Exercise

Having explained the basic framework of ESA (chapter 5), we now turn to the main practical part of the book—an exercise to give you hands-on experience with ESA so that you obtain the required technical skills to conduct your own event studies. The present chapter introduces a specific research question and demonstrates how to address it. The chapter is built as an empirical exercise; the following sections provide some necessary background points, reiterate the basic ESA framework applied to the specific case at hand, and describe the dataset and predesigned spreadsheet template. The guiding instructions will take you, hand-in-hand, through the solution process and explanations of the obtained results.

In this chapter, you are going to conduct a complete basic event study. You will start from the already provided data on events and related stock and index prices, estimate ARs employing the naïve benchmark of returns, and then estimate CAARs and assess their statistical properties, which are required for hypothesis testing. Then, you will plot the graphs of the estimated CAARs and their and confidence intervals and derive conclusions regarding the extent and timing of market reaction to the earnings announcements.

The ESA exercise in this chapter employs the process described in chapter 5, to wit, assumes that the data are not clustered. While this assumption does not completely hold in the actual dataset provided in the template, the exact clustering features of the data would not hamper our instructional purposes. In the next chapter, among other extensions to the basic setup discussed here, a walk-through with an exercise that accounts for clustering is provided.

7.1. Exercise Research Questions

The exercise investigates the market reaction to companies' earnings announcements. As pointed out in chapter 2, earnings announcements comprise the subject of a range of market reaction studies whose results, in general, are mixed. Briefly reiterating some of the findings, Aharony and Swary (1980) found that the market quickly adjusts to the new information inherent in companies' quarterly announcements, while Rendleman, Jones, and Latané (1982), using a different data sample, found that roughly half of the total reaction to the most significant earnings surprises was observed in the course of 90 days following the official announcement, a result apparently at odds with market efficiency. More results have been reported by a range of other studies of market reaction to earnings announcements, some of which may be found in Fama (1991). Attempts to explain the mixed results regarding market efficiency include refining the techniques of AR measurement or, alternatively, appealing to an inadequate understanding of quarterly announcements by market participants. More recently, Bartov, Radhakrishnan, and Krinsky (2000) found evidence that market inefficiency observed by post earnings-announcement return patterns is inversely related to the extent of institutional security holdings, suggesting that investors' sophistication may indeed be a source of observed anomalies; however, the authors note that the validity of institutional holdings as a proxy for investors' sophistication remains to be established. In either case, the question of market reaction to earnings surprises is intriguing and serves as a nontrivial basis for our exercise.

To assess market reaction to the information inherent in earnings announcements, we track down the reporting companies' stock returns around the information release. If we find slow or incomplete reaction to the event, we would interpret it as refuting EMH. Conversely, if we find an immediate, full reaction, we would interpret it as being in line with EMH, to wit, we would not reject the hypothesis of market efficiency. The practical result of market efficiency is that conditioning on the news may not provide any trading rule that enables "beating the market." Further interesting research questions also refer to the timing of market reaction. For instance, one may be interested to ask how early the reaction started; whether it continued beyond the day of announcement; how much of reaction (if at all) occurred with a delay; and how long it took for the reaction to be fully incorporated into the prices.

Recall that measuring market reaction involves defining NRs, which in turn involves defining a return benchmark against which actual stock returns are assessed. In the current chapter, we present the basic solution that employs the naïve benchmark of returns, according to which the NR is the concurrent aggregate market return, so that the AR is defined as the deviation from the market return (see subsection 3.1.1 of chapter 3).[1]

7.2. Data Description

For this hands-on exercise, we employ earnings announcement records. The sample consists of 670 individual firms' earnings announcements issued by companies belonging to the services and technology sectors between January 9, 2007, and February 28, 2007. In addition, we use daily stock prices of the firms which announced their earnings, related S&P 500 Index levels, and earnings estimates of analysts. Each firm appears in our sample only once, though there is usually more than one event per calendar date. To facilitate the solution and permit full concentration on the ESA application, we filtered, preprocessed, and organized the original records. The data for each observation include the calendar date of the earnings announcement, announcing firm's name, stock ticker, and market sector. Each earnings announcement appears in terms of earnings per share (EPS) and is accompanied by the contemporaneous analyst-consensus EPS forecast. Each firm's announced EPS and analysts' consensus forecast are normalized by dividing them by the stock price on the announcement date.[2] We employ the difference between these two normalized figures as an assessment of the surprise component of the firm's earnings announcement.

Below we provide a detailed description of the data as appearing in the predesigned electronic spreadsheet file.

7.3. Meeting the Dataset and Spreadsheet Template

To facilitate the solution process, we devised an Excel template for you to work on based on our instructions. The Excel template (http://dx.doi.org/10.6084/m9.figshare.1221836), as well as a file with the complete solution (http://dx.doi.org/10.6084/m9.figshare.1221835), may be downloaded from the book's website. You may choose to either solve the exercise using our detailed instructions and provided template, or work independently on a copy of the dataset file (http://dx.doi.org/10.6084/m9.figshare.1221834).

A list of worksheets may be found in Table 7.1. The first four worksheets contain data that we collected and processed and some descriptive information; the next ten worksheets are structured to contain your solution according to the provided guidelines; and the remaining worksheets (whose names begin with the word "GRAPH") are predesigned to show the ESA results in a graphical manner. We term these groups of worksheets as *DataSheets*, *WorkingSheets*, and *GraphSheets*, respectively. The tabs of the *DataSheets* and *GraphSheets* are red, and those of the *WorkingSheets* are green. The tab colors serve as a "traffic light," reminding you in which sheets you are allowed (green) or not allowed (red) to modify cell contents. Below we introduce the worksheets and explain their specific purposes, design, and detailed contents.

The Excel template (http://dx.doi.org/10.6084/m9.figshare.1221836) and the complete solution (http://dx.doi.org/10.6084/m9.figshare.1221835) contain all the worksheets introduced above. The dataset file (http://dx.doi.org/10.6084/m9.figshare.1221834, to be used for independent working) consists of *DataSheets* only.

A caveat regarding notation in Excel files is in place here. As Excel files have limited notation flexibility, and we want to keep the variable names concise, we apply less rigorous notation in the files than in the body of text.

We constructed the worksheets in a way that keeps the events in fixed rows up to the point where the data are split into categories according to the hypothesized direction of reaction to the event. The events' data up to that point appear in rows 2 to 671, with the first event in row 2 and the last in row 671. Subsequently, the data of each category are handled in a separate worksheet. In addition, the relative event dates are kept in fixed columns, throughout the worksheets. When relevant, the data for $t = -31$ to $t = 90$ appear in rows S to EJ, respectively. As a result, column AX contains data for the event date ($t = 0$). Additionally, the worksheets

Table 7.1 Exercise file: worksheets content and design

Worksheets	Description
DataSheets	
TOU	Terms of use: Personal and noncommercial use limitation
README	Abbreviated description of the variables contained in the dataset
STOCK DATA	Firms' characteristics and stock price records (see details below)
INDEX DATA	Market index (S&P 500) records for the event dates (the firms' characteristics appear again, for convenience)
WorkingSheets	
STOCK RETURNS	Placeholder for calculating stock returns
INDEX RETURNS	Placeholder for calculating index returns
AR	Placeholder for estimating ARs
AR GOOD / AR MET / AR BAD	Placeholders for partitioning the estimated ARs into categories according to the direction of the hypothesized reaction to the event
CAR GOOD / CAR MET / CAR BAD	Placeholders for the estimated CARs, partitioned by the categories according to the direction of the hypothesized reaction to the event
CAAR	Placeholder for estimating CAAR series
GraphSheets	
GRAPH CAAR(–30, *t*) / (0, *t*) / (1, *t*) ALL	Placeholders for graphical representation of CAAR series
GRAPH CAAR(–30, *t*) GOOD / MET / BAD	
GRAPH CAAR(0, *t*) GOOD / MET / BAD	
GRAPH CAAR(1, *t*) GOOD / MET / BAD	

Table 7.2 *DataSheet* README: basic exercise data

Basic variable	Description
ID	Firm's database identification number
EventDate	Earnings announcement calendar date ($t = 0$)
rEPS	Reported EPS normalized by stock price on event day
cEPS	Consensus EPS normalized by stock price on event day
Surprise	Difference between rEPS and cEPS
Good / Met / Bad	Dummies for Upside/Met Expectations/Downside Surprises
P(t)	Stock price on day t relative to the event date
M(t)	S&P 500 Index level on day t relative to the event date

reintroduce some observation-related data from *DataSheet* STOCK DATA in columns A to R. We find this structure helpful for understanding the relations among the various cells and preventing errors of mismatching event and date information. You may visualize this structure of the file having three dimensions: the rows for the observations, the columns for the dates, and the sheets for the data processing stages.

Table 7.2 contains definitions and concise descriptions of the basic variables in our dataset. *DataSheet* README in the Excel files describes more variables that may be used for extensions, some of which are presented in the next chapter, and also lists the variables that should be calculated while solving the exercise.

DataSheet STOCK DATA contains information on firms undergoing the event and their relevant stock price data. Recall that each row in this worksheet, from 2 to 671, comprises one observation, which is identified by the firm's database identification number (ID). Each observation contains details on the stock of one company that underwent the analyzed event (to wit, has announced its earnings figure). Table 7.3 describes the contents of *DataSheet* STOCK DATA in detail.

The event date is defined as t=0. The stock prices are recorded for the period starting from 31 days before and up to 90 days after the event, that is, from $t = -31$ to $t = 90$. We define the event and estimation windows on these data as follows (see the timeline for basic example in Figure 7.1).

$$\text{The event window: } t_{Start}^{EventWin},\ldots,t_{End}^{EventWin} = -31,\ldots,30$$

$$\text{The estimation window: } t_{Start}^{EstWin},\ldots,t_{End}^{EstWin} = 31,\ldots,90$$

Note that in this example we took the less commonly employed approach of placing the estimation window after, rather than before, the event window. While under the null hypothesis of no reaction to the studied event this approach is well specified, it is mainly used in other contexts such as long-run event studies.

The firms' EPS and the corresponding analyst-consensus EPS forecast (both normalized by dividing by the day 0 stock price) are denoted as rEPS and cEPS, respectively (see Table 7.3). The variable "Surprise" is defined as the difference between rEPS and cEPS. In the event study vocabulary,

Table 7.3 *DataSheet* STOCK DATA: individual firm characteristics and event records

Column	Column title	Data description
A	Sector	Firm's business activity area
B	ID	Firm's database identification number
C	EventDate	Earnings announcement calendar date
D	Company	Firm's full name
E	Ticker	Firm's stock exchange symbol
F	rEPS	Reported EPS normalized by stock price on event day
G	cEPS	Consensus EPS normalized by stock price on event day
H	Surprise	Difference between rEPS and cEPS
I	P(–1)	Adjusted closing price of the stock on day –1
J	P(0)	Adjusted closing price of the stock on the event day
K	R(0)	Event day stock return
L	Volume(0)	Trading volume on the event day
M	Good	Positive Surprise indicator
N	Met	Met Expectations indicator
O	Bad	Negative Surprise indicator
P	MCap	Firm's market capitalization, $ millions
Q	Beta	Single-factor benchmark slope estimate (placeholder for exercise use)
R	Alpha	Single-factor benchmark intercept estimate (placeholder for exercise use)
S – EJ	P(t)	Adjusted stock price at the closing of day *t*

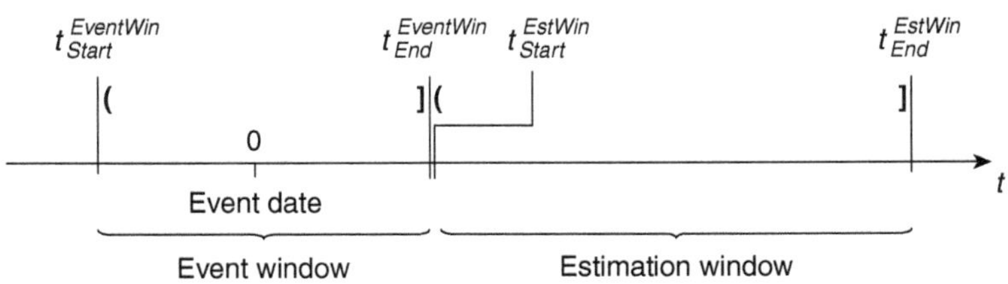

Figure 7.1 ESA basic example timeline: event window, event date, and estimation window.

"Surprise" is the "news" component, that is, the unexpected deviation of realized earnings from the forecast.

According to the "Surprise" variable, the sample contains three general categories of data: stocks with Upside Surprise (higher-than-expected earnings), Downside Surprise (lower-than-expected earnings), and Met Expectations (earnings as expected).

DataSheet INDEX DATA contains records of S&P 500 Index level matched for the calendar dates of stock prices in *DataSheet* STOCK DATA. The index records run from column S to EJ in parallel to the stock price data in *DataSheet* STOCK DATA (Table 7.3). The purpose of the index data is to provide a benchmark against which observed returns may be measured to gauge the reaction to the event.

The remaining worksheets in the exercise template are *WorkingSheets*, which are designed to contain the stages of the exercise solution. Many of them (all that contain disaggregated data) replicate the observations' characteristics in rows A to R. Columns to the right of that area, highlighted in green, are designed to contain various calculations, toward the production of the estimated CAAR series and their graphs. Generally, we highlight in green the cells that you should fill your calculations with (you may easily remember that you have a "green light" to write in these cells). We now turn to explaining the *WorkingSheets* in detail.

7.4. Putting Hands on the Data

You are now ready to process the data toward conducting the basic ESA exercise, which is built according to the path paved in chapter 5.[3] The Excel template for conducting this exercise (http://dx.doi.org/10.6084/m9.figshare.1221836) may be downloaded from the book's website.

In case you wish to solve the exercise without our intermediation, please skip the current section and use a copy of the dataset file (http://dx.doi.org/10.6084/m9.figshare.1221834) to work independently. When you finish, please rejoin in section 7.5 of this chapter for the results and discussion of the provided solution.

The instructions are given as a list of *stages*, each of which is divided into tractable *steps*, for which we detail the required calculations and designate the input data and venue for the output. In the construction of the stages and steps of the solution process, we made use of simple Excel functions and manipulations, such that technical Excel issues were kept to conceivable minimum.

Stage 1: AR Estimation

In the first stage, you start with the raw price data and arrive at estimated ARs, calculated according to the naïve benchmark of returns.

1.1 Calculate daily logarithmic return series for each stock, over the entire available data period, using the corresponding daily price series (see chapter 3 for details). Place the calculations in *WorkingSheet* STOCK RETURNS. Note that the first return to be calculated is for $t = -30$, since the earliest price available is for $t = -31$.

Input for this step: DataSheet STOCK DATA, columns S to EJ with *P(–31)... P(90)*.

Output of this step: WorkingSheet STOCK RETURNS, columns T to EJ for *R(–30)... R(90)*.

Formulas: Equation (3.2), adjusted to the current case.

$$R(l)_t^i \equiv ln\frac{P_t^i}{P_{t-1}^i} = ln\left(R(a)_t^i + 1\right);\ i = 1,\ldots,670;\ t = -30,\ldots,90. \quad (7.1)$$

Remark: For tractability, copy columns A to P of *DataSheet* STOCK DATA (with the observation characteristics) to columns A to P of *WorkingSheet* STOCK RETURNS. Note that columns Q and R are placeholders for the parameters of the single-factor model of returns, which will be estimated as part of one of the exercises in chapter 8.

1.2 Calculate daily logarithmic returns of the S&P 500 Index on the same dates as above, using the corresponding daily index series. Place the calculations in *WorkingSheet* INDEX RETURNS. Again, the first return to be calculated is for $t = -30$, since the earliest index data available are for $t = -31$.

Input for this step: DataSheet INDEX DATA, columns S to EJ with *M(–31)... M(90)*.

Output of this step: WorkingSheet INDEX RETURNS, columns T to EJ for *RM(–30)... RM(90)*.

Formulas: The same formula as in the above step, applied on the index data.

Remark: For tractability, copy columns A to P of *DataSheet* INDEX DATA (with the observation characteristics) to columns A to P of *WorkingSheet* INDEX RETURNS.

1.3 Calculate the estimated ARs for each stock, using the naïve benchmark of returns. Recall (chapter 3) that according to this model, AR is the difference between the stock's return and the contemporaneous index return. Place the calculations in *WorkingSheet* AR.

Input for this step: WorkingSheet STOCK RETURNS, columns T to EJ with *R(–30)... R(90)*; *WorkingSheet* INDEX RETURNS, columns T to EJ with *RM(–30)... RM(90)*.

Output of this step: WorkingSheet AR, columns T to EJ for *AR(–30)... AR(90)*.

Formulas: Equation (3.6), adjusted to the current case.

$$\widehat{AR}_t^i \equiv R_t^i - \widehat{NR}_t^i;\ i = 1,\dots,670;\ t = -30,\dots,90. \tag{7.2}$$

Remark: For tractability, copy columns A to P of *WorkingSheet* STOCK RETURNS (with the observation characteristics) to columns A to P of *WorkingSheet* AR.

Stage 2: Data Sorting

In this stage you partition the observations that you filled in the previous step in *WorkingSheet* AR by the Good/Met/Bad indicators, for separate analysis of each category of events. To do so, filter the data in *WorkingSheet* AR by each of the values in columns M, N, and O (Good/Met/Bad), copy the filtered data, and paste it to *WorkingSheets* AR GOOD/AR MET/AR BAD, respectively.

2.1 Filter the data in *WorkingSheet* AR by column M, to select the observations with Good=1, i.e., the observations for which there was an Upside Surprise. Copy the filtered data and paste to to *WorkingSheet* AR GOOD.

Input for this step: WorkingSheet AR, columns T to EJ with *AR(–30)...AR(90)*, rows with Good=1.

Output of this step: WorkingSheet AR GOOD, columns T to EJ for *AR(–30)...AR(90).*

Formulas: None (copy/paste step).

Remark: For tractability, copy the filtered columns A to P of *WorkingSheet* AR (with the observation characteristics) to columns A to P of *WorkingSheet* AR GOOD.

2.2 Next, filter the data in *WorkingSheet* AR by column N, to select the observations with Met=1, i.e., the observations for Met Expectations. Copy the filtered data and paste to *WorkingSheet* AR MET.

Input for this step: WorkingSheet AR, columns T to EJ with *AR(–30)...AR(90),* rows with Met=1.

Output of this step: WorkingSheet AR MET, columns T to EJ for *AR(–30)...AR(90).*

Formulas: None (copy/paste step).

Remark: For tractability, copy the filtered columns A to P of *WorkingSheet* AR (with the observation characteristics) to columns A to P of *WorkingSheet* AR MET.

2.3 Lastly, filter the data in *WorkingSheet* AR by column O, to select the observations with Bad=1, i.e., the observations for which there was a Downside Surprise. Copy the filtered data and paste to *WorkingSheet* AR BAD.

Input for this step: WorkingSheet AR, columns T to EJ with *AR(–30)...AR(90),* rows with Bad=1.

Output of this step: WorkingSheet AR BAD, columns T to EJ for *AR(–30)...AR(90).*

Formulas: None (copy/paste step).

Remark: For tractability, copy the filtered columns A to P of *WorkingSheet* AR (with the observation characteristics) to columns A to P of *WorkingSheet* AR BAD.

Stage 3: CAR Estimation

In this stage, you use each category's estimated ARs to get estimated CARs.

3.1 For each of the estimated AR categories arrived at in the previous step, calculate estimated CARs ($\widehat{CARs}$). Use *WorkingSheets* CAR GOOD, CAR MET, and CAR BAD to present the results.

Input for this step: WorkingSheets AR GOOD, AR MET, AR BAD, columns T to EJ with *AR(–30)...AR(90)*.

Output of this step: WorkingSheets CAR GOOD, CAR MET, CAR BAD, columns T to EJ for *CAR(–30)... CAR(90)*.

Formulas: Equation (5.8).

$$\widehat{CAR}^{i}_{s,t} \equiv \sum_{\tau=s}^{t} \widehat{AR}^{i}_{\tau}. \tag{7.3}$$

Remark: For tractability, copy columns A to P of the input *WorkingSheets* (with the observation characteristics) to columns A to P of the output *WorkingSheets*.

Stage 4: Averaging $\widehat{CARs}$ to Obtain $\widehat{CAARs}$

In this stage, you average each category's estimated CARs to get estimated CAARs for the whole event window ($\widehat{CAAR}_{-30,t}$) and the time period starting from the event date ($\widehat{CAAR}_{0,t}$), for each Surprise category. In the end, the series of estimated CAARs for the time period starting immediately after the event date, namely $\widehat{CAAR}_{1,t}$ along with its relevant statistics, will be generated automatically from your work.

Note that the estimated Cumulative Average Abnormal Returns ($\widehat{CAARs}$) for all categories should be placed at designated places, in *WorkngSheet* CAAR.

4.1 Start with $\widehat{CAAR}_{-30,t}$ for the Upside Surprise category. Average the estimated CARs ($\widehat{CARs}$) across all observations in the Upside Surprise category, for each relative date t = –30...90, to obtain estimated CAARs ($\widehat{CAARs}$) for that category. Post your calculations in Panel $\widehat{CAAR}_{-30,t}$ of Table CAAR GOOD in *WorkingSheet* CAAR.

Input for this step: WorkingSheet CAR GOOD, columns T to EJ with *CAR(–30)... CAR(90)*.

Output of this step: WorkingSheet CAAR, cells T7 to EJ7 for $\widehat{CAAR}_{-30,t}, t = -30,...,90$ of Table CAAR GOOD.

Formulas: Equation (5.10).

$$\widehat{CAAR}_{s,t} \equiv \frac{1}{n}\sum_{i=1}^{n}\widehat{CAR}_{s,t}^{i}. \tag{7.4}$$

4.2 Continue with $\widehat{CAAR}_{0,t}$ for the Upside Surprise category. Offset the $\widehat{CAAR}_{-30,t}$ series you generated for the Upside Surprise category in the previous step, to obtain a series with a value of zero at $t = -1$. This series, ($\widehat{CAAR}_{0,t}$) when presented graphically later on, will cross the horizontal axis (of the time relative to the event date) at $t = -1$. Post your calculations in Panel ($\widehat{CAAR}_{0,t}$) of Table CAAR GOOD in *WorkingSheet* CAAR.

Input for this step: WorkingSheet CAAR, cells T7 to EJ7 for $\widehat{CAAR}_{-30,t}$, $t = 0,...,90$ of Table CAAR GOOD.

Output of this step: WorkingSheet CAAR, cells AX19 to EJ19 for $\widehat{CAAR}_{0,t}$, $t = 0,...,90$ of Table CAAR GOOD.

Formulas:

$$\widehat{CAAR}_{0,t} = \widehat{CAAR}_{-30,t} - \widehat{CAAR}_{-30,-1},\ t = 0,...,90. \tag{7.5}$$

Remark: Note that the series here emanates from $t = -1$. For instructional purposes, the corresponding series in chapter 5 was plotted from the beginning of the event window and depicted in a dashed manner till $t = -1$.

4.3 Now it is the turn of $\widehat{CAAR}_{-30,t}$ and $\widehat{CAAR}_{0,t}$ for the Met Expectations category. Follow the two steps above (4.1 and 4.2), but for the Met Expectations (instead of Upside Surprise) category. Post your calculations in Panels $\widehat{CAAR}_{-30,t}$ and $\widehat{CAAR}_{0,t}$ of Table CAAR MET in *WorkingSheet* CAAR.

Input for this step: WorkingSheet CAR MET, columns T to EJ with *CAR(−30)... CAR(90)*.

Output of this step: WorkingSheet CAAR, cells T33 to EJ33 for $\widehat{CAAR}_{-30,t}$, $t = -30,...,90$ of Table CAAR MET; *WorkingSheet* CAAR, cells AX47 to EJ47 for $\widehat{CAAR}_{0,t}$, $t = 0,...,90$ of Table CAAR MET.

Formulas: Same as above (7.4 and 7.5).

Remark: Note that the series here emanates from $t = -1$, while the corresponding series in chapter 5 was plotted from the beginning of the event window and depicted in a dashed manner till $t = -1$.

4.4 Lastly, it is the turn of $\widehat{CAAR}_{-30,t}$ and $\widehat{CAAR}_{0,t}$ for the Downside Surprise category. Follow steps 4.1 and 4.2, but for the Downside Surprise (instead of Upside Surprise) category. Post your calculations in Panels $\widehat{CAAR}_{-30,t}$ and $\widehat{CAAR}_{0,t}$ of Table CAAR BAD in *WorkingSheet* CAAR.

Input for this step: WorkingSheet CAR BAD, columns T to EJ with *CAR(-30)... CAR(90).*

Output of this step: WorkingSheet CAAR, cells T63 to EJ63 for $\widehat{CAAR}_{-30,t}$, $t=-30,...,90$ of Table CAAR BAD; *WorkingSheet* CAAR, cells AX75 to EJ75 for $\widehat{CAAR}_{0,t}$, $t=0,...,90$ of Table CAAR BAD.

Formulas: Same as above (7.4 and 7.5).

Remark: Note that the series here emanates from $t = -1$, while the corresponding series in chapter 5 was plotted from the beginning of the event window and depicted in a dashed manner till $t = -1$.

Stage 5: Calculating Descriptive Statistics within the Surprise Categories

In this stage, you calculate descriptive statistics for the observations within each Surprise category (Good/Met/Bad). For the purpose of demonstration, we provide the path of calculating the characteristics' averages. Other statistics such as the characteristics minima and maxima may be computed in a similar manner.

5.1 Start with the averages for the Upside Surprise category. Average the observation characteristics' listed in columns F to L and P (to wit: rEPS, cEPS, Surprise, P(−1), P(0), R(0), Volume(0), and MCap), across all observations in the Upside Surprise category. Post your calculations in the designated cells in Panel $\widehat{CAAR}_{-30,t}$ of Table CAAR GOOD in *WorkingSheet* CAAR.

Input for this step: WorkingSheet CAR GOOD, columns F to L and P.

Output of this step: WorkingSheet CAAR, cells F7 to L7 and P7 of Table CAAR GOOD.

Formulas:

$$Average\ X \equiv \frac{1}{n}\sum_{i=1}^{n} X_i, \tag{7.6}$$

where X stands for the characteristic for which the average is calculated and n is the number of observations in the Upside Surprise category.

Remark: For convenience, the column letter of each observation characteristic is kept the same throughout the template.

5.2 Continue with the averages for Met Expectations and Downside Surprise categories. Similar to the step above, average the observation characteristics across all observations in Met Expectations and Downside Surprise categories. Post your calculations in the designated cells in Panels $\widehat{CAAR}_{-30,t}$ of Tables CAAR MET and CAAR BAD in *WorkingSheet* CAAR.

Input for this step: WorkingSheet CAR MET, columns F to L and P; *WorkingSheet* CAR BAD; columns F to L and P.

Output of this step: WorkingSheet CAAR, cells F33 to L33 and P33 of Table CAAR MET; *WorkingSheet* CAAR, cells F63 to L63 and P63 of Table CAAR BAD.

Formulas: Same as above (7.6).

Remark: For convenience, the averages are automatically copied by the template from the first panel of each table (panel $\widehat{CAAR}_{-30,t}$) to the second panel of the table (panel $\widehat{CAAR}_{0,t}$).

Stage 6: Calculating Statistics for the Estimated CAAR Series within the Surprise Categories

In this stage, you apply basic statistical analysis to assess the significance of the observed reaction of each Surprise category to the studied event.

Specifically, you calculate the statistical properties of $\widehat{CAAR}_{-30,t}$ and $\widehat{CAAR}_{0,t}$ for each data category (Good/Met/Bad), as a preparation for employing hypothesis testing.[4] The steps of the calculations, for each estimated CAAR series, deal with the following: variance estimators of $\widehat{CAARs}$, corresponding standard deviation estimators, TSs, their p-values, and 95 and 99 percent confidence thresholds. We henceforth demonstrate how to obtain the statistics of $\widehat{CAAR}_{-30,t}$ for the Upside Surprise category. The statistics of $\widehat{CAAR}_{0,t}$ for the Upside Surprise category, as well as the statistics of $\widehat{CAAR}_{-30,t}$ and $\widehat{CAAR}_{0,t}$ for the Met Expectations and Downside Surprise categories may be obtained in a similar manner (some necessary modifications appear below as remarks to the calculation steps).

6.1 Estimate the conditional variance $\sigma_i^2\left(\widehat{AR}_t^i\right)$ for each observation within the Upside Surprise category. Place your calculations within *WorkingSheet* AR GOOD, at column EL ("Est. Var AR") to the right of the estimated ARs.

Input for this step: WorkingSheet AR GOOD, columns CC to EJ with *AR(31)...AR(90).*

Output of this step: WorkingSheet AR GOOD, column EL.

Formulas:

$$\sigma_i^2\left(\widehat{AR}_t^i\right) = \frac{1}{60}\sum_{t=31}^{90}\left(\widehat{AR}_t^i - \frac{\sum_{\tau=31}^{90}\widehat{AR}_\tau^i}{60}\right)^2. \tag{7.7}$$

Remarks:

1. For this calculation, you may employ Excel's VAR.P function.
2. For consistency, we employ population-based formulas throughout. We also remind that the difference between population- and sample-based formulas becomes negligible for a large number of observations.

6.2 Estimate the conditional variances of $\widehat{CAAR}_{-30,t}; t=-30,\ldots,90$ for the Upside Surprise category. Place your calculations at *WorkingSheet* CAAR, within Panel CAAR (–30, *t*) of Table CAAR GOOD ("Est. Var CAAR").

Input for this step: WorkingSheet AR GOOD, column EL; *WorkingSheet* CAAR, cells T6 to EJ6 of Table CAAR GOOD.

Output of this step: WorkingSheet CAAR, cells T8 to EJ8 of Table CAAR GOOD.

Formulas: Equation (5.11).

$$Var\ \widehat{CAAR}_{s,t} \equiv \frac{1}{n^2}\sum_{i=1}^{n} Var\left(\widehat{CAR}^{i}_{s,t}\right) = \frac{(t-s+1)}{n^2}\sum_{i=1}^{n}\hat{\sigma}_i^2. \tag{7.8}$$

Remark: For convenience, row 6 ("(*t*–(–30)+1)=") calculates $(t-s+1)$ for each $\widehat{CAAR}_{-30,t}$.

6.3 Estimate the standard deviations of $\widehat{CAAR}_{-30,t}$ for the Upside Surprise category. Place your calculations at *WorkingSheet* CAAR, within Panel CAAR (-30, *t*) of Table CAAR GOOD (Row title is "Est._Sigma_CAAR").

Input for this step: WorkingSheet CAAR, cells T8 to EJ8 of Table CAAR GOOD with the estimated conditional variances of $\widehat{CAARs}$.

Output of this step: WorkingSheet CAAR, cells T9 to EJ9 of Table CAAR GOOD.

Formulas: Equation (5.12).

$$\hat{\sigma}^{CAAR}_{s,t} \equiv \left(Var\left(\widehat{CAAR}_{s,t}\right)\right)^{1/2}. \tag{7.9}$$

6.4 Calculate the TSs of $\widehat{CAAR}_{-30,t}$ for the Upside Surprise category. Place your calculations at *WorkingSheet* CAAR, within Panel CAAR (–30, *t*) of Table CAAR GOOD (Row title is "TS").

Input for this step: WorkingSheet CAAR, cells T7 to EJ7 of Table CAAR GOOD; *WorkingSheet* CAAR, cells T9 to EJ9 of Table CAAR GOOD.

Output of this step: WorkingSheet CAAR, cells T10 to EJ10 of Table CAAR GOOD.

Formulas: Equation (5.13).

$$TS_{s,t} \equiv \widehat{CAAR}_{s,t} / \hat{\sigma}^{CAAR}_{s,t} \mathrel{\dot\sim} N(0,1). \tag{7.10}$$

6.5 Calculate the upper-tail p-values of $\widehat{CAAR}_{-30,t}$ for the Upside Surprise category. Place your calculations at *WorkingSheet* CAAR, within Panel CAAR (–30, *t*) of Table CAAR GOOD (Row title is "up_tail_p_val.").

Input for this step: WorkingSheet CAAR, cells T10 to EJ10 of Table CAAR GOOD.

Output of this step: WorkingSheet CAAR, cells T11 to EJ11 of Table CAAR GOOD.

Formulas: The required p-values are computed according to the standard normal cumulative distribution function. When the null hypothesis is tested against a unidirectional alternative, such as in the case of the Upside Surprise category, one-tail p-values may be practiced. Specifically, for this category, the upper-tail p-value should be used. It is obtained by integrating the standard normal density function from the calculated value of TS till $(+\infty)$:

$$up\_\_tail\_p\_val.\left(TS_{s,t}\right) \equiv 1-\Phi\left(TS_{s,t}\right) = 1-\frac{1}{\sqrt{2\pi}}\int_{-\infty}^{TS_{s,t}} e^{-\frac{z^2}{2}}dz = \frac{1}{\sqrt{2\pi}}\int_{TS_{s,t}}^{\infty} e^{-\frac{z^2}{2}}dz. \tag{7.11}$$

Remarks:

1. You may employ Excel's NORM.S.DIST function to calculate $\Phi(TS_{s,t})$.
2. For the Met Expectations category, the null hypothesis may be tested against a bidirectional alternative, thus two-tail p-values are appropriate. The two-tail p-value is obtained by integrating the standard normal density function, from the absolute value of TS till $(+\infty)$ and multiplying by 2:

$$two\_tail\_p\_val.\left(TS_{s,t}\right) \equiv 2\left[1-\Phi\left(\left|TS_{s,t}\right|\right)\right]. \tag{7.12}$$

3. For the Downside Surprise category, the lower-tail p-value should be used. It is obtained by integrating the standard normal density function from $(-\infty)$ till the calculated value of the TS, that is:

$$low\_tail\_p\_val.\left(TS_{s,t}\right) \equiv \Phi\left(TS_{s,t}\right). \tag{7.13}$$

4. Note that the whole empirical picture here is portrayed by testing both unidirectional and bidirectional alternative hypotheses, so one-tail as well as two-tail tests are employed. When reporting research results, one should draw the attention of readers to that point in order to prevent confusion.

6.6 Estimate 95 and 99 percent confidence thresholds for $\widehat{CAAR}_{-30,t}$ of the Upside Surprise category. Place your calculations at *WorkingSheet* CAAR, within Panel CAAR (–30, *t*) of Table CAAR GOOD (Row titles are "95% confidence" and "99% confidence," respectively).

Input for this step: WorkingSheet CAAR, cells T9 to EJ9 of Table CAAR GOOD.

Output of this step: WorkingSheet CAAR, cells T12 to EJ12 of Table CAAR GOOD; *WorkingSheet* CAAR, cells T13 to EJ13 of Table CAAR GOOD.

Formulas: The required (1–α) confidence threshold (significance of size α) is computed according to the inverse of the standard normal cumulative distribution function. You may employ Excel's NORM.INV function. For the Upside Surprise category, calculate $NORM.INV(1-\alpha, 0, Est.\_Sigma\_CAAR)$.

Remarks:

1. Recall that for Met Expectations, two-tailed tests are appropriate, thus the confidence intervals have upper and lower bounds, for which the two respective calculations are $NORM.INV(1-\alpha/2, 0, Est.\_Sigma\_CAAR)$ and $NORM.INV(\alpha/2, 0, Est.\_Sigma\_CAAR)$.
2. For Downside Surprise, calculate $NORM.INV(\alpha, 0, Est.\_Sigma\_CAAR)$.

7.5. Results and Discussion

We are now ready to view the results and discuss the solution of the exercise. At this point, you are encouraged to check your work vis-à-vis the provided solution. Recall that the complete solution file (http://dx.doi.org/10.6084/m9.figshare.1221835) may be downloaded from the book's website.

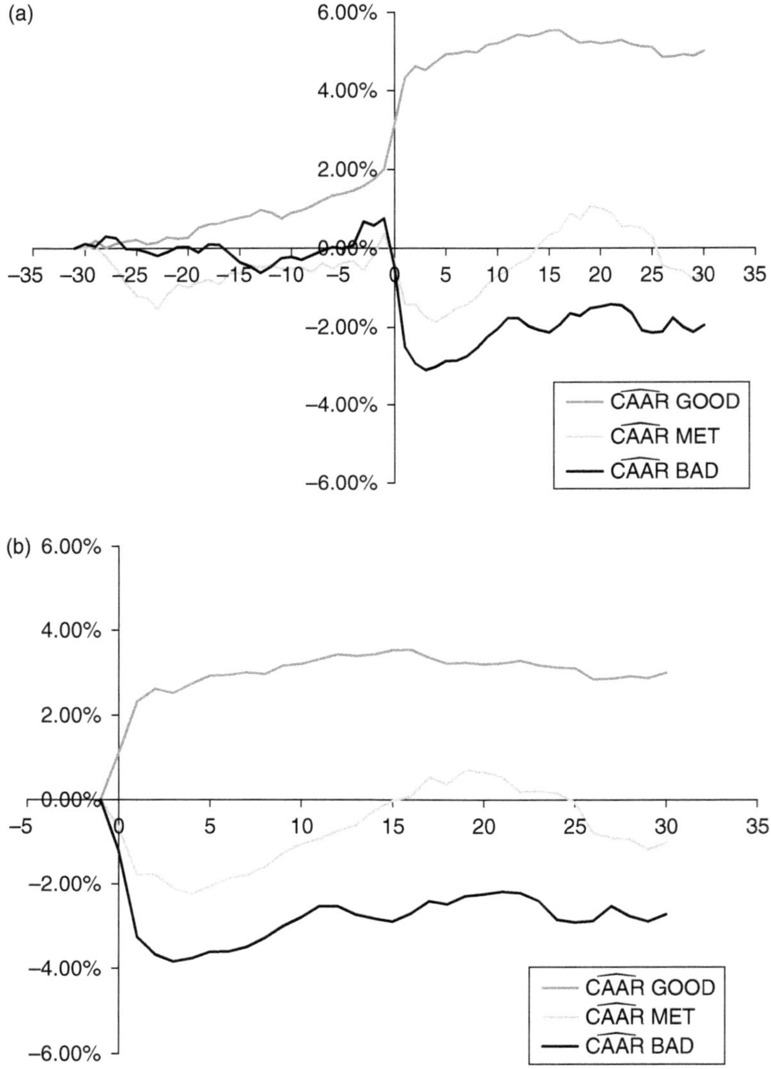

Figure 7.2 Basic exercise: $\widehat{CAAR}_{-30,t}$ and $\widehat{CAAR}_{0,t}$ for the three Surprise categories. (a) $\widehat{CAAR}_{-30,t}$ for all Surprise categories and (b) $\widehat{CAAR}_{0,t}$ for all Surprise Categories.

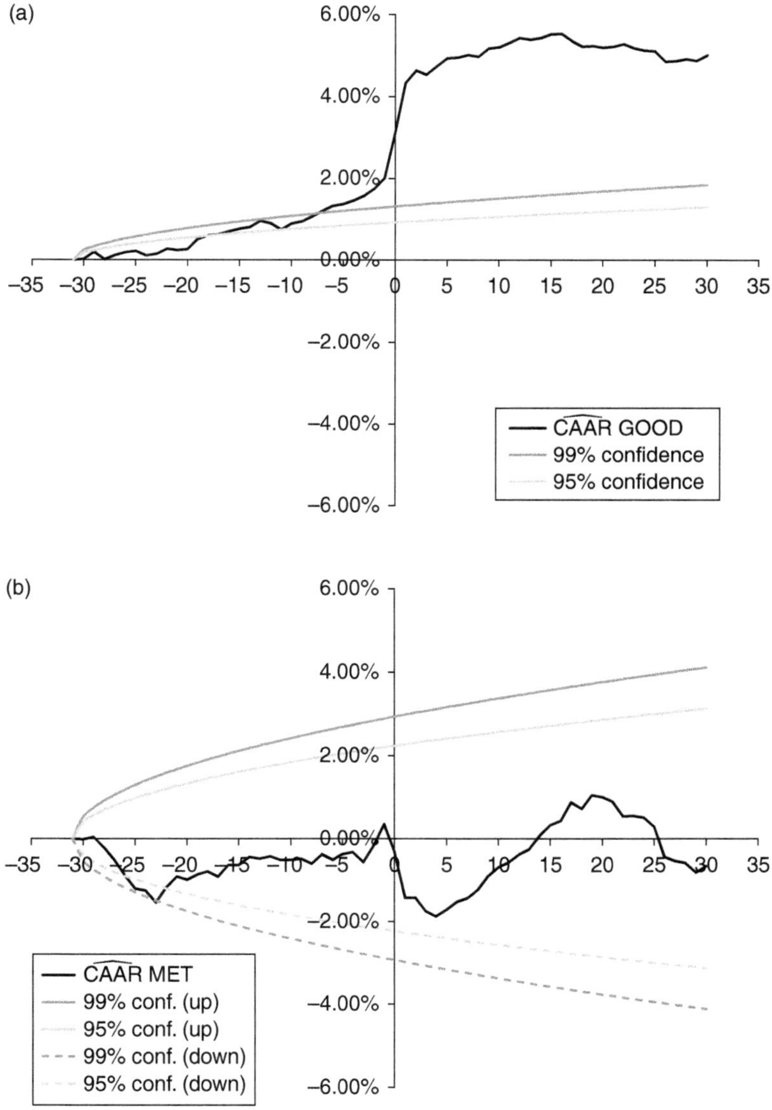

Figure 7.3 Continued on next page.

(c)

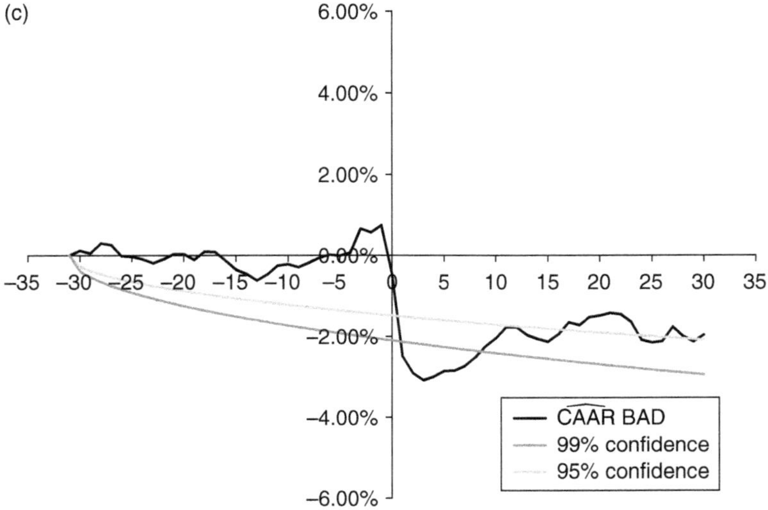

Figure 7.3 Basic exercise: $\widehat{CAAR}_{-30,t}$ for the three Surprise categories. (a) $\widehat{CAAR}_{-30,t}$ for the Upside Surprise category, (b) $\widehat{CAAR}_{-30,t}$ for the Met Expectations category, and (c) $\widehat{CAAR}_{-30,t}$ for the Downside Surprise category.

As a result of your spreadsheet manipulation, the $\widehat{CAARs}$ and their confidence threshold curves have been graphed.

In the Excel file, the first three *GraphSheets*—GRAPH CAAR(–30, *t*) ALL, GRAPH CAAR(0, *t*) ALL, and GRAPH CAAR(1, *t*) ALL—present the respective estimated CAAR series for the three Surprise categories: whole event window ($\widehat{CAAR}_{-30,t}$); time period starting from the event date ($\widehat{CAAR}_{0,t}$); and ime period starting immediately after the event date ($\widehat{CAAR}_{1,t}$). The Surprise categories' graphs—CAAR GOOD, CAAR MET, CAAR BAD—are green, orange, and red, respectively (in the book they are in greyscale).

The remaining 9 (=3×3) *GraphSheets* depict the estimated CAARs of each Surprise category (Good/Met/Bad), for each of the time periods (from $t = -30$ / $t = 0$ / $t = 1$), along with their 95 and 99 percent confidence thresholds, which are portrayed in light and dark purple, respectively.

Please review the graphs and express in your own words the story told by the data. You may structure your report according to the following

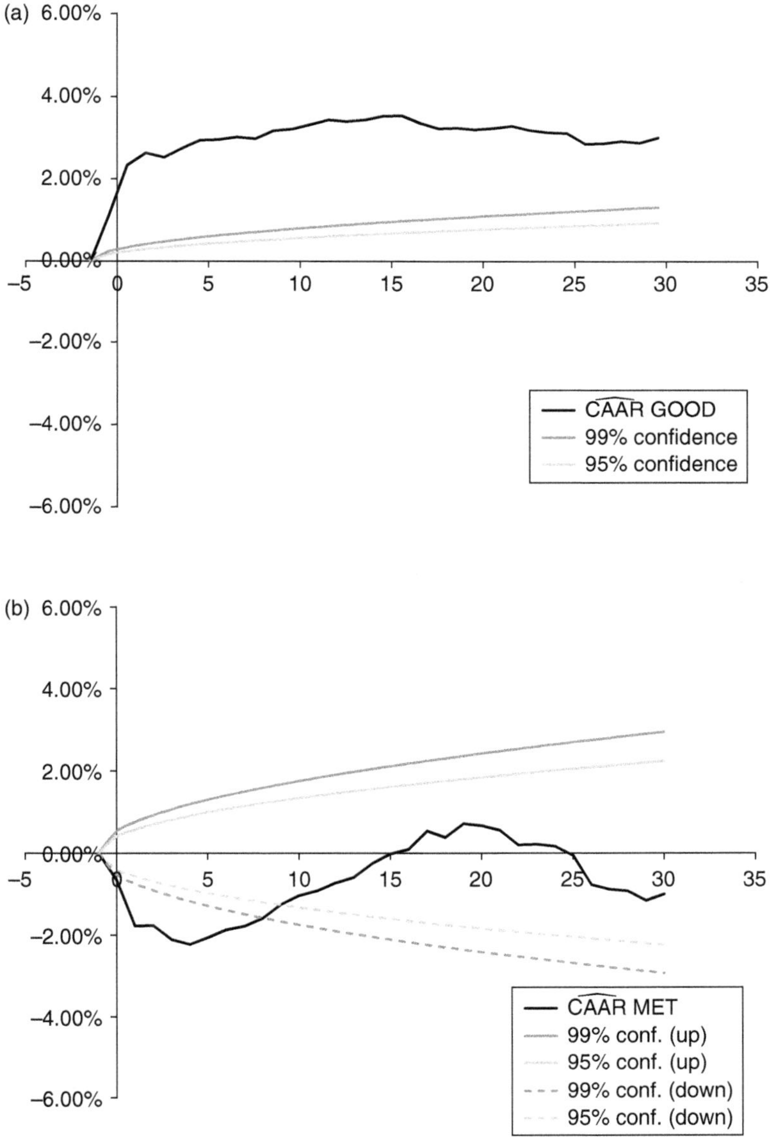

Figure 7.4 Continued on next page.

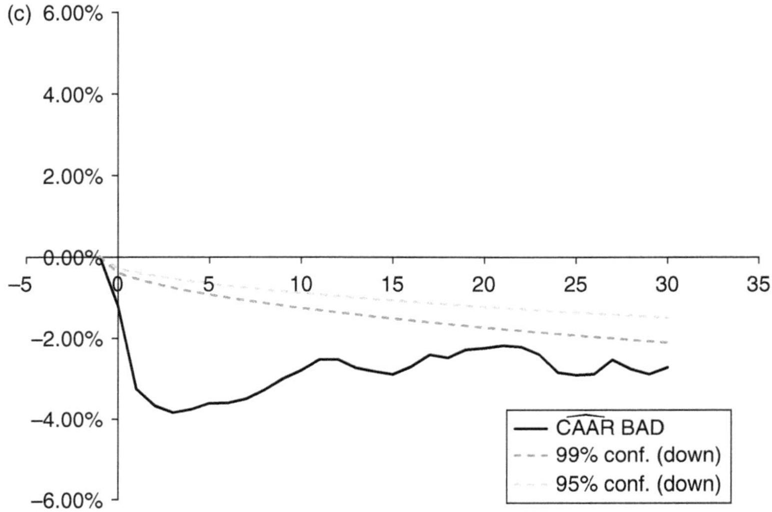

Figure 7.4 Basic exercise: $\widehat{CAAR}_{0,t}$ for the three Surprise categories. (a) $\widehat{CAAR}_{0,t}$ for the Upside Surprise category, (b) $\widehat{CAAR}_{0,t}$ for the Met Expectations category, and (c) $\widehat{CAAR}_{0,t}$ for the Downside Surprise category.

questions. Substantiate your reply by pointing to the empirical results depicted in the graphs. Make note to refer to the significance of the results, using the plotted confidence thresholds.

Question 1: What can you say regarding the information content of the analyzed event?
Question 2: Was there any market reaction *before* the release of earnings figures? If yes, in what direction?
Question 3: Was there any market reaction *upon* the release of earnings figures? If yes, in what direction?
Question 4: Was there any market reaction *after* the release of earnings figures? If yes, in what direction?
Question 5: What can you say regarding market efficiency?

Henceforth we present a report of the results structured according to the questions above.

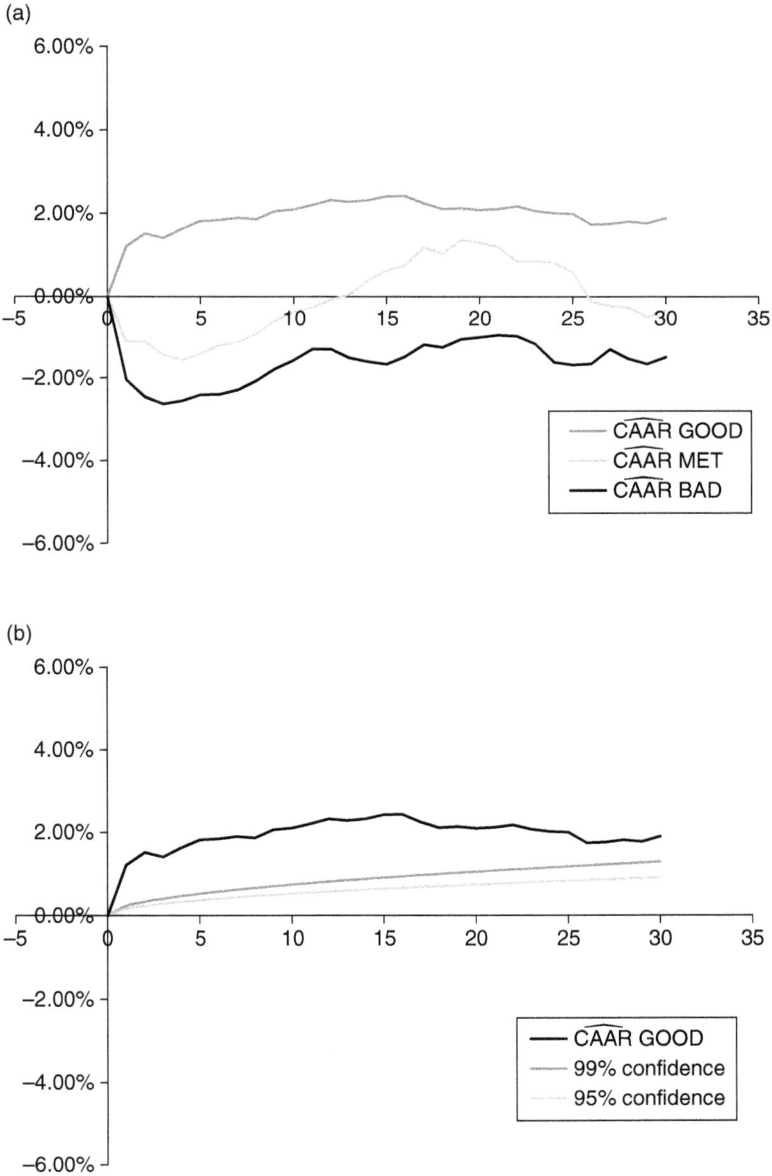

Figure 7.5 Continued on next page.

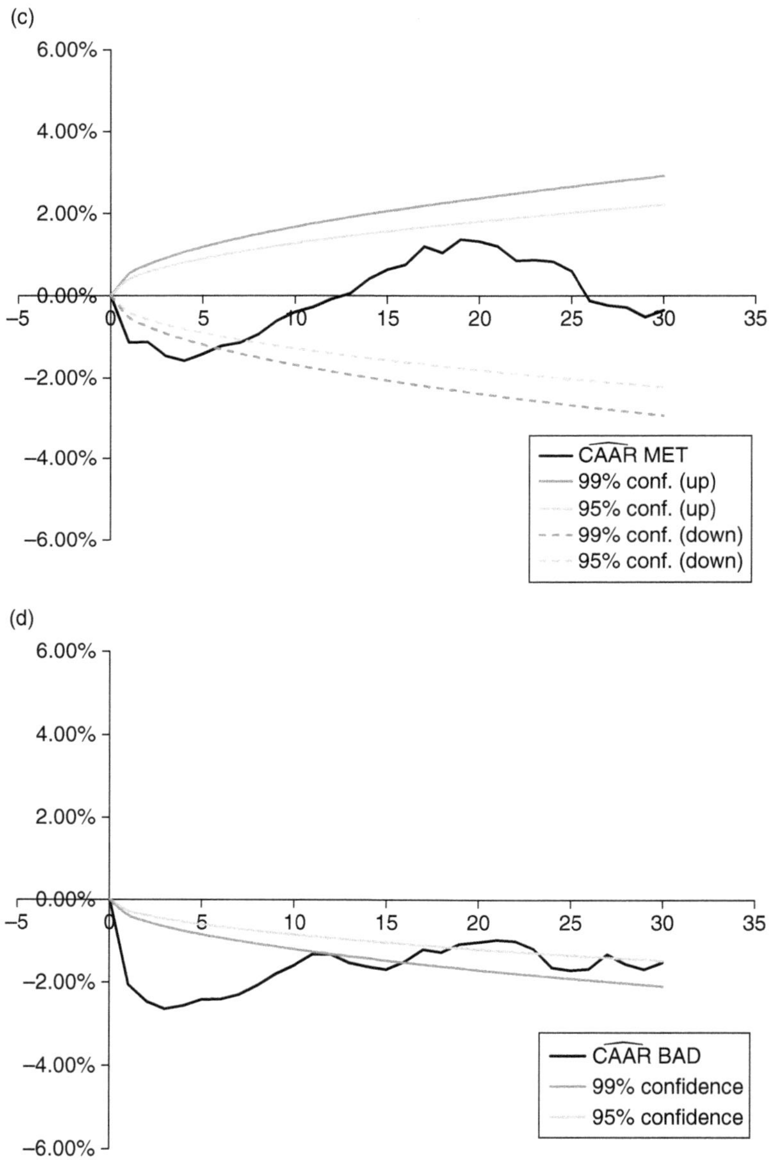

Figure 7.5 Basic exercise: $\widehat{CAAR}_{1,t}$ for the three Surprise categories. (a) $\widehat{CAAR}_{1,t}$ for all Surprise categories, (b) $\widehat{CAAR}_{1,t}$ for the Upside Surprise category, (c) $\widehat{CAAR}_{1,t}$ for the Met Expectations category, and (d) $\widehat{CAAR}_{1,t}$ for the Downside Surprise category.

Question 1: What can you say regarding the information content of the analyzed event?

On the general level, from Figure 7.2, it is evident that there has been considerable reaction to the analyzed event.

The emerging picture is also statistically significant, as seen from the graphs that employ the whole event window (Figure 7.3), as well as the graphs of $\widehat{CAAR}_{0,t}$ (Figure 7.4). The considerable $\widehat{CAAR}$ irregularities, which are clearly observed, are substantiated by all series crossing their respective confidence thresholds.

Question 2: Was there any market reaction *before* the release of earnings figures? If yes, in what direction?

Investigating $\widehat{CAAR}_{-30,t}$, an early, positive, and persistent reaction is clearly observed for the Upside Surprise category; no early reaction in any direction is observed for the Downside Surprise category; and an early, negative reaction is observed for the Met Expectation category.

Question 3: Was there any market reaction *upon* the release of earnings figures? If yes, in what direction?

As revealed by the $\widehat{CAAR}_{0,t}$ series, substantial market reaction was observed upon the release of the news for all the categories. In particular, there was a sharp increase in the estimated CAARs of the Upside Surprise category on day zero, implying that the "Good news" embedded in above-forecast earnings was appreciated by market participants, who (further) rewarded the stocks of the reporting firms during the day of news announcement. In the case of the Downside Surprise category, there was a decline in the estimated CAARs on day zero, implying that the "Bad news" in below-forecast earnings was not welcomed in the market.

Thus far, the results are in line with straightforward hypotheses regarding market reaction to the firms' earnings figures. Possibly more surprising is the behavior of the Met Expectations category, which appears, at least on the day of news release, very similar to the Downside Surprise category. The observed effect may suggest that meeting earnings expectations is negatively interpreted by the market.

Question 4: Was there any market reaction *after* the release of earnings figures? If yes, in what direction?

Inspecting the $\widehat{CAAR}_{1,t}$ series (Figure 7.5) indicates immediate continuation of the initially observed reactions. For the Upside Surprise category, the upward irregularity is continued, while a downward irregularity is evident in both Downside Surprise and Met Expectations categories.

Looking a bit further toward the continuation of the event window reveals that the estimated effect is sustained for the Upside Surprise category, more or less so for the Downside surprise category, and is reverted for the Met Expectations category; the latter suggests that the initial negative market reaction observed for the firms that have been meeting their earnings expectations was temporary.

Question 5: What can you say regarding market efficiency?

According to the answer to question 4, semistrong market efficiency is rejected. In all cases, the market reactions have not been fully incorporated upon the news release.

Chapter 8

Further Hands-on Exercises

This chapter extends the basic exercise you worked through in chapter 7. Using the same dataset, we address here some of the further relevant practical issues discussed in previous chapters. The core issues are accompanied by Excel templates, some of them with fully detailed walk-through instructions, and others with more general guiding. The Excel templates, as well as the files with complete solutions, may be downloaded from the book's website.

We start the chapter with a walk-through (section 8.1) of the steps of conducting ESA in a way that accounts for time clustering. Recall that when the observations are clustered, there may be interdependencies among the estimated ARs, which could affect the distributional properties of the TSs. The procedure we show takes this into account, while not affecting the estimated CAARs.

In section 8.2, we apply nonparametric tests. We employ the versions of these tests presented in section 6.2 of chapter 6. These tests are valid under the "regular" conditions, inter alia, they require independence among the returns of the securities comprising the sample.

In section 8.3, we assess the robustness of the results to the selected benchmark of NRs. To demonstrate how this may be done, we reevaluate the estimated CAARs using the single-factor model of NRs and compare the results to those obtained in the basic setup, with the naïve benchmark.

In section 8.4, we employ a finer partition of the data to investigate the effect of the magnitude of the surprise embedded in the disseminated information.

In section 8.5, we explore possible differential effects by the companies' sectors.

In section 8.6 we conclude the chapter by raising some further data analysis ideas.

The issues we discuss in this chapter share the same research goal, underlying assumptions, and data with the basic exercise discussed in chapter 7. Thus, we do not replicate here the background to the research question, nor do we reintroduce the dataset.[1] The structures of the exercise templates and solution files are kept as similar as possible to their counterparts in chapter 7. Specifically, the *DataSheets* are identical to those presented in chapter 7, and the *WorkingSheets* are different only in aspects that are necessary for the issue at hand.[2] Lastly, for the purpose of the exercises presented in this chapter, when estimating the statistical properties of random variables and TSs, assume that the asymptotical properties described in chapter 5 hold.

The exercises in sections 8.1 and 8.2, to wit, conducting ESA in a way that accounts for time clustering and applying nonparametric tests, are presented in a detailed manner, with step-by-step instructions in the same way as the basic hands-on exercise in chapter 7. The exercises in sections 8.3, 8.4, and 8.5 (applying the single-factor model, analyzing the effect of the magnitude of surprise, and analyzing differential effects across sectors), are provided with succinct directions. In section 8.6 we sketch out possible additional extensions to the exercise, suggested as open-ended questions.

8.1. Clustering-Adjusted Procedure

In this section we apply the clustering-adjusted procedure introduced in section 6.1 of chapter 6. The Excel template for the exercise presented in this section (http://dx.doi.org/10.6084/m9.figshare.1221838) may be downloaded from the book's website.

In case you wish to solve the exercise without our intermediation, skip the instructions below, download a copy of the dataset file (http://dx.doi.org/10.6084/m9.figshare.1221834), consisting of *DataSheets* only, create your own *WorkingSheets*, and work independently. When you finish, please rejoin in the last subsection of this section, "Results and Discussion," to view the results of the provided solution and related discussion.

As evident from the calendar dates of the event, there is a substantial overlap in the event windows of different stocks. As a result, the assumption of return independence across different stocks, underlying the "regular" ESA application, does not hold. As explained in chapter 6, the issue may be addressed by forming a portfolio of ARs that accounts for cross-sectional correlations of its constituents, and using its estimated variability for hypothesis testing.[3]

Table 8.1 Clustering-adjusted exercise template

Worksheets	Description
DataSheets	
TOU	Terms of use: Personal and noncommercial use limitation
README	Abbreviated description of the variables contained in the dataset
STOCK DATA	Firms' characteristics and stock price records (see details below)
INDEX DATA	Market index (S&P 500) records for the event dates (the firms' characteristics appear again, for convenience)
WorkingSheets	
STOCK RETURNS	Placeholder for calculating stock returns
INDEX RETURNS	Placeholder for calculating index returns
AR	Placeholder for estimating ARs
AR GOOD / AR MET / AR BAD	Placeholders for partitioning the estimated ARs into categories according to the direction of the hypothesized reaction to the event
CAAR	Placeholder for estimating CAAR series
GraphSheets	
GRAPH CAAR (–30,*t*) / (0,*t*) / (1,*t*) ALL	Placeholders for graphical representation of CAAR series
GRAPH CAAR (–30,*t*) GOOD / MET / BAD	
GRAPH CAAR(0,*t*) GOOD / MET / BAD	
GRAPH CAAR(1,*t*) GOOD / MET / BAD	

We start by introducing the spreadsheet template, which was predesigned to accommodate the clustering-adjusted solution. Table 8.1 enumerates the worksheets contained in the clustering-adjusted template.

Now the stage is set to process the data toward conducting the event study exercise using the clustering-adjusted design. In order to proceed, open the clustering-adjusted exercise template (http://dx.doi.org/10.6084/m9.figshare.1221838) and work according to the following guidelines. As in chapter 7, the instructions are given as a list of *stages*, each divided into tractable *steps* for which we detail the required calculations and designate the input data and venue for the output. The instructions in stages 1 and 2, namely ARs estimation and data sorting, are identical to those given in chapter 7 for the basic ESA. The instructions in stages 3 and 4 (the way from $\widehat{ARs}$ to $\widehat{CAARs}$) are different here, in order to take into account the cross-correlations due to data clustering, by estimating the AARs over the estimation window and eliciting their distributional properties (cf. the "portfolio approach" explained in chapter 6). The instructions in stages 5 (descriptive statistics) and 6 (statistics for the estimated CAAR series) are identical to those given in chapter 7, except for the estimation of conditional variances of the $\widehat{AAR}$ series, which now accounts for clustering in the data.

Stage 1: AR Estimation

In the first stage, you start with the raw price data and arrive at estimated ARs, calculated according to the naïve benchmark of returns.

1.1 Calculate daily logarithmic return series for each stock, over the entire available data period, using the corresponding daily price series (see chapter 3 for details). Place the calculations in *WorkingSheet* STOCK RETURNS. Note that the first return to be calculated is for $t = -30$, since the earliest price available is for $t = -31$.

Input for this step: DataSheet STOCK DATA, columns S to EJ with *P(–31)... P(90)*.

Output of this step: WorkingSheet STOCK RETURNS, columns T to EJ for *R(–30)... R(90)*.

Formulas: Equation (3.2), adjusted to the current case.

$$R(l)_t^i \equiv ln\frac{P_t^i}{P_{t-1}^i} = ln\left(R(a)_t^i + 1\right);\ i = 1,\ldots,670;\ t = -30,\ldots,90. \quad (8.1)$$

Remark: For tractability, copy columns A to P of *DataSheet* STOCK DATA (with the observation characteristics) to columns A to P of *WorkingSheet* STOCK RETURNS. Note that columns Q and R are placeholders for the parameters of the single-factor model of returns, which will be dealt with in the sequel.

1.2 Calculate daily logarithmic returns of the S&P 500 Index on the same dates as above using the corresponding daily index series. Place the calculations in *WorkingSheet* INDEX RETURNS. Again, the first return to be calculated is for $t = -30$, since the earliest index data available are for $t = -31$.

Input for this step: DataSheet INDEX DATA, columns S to EJ with *M(–31)... M(90).*

Output of this step: WorkingSheet INDEX RETURNS, columns T to EJ for *RM(–30)... RM(90).*

Formulas: The same formula as in the above step, applied on the index data.

Remark: For tractability, copy columns A to P of *DataSheet* INDEX DATA (with the observation characteristics) to columns A to P of *WorkingSheet* INDEX RETURNS.

1.3 Compute the estimated ARs for each stock using the naïve benchmark of returns. Recall (chapter 3) that according to this model, AR is the difference between the stock's return and the contemporaneous index return. Place the calculations in *WorkingSheet* AR.

Input for this step: WorkingSheet STOCK RETURNS, columns T to EJ with *R(–30)... R(90)*; *WorkingSheet* INDEX RETURNS, columns T to EJ with *RM(–30)... RM(90).*

Output of this step: WorkingSheet AR; columns T to EJ for *AR(–30)... AR(90).*

Formulas: Equation (3.6), adjusted to the current case.

$$\widehat{AR}_t^i \equiv R_t^i - \widehat{NR}_t^i;\ i{=}1,\ldots,670;\ t{=}-30,\ldots,90. \tag{8.2}$$

Remark: For tractability, copy columns A to P of *WorkingSheet* STOCK RETURNS (with the observation characteristics) to columns A to P of *WorkingSheet* AR.

Stage 2: Data Sorting

In this stage you partition the observations that you filled in the previous step in *WorkingSheet* AR by the Good/Met/Bad indicators, for separate analysis of each category of events. To do so, filter the data in *WorkingSheet* AR by each of the values in columns M, N, and O (Good/Met/Bad), copy the filtered data, and paste it to WorkingSheets AR GOOD / AR MET / AR BAD, respectively.

2.1 Filter the data in WorkingSheet AR by column M, to select the observations with Good=1, i.e., the observations for which there was an Upside Surprise. Copy the filtered data and paste to *WorkingSheet* AR GOOD.

Input for this step: WorkingSheet AR, columns T to EJ with *AR(–30)…AR(90)*, rows with Good=1.
Output of this step: WorkingSheet AR GOOD, columns T to EJ for *AR(–30)…AR(90)*.

Formulas: None (copy/paste step).

Remark: For tractability, copy the filtered columns A to P of *WorkingSheet* AR (with the observation characteristics) to columns A to P of *WorkingSheet* AR GOOD.

2.2 Next, filter the data in *WorkingSheet* AR by column N, to select the observations with Met=1, i.e., the observations for Met Expectations. Copy the filtered data and paste to *WorkingSheet* AR MET.

Input for this step: WorkingSheet AR, columns T to EJ with *AR(–30)…AR(90)*, rows with Met=1.

Output of this step: WorkingSheet AR MET, columns T to EJ for *AR(–30)…AR(90)*.

Formulas: None (copy/paste step).

Remark: For tractability, copy the filtered columns A to P of *WorkingSheet* AR (with the observation characteristics) to columns A to P of *WorkingSheet* AR MET.

2.3 Lastly, filter the data in *WorkingSheet* AR by column O, to select the observations with Bad=1, i.e., the observations for which there was a Downside Surprise. Copy the filtered data and paste to *WorkingSheet* AR BAD.

Input for this step: WorkingSheet AR, columns T to EJ with *AR(–30)…AR(90)*, rows with Bad=1.

Output of this step: WorkingSheet AR BAD, columns T to EJ for *AR(–30)…AR(90)*.

Formulas: None (copy/paste step).

Remark: For tractability, copy the filtered columns A to P of *WorkingSheet* AR (with the observation characteristics) to columns A to P of *WorkingSheet* AR BAD.

Stage 3: Averaging $\widehat{ARs}$ to Obtain $\widehat{AARs}$

In this stage, you average each category's estimated ARs to get its estimated AARs.

3.1 For each of the estimated AR categories, calculate estimated AARs ($\widehat{AARs}$). Use rows 398, 101, and 180 (see below the AR tables) of *WorkingSheets* AR GOOD, AR MET, and AR BAD, respectively, to place your calculations.

Input for this step: WorkingSheets AR GOOD, AR MET, AR BAD, columns T to EJ with *AR(–30)…AR(90)*.

Output of this step: WorkingSheets AR GOOD, AR MET, AR BAD, rows 398, 101, and 180 (below the AR tables), respectively, for *AAR(–30)…AAR(90)*.

Formulas: Equation (6.2).

$$\widehat{AAR}_t = \frac{\sum_{i=1}^{n} \widehat{AR}_t^i}{n};\ i=1,\ldots,n; \begin{cases} t = t_{Start}^{EstWin}+1,\ldots,t_{End}^{EstWin} \\ t = t_{Start}^{EventWin}+1,\ldots,t_{End}^{EventWin} \end{cases}. \tag{8.3}$$

Stage 4: Accumulating $\widehat{AARs}$ to Obtain $\widehat{CAARs}$

In this stage, you use each category's estimated AARs to get its estimated CAARs for the whole event window ($\widehat{CAAR}_{-30,t}$) and for the time period starting from the event date ($\widehat{CAAR}_{0,t}$), for each Surprise category. In the end, the series of estimated CAARs for the time period starting immediately after the event date, namely ($\widehat{CAAR}_{1,t}$) along with its relevant statistics, will be generated automatically from your work.

Note that the estimated CAARs for all categories should be placed at designated places, in *WorkngSheet* CAAR.

4.1 Start with $\widehat{CAAR}_{-30,t}$ for the Upside Surprise category. Accumulate $\widehat{AAR}$s at the bottom of AR GOOD from t = –30 till each date over the event window. Post your calculations in Panel $\widehat{CAAR}_{-30,t}$ of Table CAAR GOOD in *WorkingSheet* CAAR.

Input for this step: WorkingSheet AR GOOD, row 398 (below the AR table), with *AAR(–30)*. . .*AAR(90).*

Output of this step: WorkingSheet CAAR, cells T7 to EJ7 for $\widehat{CAAR}_{-30,t}$, t = –30,...,90 of Table CAAR GOOD.

Formulas: Equation (6.6).

$$\widehat{CAAR}_{s,t} \equiv \sum_{\tau=s}^{t} \widehat{AAR}_{\tau}. \tag{8.4}$$

4.2 Continue with $\widehat{CAAR}_{0,t}$ for the Upside Surprise category. Offset the $\widehat{CAAR}_{-30,t}$ series you generated for the Upside Surprise category in the previous step, to obtain a series with a value of zero on t = –1. This series, ($\widehat{CAAR}_{0,t}$) when presented graphically later on, will cross the horizontal axis (of the time relative to the event date) at t = –1. Post your calculations in Panel ($\widehat{CAAR}_{0,t}$) of Table CAAR GOOD in *WorkingSheet* CAAR.

Input for this step: WorkingSheet CAAR, cells T7 to EJ7 for $\widehat{CAAR}_{-30,t}$, t = 0,...,90 of Table CAAR GOOD.

Output of this step: WorkingSheet CAAR, cells AX19 to EJ19 for $\widehat{CAAR}_{0,t}$, t = 0,...,90 of Table CAAR GOOD.

Formulas:

$$\widehat{CAAR}_{0,t} = \widehat{CAAR}_{-30,t} - \widehat{CAAR}_{-30,-1}, t = 0,...,90. \tag{8.5}$$

Remark: Note that the series here emanates from t = –1. For instructional purposes, the corresponding series in chapter 5 was plotted from the beginning of the event window and depicted in a dashed manner till t = –1.

4.3 Now it is the turn of $\widehat{CAAR}_{-30,t}$ and $\widehat{CAAR}_{0,t}$ for the Met Expectations category. Follow the two steps above (4.1 and 4.2), but for the Met Expectations (instead of Upside Surprise) category. Post your calculations in Panels $\widehat{CAAR}_{-30,t}$ and $\widehat{CAAR}_{0,t}$ of Table CAAR MET in *WorkingSheet* CAAR.

Input for this step: WorkingSheet AR MET, row 101 (below the AR table), with *AAR(–30)*. . .*AAR(90)*.

Output of this step: WorkingSheet CAAR, cells T33 to EJ33 for $\widehat{CAAR}_{-30,t}$, $t = -30,...,90$ of Table CAAR MET; *WorkingSheet* CAAR, cells AX47 to EJ47 for $\widehat{CAAR}_{0,t}$, $t = 0,...,90$ of Table CAAR MET.

Formulas: Same as above (8.4 and 8.5).

Remark: Note that the series here emanates from $t = -1$, while the corresponding series in chapter 5 was plotted from the beginning of the event window and depicted in a dashed manner till $t = -1$.

4.4 Lastly, it is the turn of $\widehat{CAAR}_{-30,t}$ and $\widehat{CAAR}_{0,t}$ for the Downside Surprise category. Follow steps 4.1 and 4.2, but for the Downside Surprise (instead of Upside Surprise) category. Post your calculations in Panels $\widehat{CAAR}_{-30,t}$ and $\widehat{CAAR}_{0,t}$ of Table CAAR BAD in *WorkingSheet* CAAR.

Input for this step: WorkingSheet AR BAD, row 180 (below the AR table), with *AAR(–30)*. . .*AAR(90)*.

Output of this step: WorkingSheet CAAR, cells T63 to EJ63 for $\widehat{CAAR}_{-30,t}$, $t = -30,...,90$ of Table CAAR BAD; *WorkingSheet* CAAR, cells AX75 to EJ75 for $\widehat{CAAR}_{0,t}$, $t = 0,...,90$ of Table CAAR BAD.

Formulas: Same as above (8.4 and 8.5).

Remark: Note that the series here emanates from $t = -1$, while the corresponding series in chapter 5 was plotted from the beginning of the event window and depicted in a dashed manner till $t = -1$.

Stage 5: Calculating Descriptive Statistics within the Surprise Categories

In this stage, you calculate descriptive statistics for the observations within each Surprise category (Good/Met/Bad). For the purpose of demonstration, we provide the path of calculating the characteristics' averages. Other statistics such as the characteristics' minima and maxima may be computed in a similar manner.

5.1 Start with the averages for the Upside Surprise category. Average the observation characteristics listed in columns F to L and P (to wit: rEPS, cEPS, Surprise, P(–1), P(0), R(0), Volume(0), and MCap), across all observations in the Upside Surprise category. Post your calculations in the designated cells in Panel $\widehat{CAAR}_{-30,t}$ of Table CAAR GOOD in *WorkingSheet* CAAR.

Input for this step: WorkingSheet AR GOOD, columns F to L and P.

Output of this step: WorkingSheet CAAR, cells F7 to L7 and P7 of Table CAAR GOOD.

Formulas:

$$Average\ X \equiv \frac{1}{n}\sum_{i=1}^{n} X_i, \tag{8.6}$$

where X stands for the characteristic for which the average is calculated and n is the number of observations in the Upside Surprise category.

Remark: For convenience, the column letter of each observation characteristic is kept the same throughout the template.

5.2 Continue with the averages for Met Expectations and Downside Surprise categories. Similar to the step above, average the observation characteristics across all observations in Met Expectations and Downside Surprise categories. Post your calculations in the designated cells in Panels $\widehat{CAAR}_{-30,t}$ of Tables CAAR MET and CAAR BAD in *WorkingSheet* CAAR.

Input for this step: WorkingSheet AR MET, columns F to L and P; *WorkingSheet* AR BAD, columns F to L and P.

Output of this step: WorkingSheet CAAR, cells F33 to L33 and P33 of Table CAAR MET; *WorkingSheet* CAAR, cells F63 to L63 and P63 of Table CAAR BAD.

Formulas: Same as above (8.6).

Remark: For convenience, the averages are automatically copied by the template from the first panel of each table (panel $\widehat{CAAR}_{-30,t}$) to the second panel of the table (panel $\widehat{CAAR}_{0,t}$).

Stage 6: Calculating Statistics for the Estimated CAAR Series within the Surprise Categories

In this stage, you apply statistical analysis to assess the significance of the observed reaction of each Surprise category to the studied event.

Specifically, you calculate the statistical properties of $\widehat{CAAR}_{-30,t}$ and $\widehat{CAAR}_{0,t}$ for each data category (Good/Met/Bad), as a preparation for employing hypothesis testing.[4] The steps of the calculations, for each estimated CAAR series, deal with the following: variance estimators of $\widehat{CAARs}$, corresponding standard deviation estimators, TSs, their p-values, and 95 and 99 percent confidence thresholds. We henceforth demonstrate how to obtain the statistics of $\widehat{CAAR}_{-30,t}$ for the Upside Surprise category. The statistics of $\widehat{CAAR}_{0,t}$ for the Upside Surprise category, as well as the statistics of $\widehat{CAAR}_{-30,t}$ and $\widehat{CAAR}_{0,t}$ for the Met Expectations and Downside Surprise categories may be obtained in a similar manner (some necessary modifications appear below as remarks to the calculation steps).

6.1 Estimate the conditional variance of $\widehat{AAR}_t$ within the Upside Surprise category, namely $\sigma^2\left(\widehat{AAR}_t\right)$, using $\widehat{AARs}$ in the estimation window starting at t = 31. Place your calculation within *WorkingSheet* AR GOOD at cell EL398 ("Est._Var_AAR") to the right of the estimated AARs.

Input for this step: WorkingSheet AR GOOD, cells CC398 to EJ398 with *AAR(31)...AAR(90).*

Output of this step: WorkingSheet AR GOOD, cell EL398.

Formulas: Equations (6.4) and (6.5).

$$\sigma^2\left(\widehat{AAR}_t\right) = \frac{1}{t_{End}^{EstWin} - t_{Start}^{EstWin}} \sum_{t=t_{Start}^{EstWin}}^{t_{End}^{EstWin}} \left[\widehat{AAR}_t - \overline{AAR}\right]^2, \tag{8.7}$$

where

$$\overline{AAR} \equiv \sum_{t=t_{Start}^{EstWin}}^{t_{End}^{EstWin}} \widehat{AAR}_t \,/\, (t_{End}^{EstWin} - t_{Start}^{EstWin}). \tag{8.8}$$

Remarks:

1. For this calculation, you may employ Excel's VAR.P function.
2. For consistency, we employ population-based formulas throughout. We also remind that the difference between population- and sample-based formulas becomes negligible for a large number of observations.
3. For details on the the event- and estimation-windows see section 7.3 and timeline in Figure 7.1 there.

6.2 Estimate the conditional variances of $\widehat{CAAR}_{-30,t}$; $t = -30,\ldots,90$ for the Upside Surprise category. Place your calculations at *WorkingSheet* CAAR, within Panel CAAR (–30, t) of Table CAAR GOOD (Row title is "Est. Var CAAR").

Input for this step: WorkingSheet AR GOOD, cell EL398.

WorkingSheet CAAR, cells T6 to EJ6 of Table CAAR GOOD.

Output of this step: WorkingSheet CAAR, cells T8 to EJ8 of Table CAAR GOOD.

Formulas: Equation (6.7).

$$\sigma^2\left(\widehat{CAAR}_{s,t}\right) = (t - s + 1)\sigma^2\left(\widehat{AAR}_t\right). \tag{8.9}$$

Remark: For convenience, row 6 ("(t–(–30)+1)=") calculates $(t - s + 1)$ for each $\widehat{CAAR}_{-30,t}$.

6.3 Estimate the standard deviations of $\widehat{CAAR}_{-30,t}$ for the Upside Surprise category. Place your calculations at *WorkingSheet* CAAR, within Panel CAAR (–30, t) of Table CAAR GOOD (Row title is "Est._Sigma_CAAR").

Input for this step: WorkingSheet CAAR, cells T8 to EJ8 of Table CAAR GOOD with the estimated conditional variances of $\widehat{CAARs}$.

Output of this step: WorkingSheet CAAR, cells T9 to EJ9 of Table CAAR GOOD.

Formulas: Equation (6.8).

$$\hat{\sigma}_{s,t}^{CAAR} \equiv \sqrt{\sigma^2\left(\widehat{CAAR}_{s,t}\right)} = \sqrt{t - s + 1}\,\sigma\left(\widehat{AAR}_t\right). \tag{8.10}$$

6.4 Calculate the TSs of $\widehat{CAAR}_{-30,t}$ for the Upside Surprise category. Place your calculations at *WorkingSheet* CAAR, within Panel CAAR (-30, *t*) of Table CAAR GOOD (Row title is "TS").

Input for this step: WorkingSheet CAAR, cells T7 to EJ7 of Table CAAR GOOD; *WorkingSheet* CAAR, cells T9 to EJ9 of Table CAAR GOOD.

Output of this step: WorkingSheet CAAR, cells T10 to EJ10 of Table CAAR GOOD.

Formulas: Equation (6.9).

$$TS_{s,t} \equiv \widehat{CAAR}_{s,t} \,/\, \hat{\sigma}_{s,t}^{CAAR} \,\dot{\sim}\, N(0,1). \tag{8.11}$$

6.5 Calculate the upper-tail p-values of $\widehat{CAAR}_{-30,t}$ for the Upside Surprise category. Place your calculations at *WorkingSheet* CAAR, within Panel CAAR (-30, *t*) of Table CAAR GOOD (Row title is "up_tail_p_val.").

Input for this step: WorkingSheet CAAR, cells T10 to EJ10 of Table CAAR GOOD.

Output of this step: WorkingSheet CAAR, cells T11 to EJ11 of Table CAAR GOOD.

Formulas: The required p-values are computed according to the standard normal cumulative distribution function. When the null hypothesis is tested against a unidirectional alternative, such as in the case of the Upside Surprise category, one-tail p-values may be practiced. Specifically, for this category, the upper-tail p-value should be used. It is obtained by integrating the standard normal density function from the calculated value of TS till $(+\infty)$:

$$\begin{aligned} up\_tail\_p\_val.(TS_{s,t}) &\equiv 1-\Phi(TS_{s,t}) = 1-\frac{1}{\sqrt{2\pi}}\int_{-\infty}^{TS_{s,t}} e^{-\frac{z^2}{2}}\,dz \\ &= \frac{1}{\sqrt{2\pi}}\int_{TS_{s,t}}^{\infty} e^{-\frac{z^2}{2}}\,dz. \end{aligned} \tag{8.12}$$

Remarks:

1. You may employ Excel's NORM.S.DIST function to calculate $\Phi(TS_{s,t})$.

2. For the Met Expectations category, the null hypothesis may be tested against a bidirectional alternative, thus two-tail p-values are appropriate. The two-tail p-value is obtained by integrating the standard normal density function, from the absolute value of TS till $(+\infty)$ and multiplying by 2:

$$two\_tail\_p\_val.(TS_{s,t}) \equiv 2\left[1 - \Phi\left(\left|TS_{s,t}\right|\right)\right]. \tag{8.13}$$

3. For the Downside Surprise category, the lower-tail p-value should be used. It is obtained by integrating the standard normal density function from $(-\infty)$ till the calculated value of TS, that is:

$$low\_\_tail\_p\_val.(TS_{s,t}) \equiv \Phi(TS_{s,t}). \tag{8.14}$$

4. Note that the whole empirical picture here is portrayed by testing both unidirectional and bidirectional alternative hypotheses, so one-tail as well as two-tail tests are employed. When reporting research results, one should draw the attention of readers to that point in order to prevent confusion.

6.6 Estimate the 95 and 99 percent confidence thresholds for $\widehat{CAAR}_{-30,t}$ of the Upside Surprise category. Place your calculations at *WorkingSheet* CAAR, within Panel CAAR (–30, *t*) of Table CAAR GOOD ("95% confidence" and "99% confidence," respectively).

Input for this step: WorkingSheet CAAR, cells T9 to EJ9 of Table CAAR GOOD.

Output of this step: WorkingSheet CAAR, cells T12 to EJ12 of Table CAAR GOOD; *WorkingSheet* CAAR, cells T13 to EJ13 of Table CAAR GOOD.

Formulas: The required $(1-\alpha)$ confidence threshold (significance of size α) is computed according to the inverse of the standard normal cumulative distribution function. You may employ Excel's NORM.INV function. For the Upside Surprise category, calculate $NORM.INV(1-\alpha, 0, Est.\_Sigma\_CAAR)$.

Remarks:

1. Recall that for Met Expectations, two-tailed tests are appropriate, thus the confidence intervals have upper and lower bounds, for which the two respective calculations are $NORM.INV(1-\alpha/2, 0, Est.\_Sigma\_CAAR)$ and $NORM.INV(\alpha/2, 0, Est.\_Sigma\_CAAR)$.

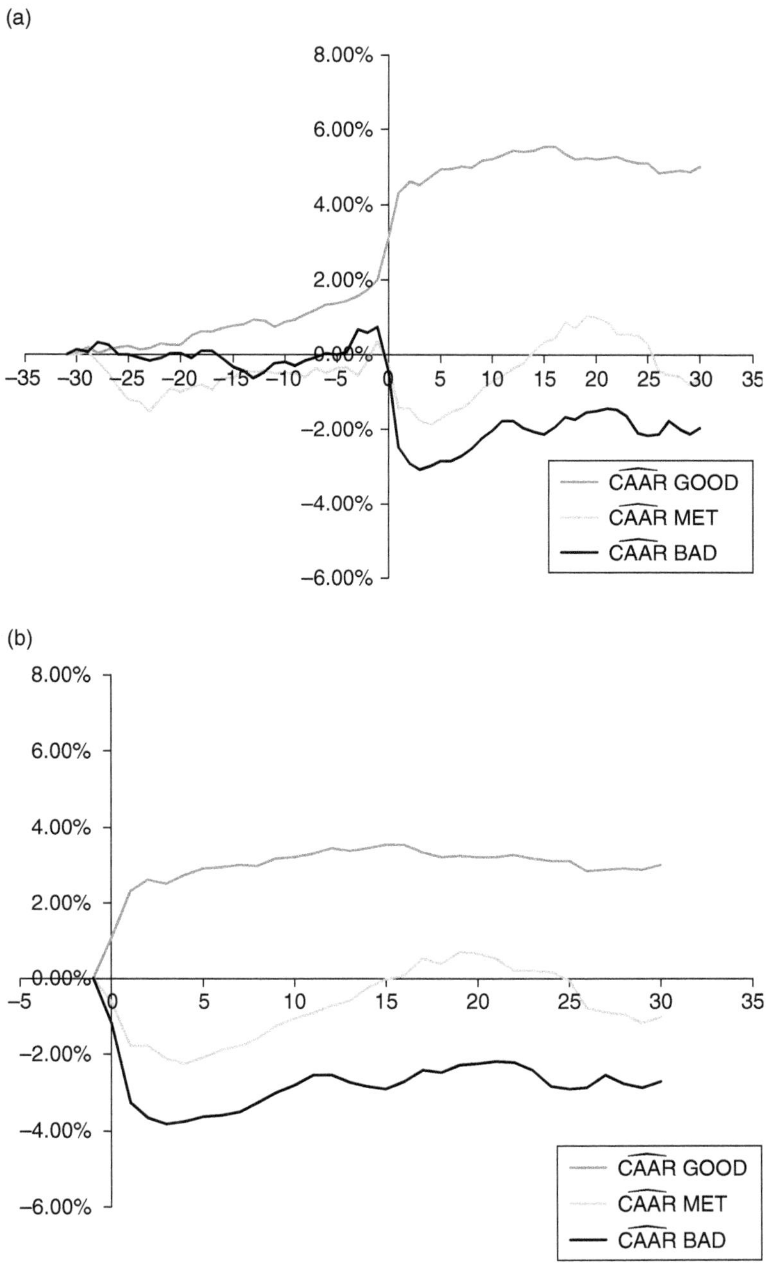

Figure 8.1 Continued on next page.

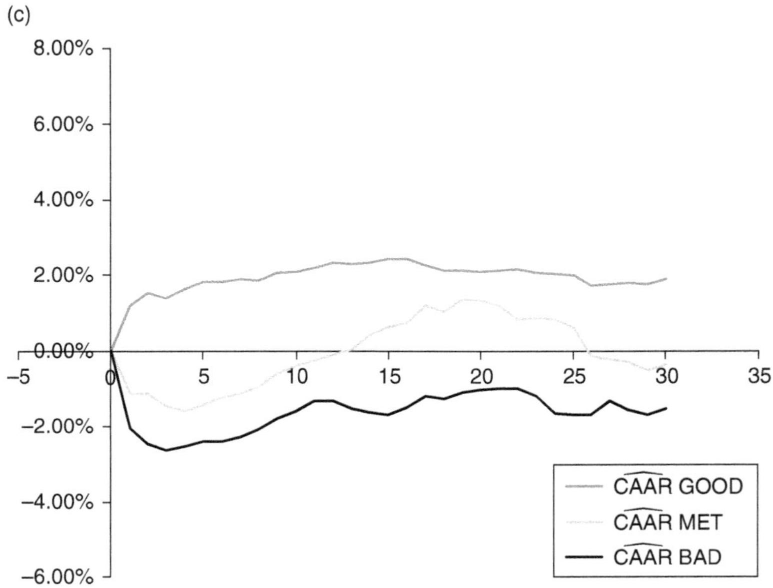

Figure 8.1 Extended exercise, clustering-adjusted procedure: $\widehat{CAAR}_{-30,t}$, $\widehat{CAAR}_{0,t}$, and $\widehat{CAAR}_{1,t}$ for the three Surprise categories. (a) $\widehat{CAAR}_{-30,t}$ for all Surprise categories, (b) $\widehat{CAAR}_{0,t}$ for all Surprise categories, and (c) $\widehat{CAAR}_{1,t}$ for all Surprise categories.

2. For Downside Surprise, calculate

$$NORM.INV(\alpha, 0, Est.\_Sigma\_CAAR).$$

8.1.1. Results and Discussion

We are now ready to view the results of the clustering-adjusted process and compare them to the solution of the basic exercise presented in chapter 7. Before you can continue, you need to equalize your work with the provided solution (http://dx.doi.org/10.6084/m9.figshare.1221837), which may be downloaded from the book's website.

The global picture emerging from the exercise is depicted in Figure 8.1. Note that, compared to the basic analysis presented in chapter 7, the clustering adjustment does not affect the estimated CAAR series.

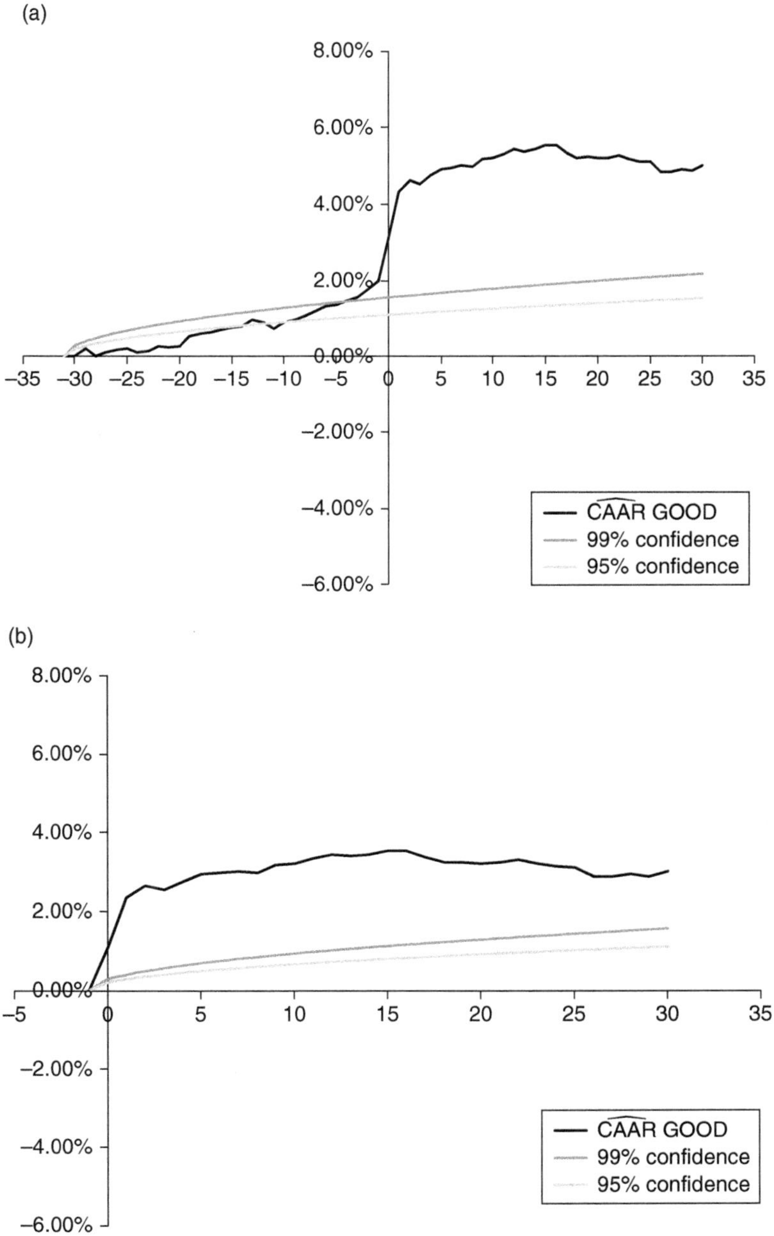

Figure 8.2 Continued on next page.

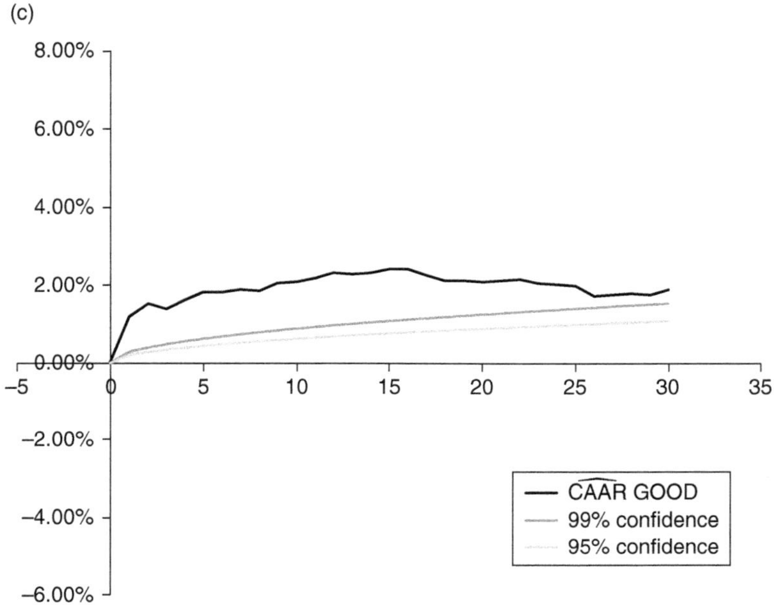

Figure 8.2 Extended exercise, clustering-adjusted procedure: $\widehat{CAAR}_{-30,t}$, $\widehat{CAAR}_{0,t}$, and $\widehat{CAAR}_{1,t}$ for the Upside Surprise category. (a) $\widehat{CAAR}_{-30,t}$ for the Upside Surprise category, (b) $\widehat{CAAR}_{0,t}$ for the Upside Surprise category, and (c) $\widehat{CAAR}_{1,t}$ for the Upside Surprise category.

Inspecting the graph of each surprise category separately (Figures 8.2, 8.3, and 8.4, which contain their confidence thresholds) reveals that statistical conclusions remain intact as well. Thus, while the example served well for demonstrating the clustering adjustment recipe of chapter 6, the effect of clustering on TSs in this specific case is not crucial.

8.2. Nonparametric Testing

In this section we employ nonparametric event study tests using the TSs introduced in section 6.2 of chapter 6. The Excel template for this exercise (http://dx.doi.org/10.6084/m9.figshare.1221840) may be downloaded

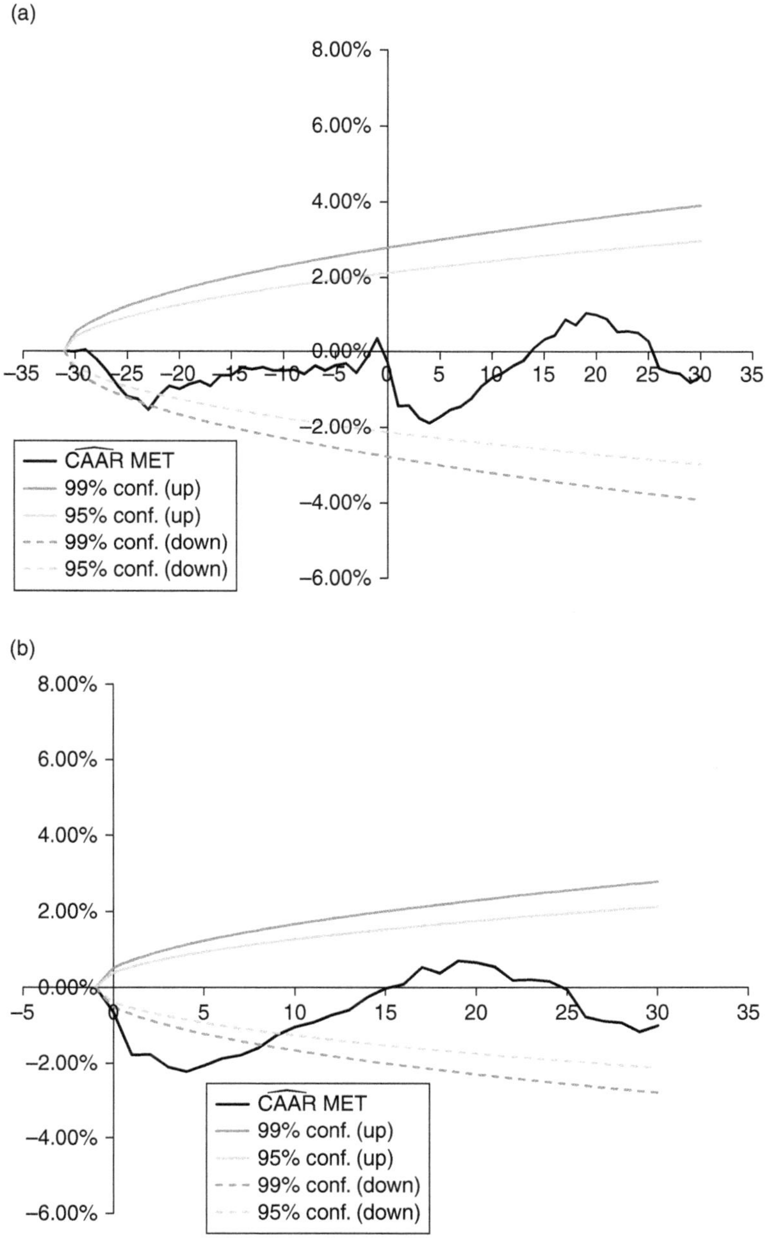

Figure 8.3 Continued on next page.

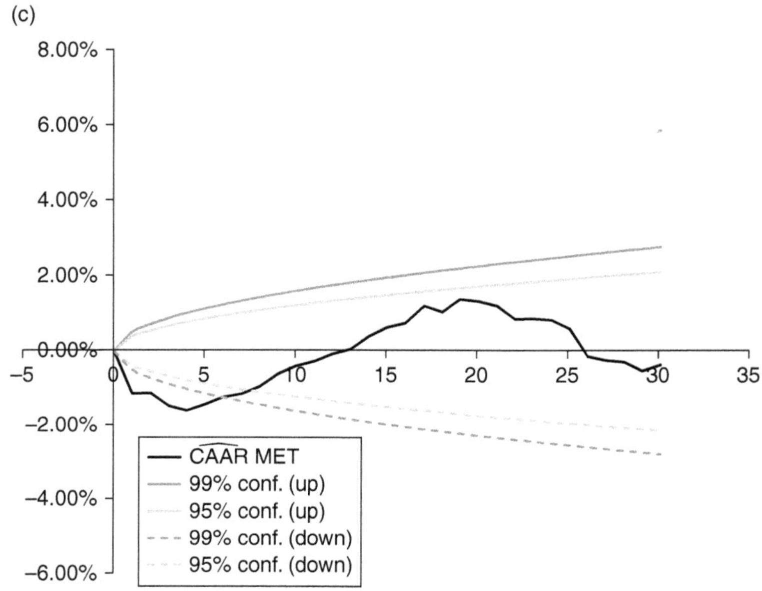

Figure 8.3 Extended exercise, clustering-adjusted procedure: $\widehat{CAAR}_{-30,t}$, $\widehat{CAAR}_{0,t}$, and $\widehat{CAAR}_{1,t}$ for the Met Expectations category. (a) $\widehat{CAAR}_{-30,t}$ for the Met Expectations category, (b) $\widehat{CAAR}_{0,t}$ for the Met Expectations category, and (c) $\widehat{CAAR}_{1,t}$ for the Met Expectations category.

from the book's website. Specifically, we use here a couple of nonparametric test approaches: the sign test and the rank test.

In case you wish to solve the exercise without our intermediation, skip the instructions below, use a copy of the dataset file (http://dx.doi.org/10.6084/m9.figshare.1221834) and work independently. When you finish, please rejoin in the last subsection of this section, "Results and Discussion", to view the results and discuss the provided solution.

In a nutshell, the sign test is built on the signs of $\widehat{AR}s$, which, under the null hypothesis of no reaction to the studied event, are presumed to be positive or negative with equal probabilities. Although the sign test is nonparametric in nature, it still requires symmetry of the underlying distribution, as well as cross-sectional independence.[5] Therefore, it is misspecified inasmuch the ARs are skewed. The rank test overpowers this obstacle, by

(a)

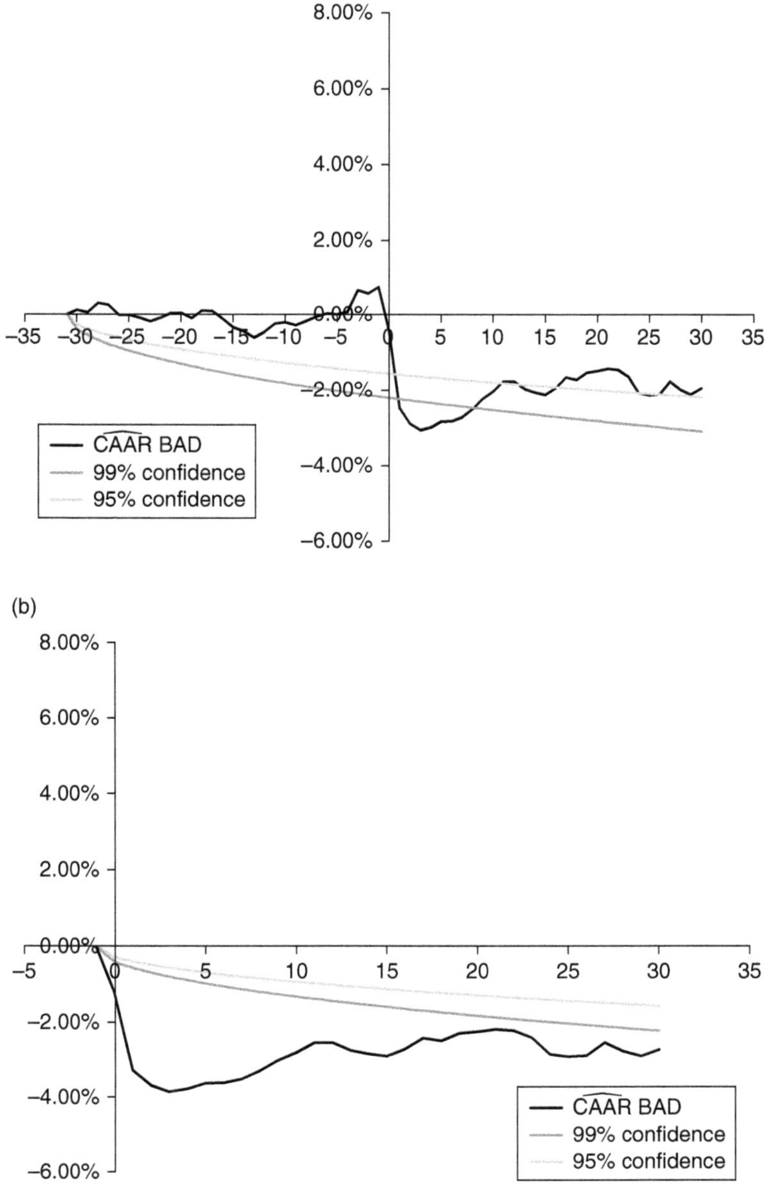

Figure 8.4 Continued on next page.

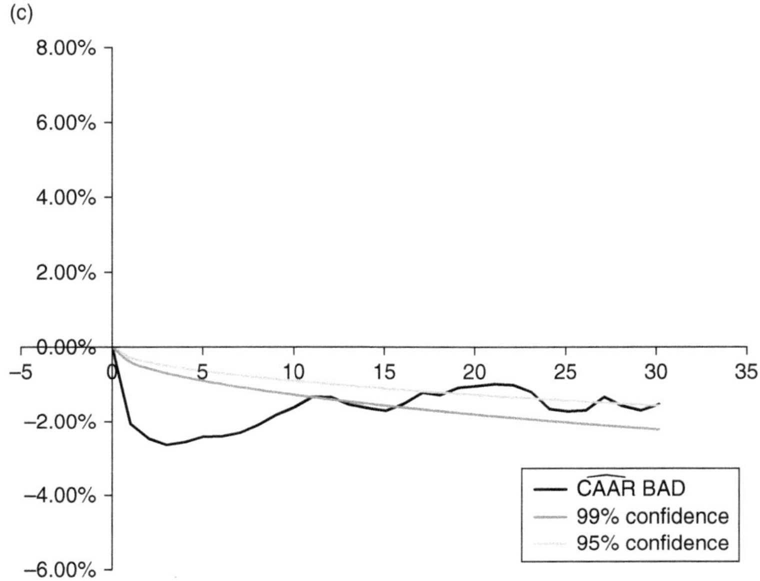

Figure 8.4 Extended exercise, clustering-adjusted procedure: $\widehat{CAAR}_{-30,t}$, $\widehat{CAAR}_{0,t}$, and $\widehat{CAAR}_{1,t}$ for the Downside Surprise category. (a) $\widehat{CAAR}_{-30,t}$ for the Downside Surprise category, (b) $\widehat{CAAR}_{0,t}$ for the Downside Surprise category, and (c) $\widehat{CAAR}_{1,t}$ for the Downside Surprise category.

inspecting the ranks of $\widehat{ARs}$, thus allowing for unequal proportions of positive and negative values.

The worksheets contained in the spreadsheet template for nonparametric testing are presented in Table 8.2.

Now we are ready to work on the nonparametric event study exercise. To do so, open the nonparametric testing exercise template (http://dx.doi.org/10.6084/m9.figshare.1221840) and follow the guidelines. As before, the instructions are listed by *stages* that comprise detailed *steps*. The preparation of data in the form of $\widehat{ARs}$ (stage 1 and stage 2) is the same as in the parametric procedure presented in chapter 7 (reintroduced in the clustering-adjusted exercise of the previous section). Subsequently, most of the instructions are unique for the nonparametric example. Thus, in the list of stages, we refer to the former lists for specific instructions, instead of repeating them verbatim.

Table 8.2 Nonparametric testing exercise template

Worksheets	Description
DataSheets	
TOU	Terms of use: Personal and noncommercial use limitation
README	Abbreviated description of the variables contained in the dataset
STOCK DATA	Firms' characteristics and stock price records (see details below)
INDEX DATA	Market index (S&P 500) records for the event dates (the firms' characteristics appear again, for convenience)
WorkingSheets	
STOCK RETURNS	Placeholder for calculating stock returns
INDEX RETURNS	Placeholder for calculating index returns
AR	Placeholder for estimating ARs
AR GOOD / AR MET / AR BAD	Placeholders for partitioning the estimated ARs into categories according to the direction of the hypothesized reaction to the event
TS(Sign) / TS(Rank)	Placeholders for computing the sign and rank nonparametric test statistics
GraphSheets	
GRAPH TS(Sign) ALL / GOOD / MET / BAD	Placeholders for graphical representation of CAAR series
GRAPH TS(Rank) ALL / GOOD / MET / BAD	

Stage 1: AR Estimation

See section 7.4. in chapter 7 or section 8.1 in the current chapter.

Stage 2: Data sorting

See Section 7.4. in chapter 7 or section 8.1 in the current chapter.

Stage 3: Computing the Sign Test-Statistic, TS(Sign)

In this stage, you use each Surprise category's $\widehat{AR}s$ to arrive at the Sign-Test Statistics. The instructions are specified for the Upside Surprise category. After completing each step, replicate them with required modifications on Met Expectations and Downside Surprise categories.

3.1 For each time relative to the event, count the number of positive, zero, and negative $\widehat{AR}s$. Use cells EN2 to JD4 of *WorkingSheet* AR GOOD to enter your calculations.

Input for this step: WorkingSheet AR GOOD, columns T to EJ with *AR(–30)...AR(90).*

Output of this step: WorkingSheet AR GOOD, cells EN2 to JD4 (to the right of the AR table).

Formulas: Employ Excel's COUNTIF function, with each of the three conditions: ">0," "=0," "<0."

Remarks:

1. The number of securities with positive $\widehat{AR}_t^i$, n_t^+ is counted with ">0."
2. The number of observations in the subsample, n, is the total count (which is 395 in this case).
3. The number of observations counted with "=0" may reveal if there are any "ties" (no such in this case).
4. We focus on the TSs for AR(–30)...AR(30), but the instructions help you build them for the whole sampling period.
5. Repeat the step with required modifications for Met Expectations and Downside Surprise categories.

3.2 For each time relative to the event, compute TS(Sign). Place your formulas at cells EN5 to JD5 of *WorkingSheet* AR GOOD.

Input for this step: WorkingSheet AR GOOD, cells EN2 to JD4.

Output of this step: WorkingSheet AR GOOD, cells EN5 to JD5.
Formulas: Equation (6.11).

$$TS_t^{sign} \equiv \left(\frac{n_t^+}{n} - 0.5\right)\frac{\sqrt{n}}{0.5} \overset{.}{\sim} N(0,1). \tag{8.15}$$

Remark: Repeat the step with required modifications for Met Expectations and Downside Surprise categories.

Stage 4: Computing the Rank Test-Statistic, TS(Rank)

In this stage, you compute the Rank Test-Statistics for each Surprise category's $\widehat{AR}s$. As in stage 3, the instructions are specified for the Upside Surprise category, and you should replicate them with required modifications for the Met Expectations and Downside Surprise categories.

4.1 For each observation in the Upside Surprise category, compute the ranks of $\widehat{AR}s$ within the event window. Place your calculations in columns JG to LO of *WorkingSheet* AR GOOD.

Input for this step: WorkingSheet AR GOOD, columns T to CB with *AR(–30)... AR(30).*

Output of this step: WorkingSheet AR GOOD, columns JG to LO for the ranks of $\widehat{AR}s$ (to the right of the TS(Sign) table).
Formulas: Employ Excel's RANK.AVG function.

Remarks:

1. Rank $\widehat{AR}s$ in the list sorted ascending;
2. Repeat the step with required modifications for Met Expectations and Downside Surprise categories.

4.2 For each time relative to the event, compute the TS(Rank). Place your formulas at columns LS to OA, rows 2, 3, and 5 of *WorkingSheet* AR GOOD.

Input for this step: WorkingSheet AR GOOD, columns JG to LO for the ranks of $\widehat{AR}s$ (to the right of the TS(Sign) table).

Output of this step: WorkingSheet AR GOOD, columns LS to OA, rows 2, 3, and 5.

Formulas: Equations (6.12) and (6.13).

$$TS_t^{rank} = \frac{1}{n}\sum_{i=1}^{n}\left(K_t^i - \frac{t_{End}^{EventWin} - t_{Start}^{EventWin} + 1}{2}\right) / \, s(K) \stackrel{\sim}{\sim} N(0,1), \quad (8.16)$$

$$s(K)=\sqrt{\frac{1}{t_{End}^{EventWin}-t_{Start}^{EventWin}}\sum_{\tau=t_{Start}^{EventWin}}^{t_{End}^{EventWin}}\left[\frac{1}{n}\sum_{i=1}^{n}\left(K_{\tau}^{i}-\frac{t_{End}^{EventWin}-t_{Start}^{EventWin}+1}{2}\right)\right]^{2}}\,. \tag{8.17}$$

Remarks:

1. For convenience, the TS formula is divided into two separate calculations, of its numerator and denominator. Use row 5 for the quotient.
2. Equation (8.17) is the denominator of TS(Rank). Use row 3 to compute it.
3. Place the numerator of TS(Rank) in row 2.
4. Repeat the step with required modifications for Met Expectations and Downside Surprise categories.

Stage 5: Calculating Descriptive Statistics within the Surprise Categories

This stage is essentially identical to stage 5 of section 7.4. in chapter 7 (or section 8.1 in the current chapter). Please see details there.

Stage 6: Conducting Statistical Inference for TS(Sign) and TS(Rank) within the Surprise Categories

In this stage, you apply nonparametric statistical analysis to assess the significance of the observed reaction of each Surprise category to the studied event. Specifically, you calculate the p-values and 95 and 99 percent confidence thresholds for TS(Sign) and TS(Rank) for each data category (Good/Met/Bad). We henceforth demonstrate how to do so for the Upside Surprise category. The statistics of Met Expectations and Downside Surprise categories may be obtained in a similar manner (some necessary modifications appear below as remarks to the calculation steps). The format of predesigned tables for placing your calculations is kept as similar as possible to the tables in other exercises (this is the reason to the grayed areas you will see there, with some obvious values and formulas).

6.1 Copy TS(Sign) and TS(Rank) from *WorkingSheet* AR GOOD to Tables TS(Sign) GOOD and TS(Rank) GOOD in *WorkingSheets* TS(Sign) and TS(Rank), respectively.

Input for this step: WorkingSheet AR GOOD, cells EN5 to JD5 with TS(Sign); *WorkingSheet* AR GOOD, cells LS5 to OA5 with TS(Rank).

Output of this step: WorkingSheet TS(Sign), cells T7 to EJ7 of Table TS(Sign) GOOD; *WorkingSheet* TS(Rank), cells T7 to EJ7 of Table TS(Rank) GOOD.

Formulas: None (copy/paste step).

6.2 Calculate the upper-tail p-values of TS(Sign) and TS(Rank) for the Upside Surprise category. Place your calculations at Tables TS(Sign) GOOD and TS(Rank) GOOD in *WorkingSheets* TS(Sign) and TS(Rank), respectively (Row title is "up_tail_p_val.").

Input for this step: WorkingSheet TS(Sign), cells T7 to EJ7 of Tables TS(Sign) GOOD; *WorkingSheet* TS(Rank), cells T7 to EJ7 of Tables TS(Rank) GOOD.

Output of this step: WorkingSheet TS(Sign), cells T11 to EJ11 of Table TS(Sign) GOOD; *WorkingSheet* TS(Rank), cells T11 to EJ11 of Table TS(Rank) GOOD.

Formulas: The required p-values are computed according to the standard normal cumulative distribution function. When the null hypothesis is tested against a unidirectional alternative, such as in the case of the Upside Surprise category, one-tail p-values may be practiced. Specifically, for this category, the upper-tail p-value should be used. It is obtained by integrating the standard normal density function from the calculated value of TS till (+∞):

$$up\_\_tail\_p\_val.\left(TS_{s,t}\right) \equiv 1 - \Phi\left(TS_{s,t}\right)$$
$$= 1 - \frac{1}{\sqrt{2\pi}} \int_{-\infty}^{TS_{s,t}} e^{-\frac{z}{2}} dz = \frac{1}{\sqrt{2\pi}} \int_{TS_{s,t}}^{\infty} e^{-\frac{z}{2}} dz. \quad (8.18)$$

Remarks:

1. You may employ Excel's NORM.S.DIST function to calculate $\Phi(TS_{s,t})$.

2. For the Met Expectations category, the null hypothesis may be tested against a bidirectional alternative, thus two-tail p-values are appropriate. The two-tail p-value is obtained by integrating the standard normal density function from the absolute value of *TS* till ($+\infty$) and multiplying by 2:

$$two\_tail\_p\_val.\left(TS_{s,t}\right) \equiv 2\left[1-\Phi\left(\left|TS_{s,t}\right|\right)\right]. \tag{8.19}$$

3. For the Downside Surprise category, the lower-tail p-value should be used. It is obtained by integrating the standard normal density function from ($-\infty$) till the calculated value of TS, that is:

$$low\_\_tail\_p\_val.\left(TS_{s,t}\right) \equiv \Phi\left(TS_{s,t}\right). \tag{8.20}$$

4. Note that the whole empirical picture here is portrayed by testing both unidirectional and bidirectional alternative hypotheses, so one-tail as well as two-tail tests are employed. When reporting research results, one should draw the attention of readers to that point in order to prevent confusion.

6.3 Estimate 95 and 99 percent confidence thresholds for TS(Sign) and TS(Rank) of the Upside Surprise category. Place your calculations at tables TS(Sign) GOOD and TS(Rank) GOOD in *WorkingSheets* TS(Sign) and TS(Rank) (Row titles are "95% confidence" and "99% confidence," respectively).

Input for this step: WorkingSheet TS(Sign), cells T9 to EJ9 of Table TS(Sign) GOOD; *WorkingSheet* TS(Rank), cells T9 to EJ9 of Table TS(Rank) GOOD.

Output of this step: WorkingSheet TS(Sign), cells T12 to EJ13 of Table TS(Sign) GOOD; *WorkingSheet* TS(Rank), cells T12 to EJ13 of Table TS(Rank) GOOD.

Formulas: The required $(1-\alpha)$ confidence threshold (significance of size α) is computed according to the inverse of the standard normal cumulative distribution function. You may employ Excel's NORM.INV function. For the Upside Surprise category, calculate $NORM.INV\left(1-\alpha,0,1\right)$.

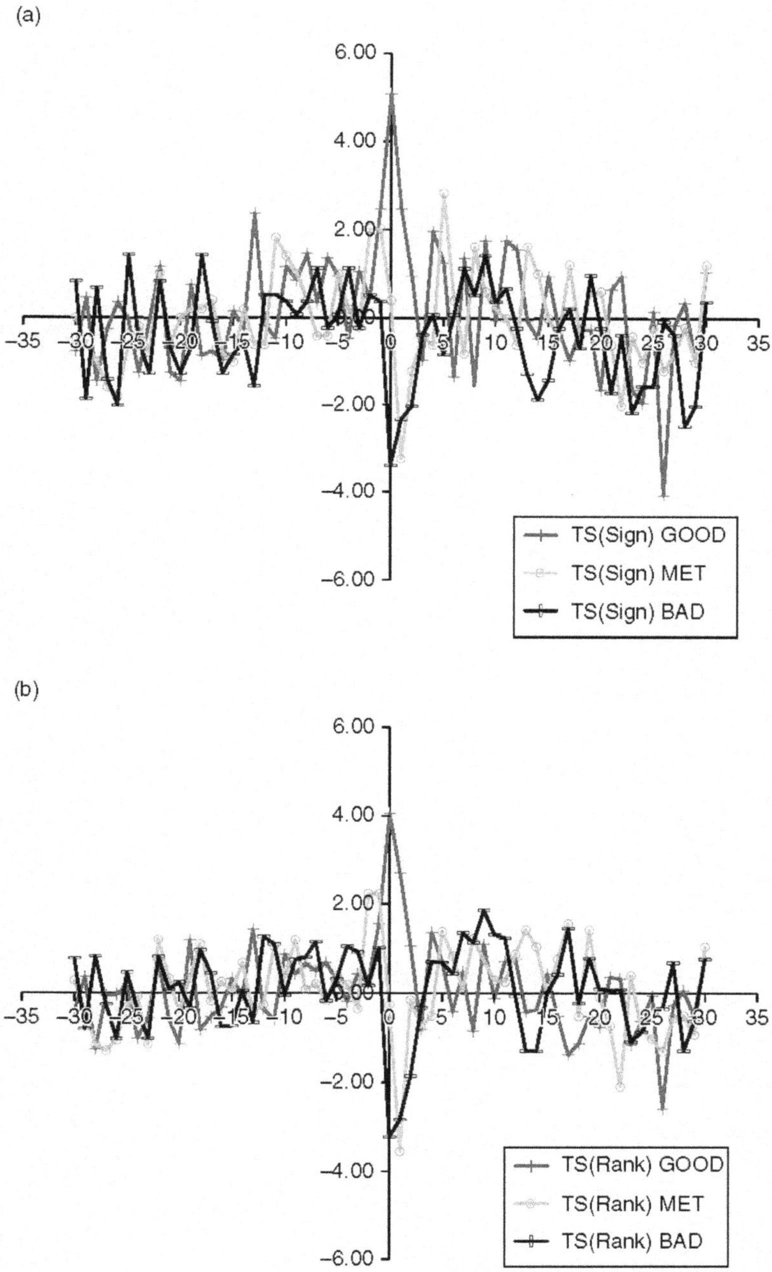

Figure 8.5 Extended exercise, nonparametric testing: TS(Sign) and TS(Rank) for the three Surprise categories. (a) TS(Sign) for all Surprise categories and (b) TS(Rank) for all Surprise categories.

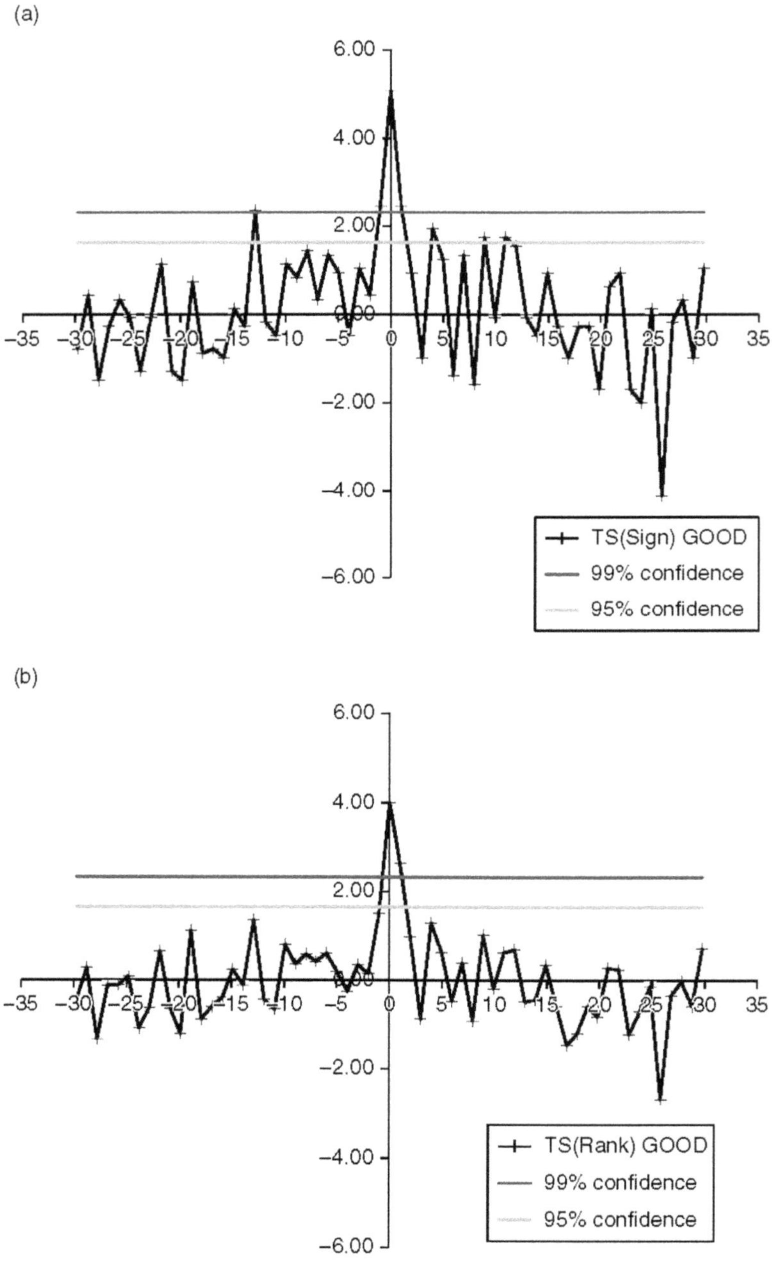

Figure 8.6 Extended exercise, nonparametric testing: TS(Sign) and TS(Rank) for the Upside Surprise category. (a) TS(Sign) for the Upside Surprise category and (b) TS(Rank) for the Upside Surprise category.

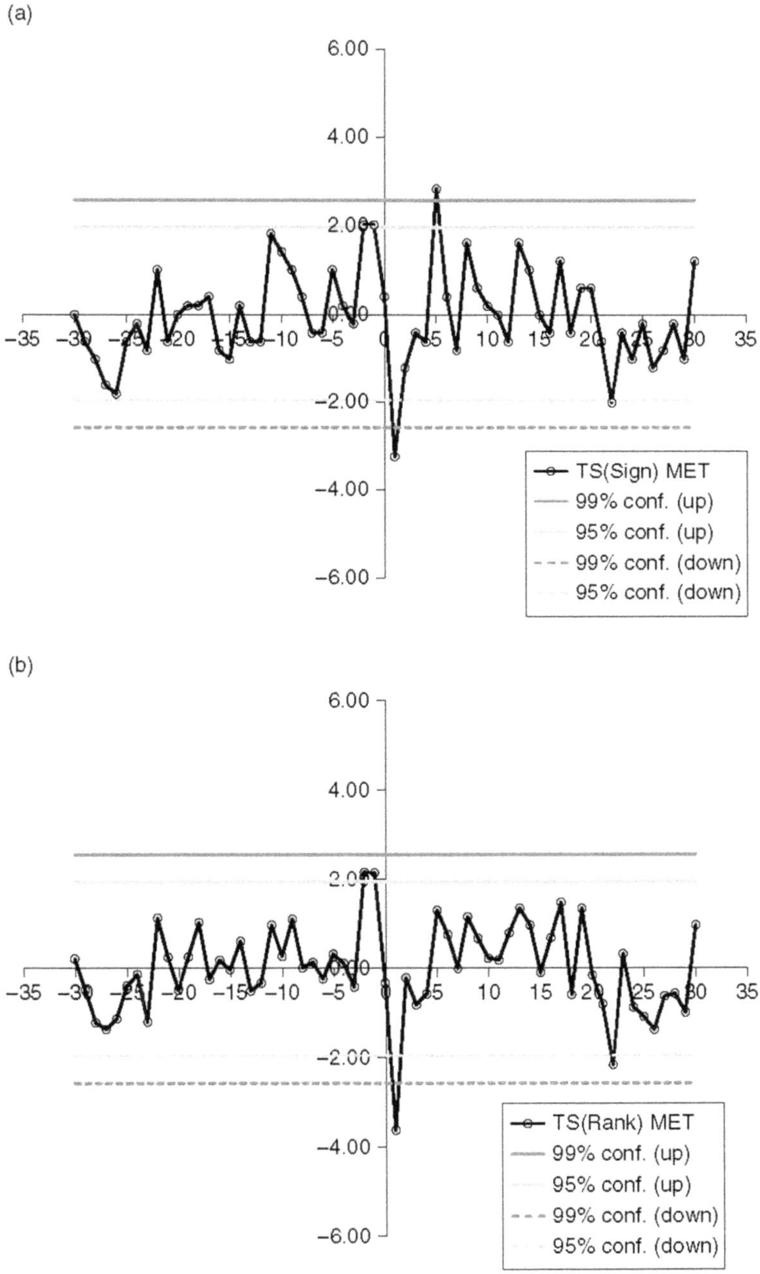

Figure 8.7 Extended exercise, nonparametric testing: TS(Sign) and TS(Rank) for the Met Expectations category. (a) TS(Sign) for the Met Expectations category and (b) TS(Rank) for the Met Expectations category.

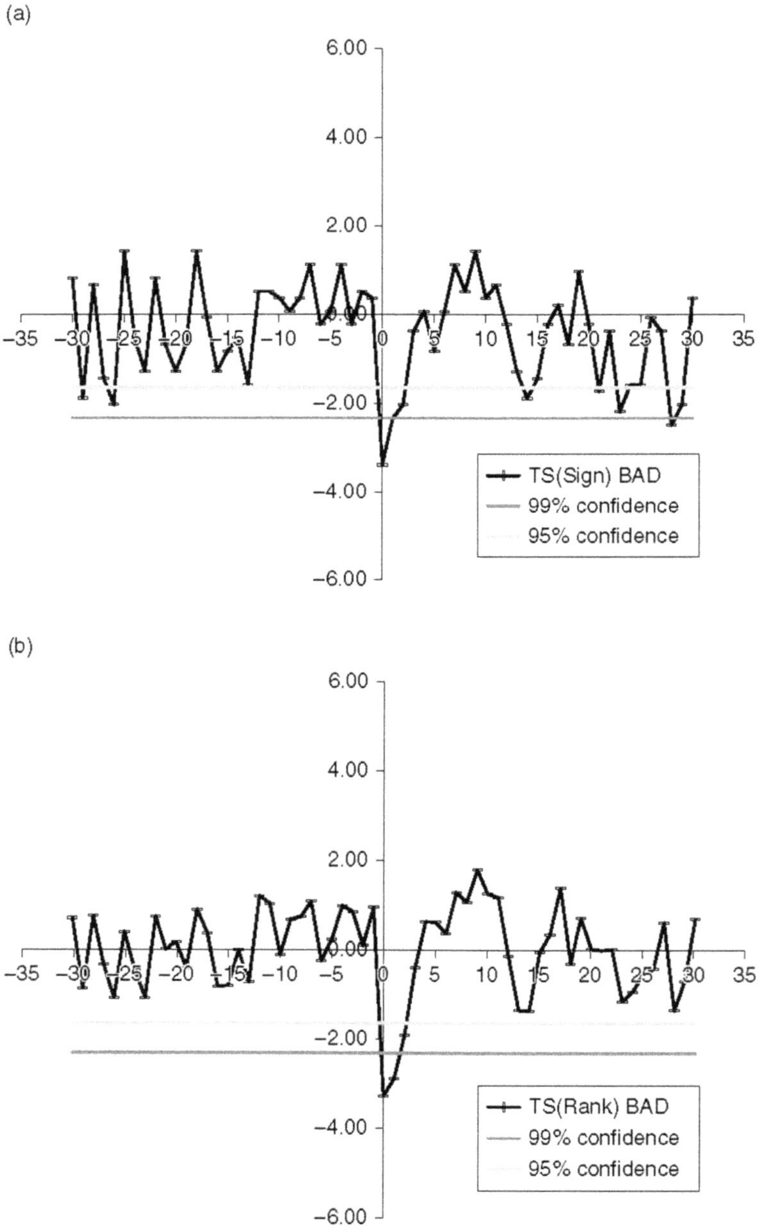

Figure 8.8 Extended exercise, nonparametric testing: TS(Sign) and TS(Rank) for the Downside Surprise category. (a) TS(Sign) for the Downside Surprise category and (b) TS(Rank) for the Downside Surprise category.

Remarks:

1. Recall that for Met Expectations, two-tailed tests are appropriate, thus the confidence intervals have upper and lower bounds, for which the two respective calculations are $NORM.INV(1-\alpha/2,0,1)$ and $NORM.INV(\alpha/2,0,1)$.
2. For Downside Surprise, calculate $NORM.INV(\alpha,0,1)$.

8.2.1. Results and Discussion

We are now ready to view the results of the nonparametric statistical inference process, draw conclusions, and compare them to those of the basic exercise presented in chapter 7. Before you can continue, you need to equalize your work with the provided solution (http://dx.doi.org/10.6084/m9.figshare.1221839), which may be downloaded from the book's website.

The general results of the nonparametric statistical inference are depicted in Figure 8.5, combining all three categories. Evidently, the results corroborate the conclusions stemming from the basic analysis presented in chapter 7.

Specifically, for the Upside Surprise category, there is a significant positive reaction on the day of the announcement, as well as on the following day, according to both sign and rank tests. According to the rank test, there is also evidence of a positive reaction on the day before the announcement ($t = -1$).

For the Met Expectations category, there is a significant negative reaction on the day following the event ($t = 1$), according to both tests, and for the Downside Surprise category, there is a significant negative reaction on the event day, and possibly also shortly afterwards. Separate results for each Surprise category are depicted in Figures 8.6, 8.7, and 8.8.

8.3. Applying the Single-Factor Benchmark of Returns

As explained in chapter 3, employing alternative models of returns may help in testing the robustness of ESA results to the selected benchmark of NRs. To address this issue in the present context, we devised the current exercise of reevaluating the estimated CAARs using the single-factor

(a)

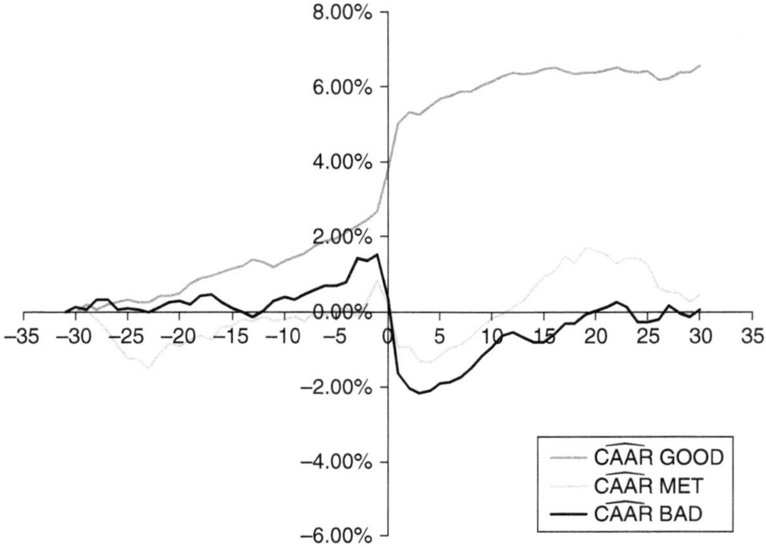

(b)

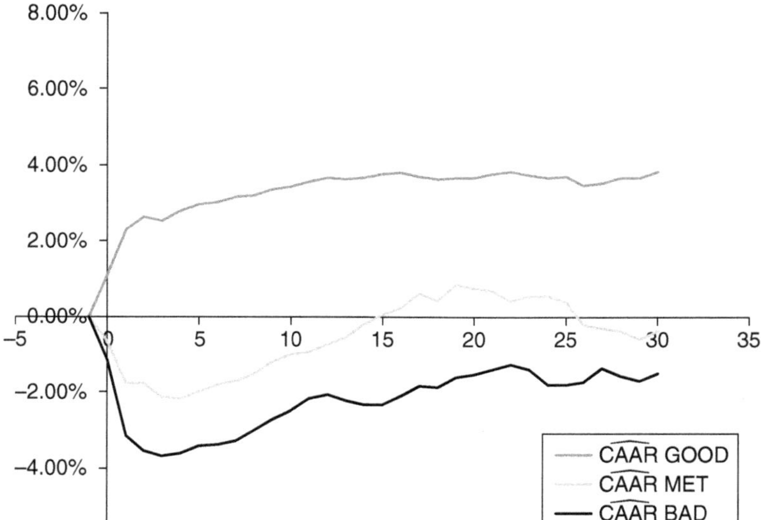

Figure 8.9 Continued on next page.

(c)

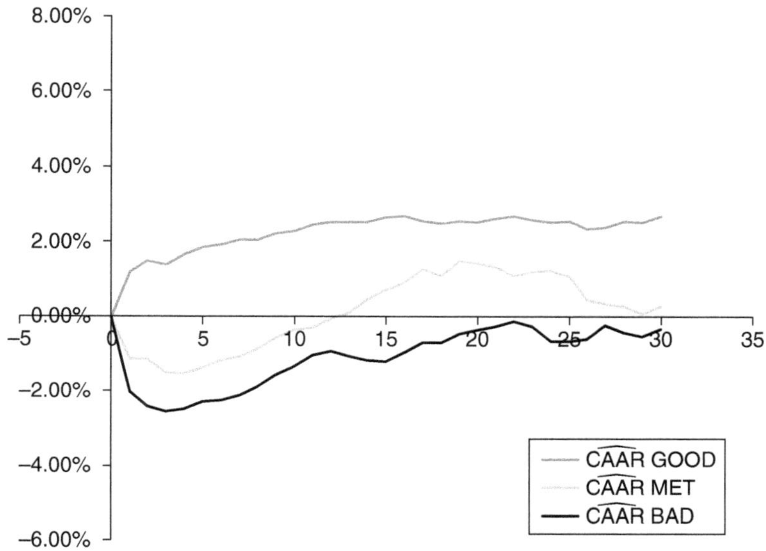

Figure 8.9 Extended exercise, applying the single-factor benchmark of returns: $\widehat{CAAR}_{-30,t}$, $\widehat{CAAR}_{0,t}$, and $\widehat{CAAR}_{1,t}$ for the three Surprise categories. (a) $\widehat{CAAR}_{-30,t}$ for all Surprise categories, (b) $\widehat{CAAR}_{0,t}$ for all Surprise categories, and (c) $\widehat{CAAR}_{1,t}$ for all Surprise categories.

model of NRs and comparing the results to those obtained in the basic setup, with the naïve benchmark.

The single-factor exercise template and solution (http://dx.doi.org/10.6084/m9.figshare.1221843 and http://dx.doi.org/10.6084/m9.figshare.1221841, respectively) may be downloaded from the book's website. If you wish to solve the exercise without using the predesigned template, feel free to use a copy of the dataset file (http://dx.doi.org/10.6084/m9.figshare.1221834) and stylize your own format.

The exercise follows similar lines as those of the basic (clustering-unadjusted) procedure of chapter 7. The difference between them is in the estimation of ARs (step 1.3 in stage 1 of chapter 7 instructions). Afterwards, the two exercises are back on the same track, with the necessary exercise-specific modifications.

For the estimation of ARs, you should apply here the single-factor benchmark, introduced in subsection 3.1.2 of chapter 3. The single-factor benchmark parameters, namely, Alpha and Beta of each stock's

(a)

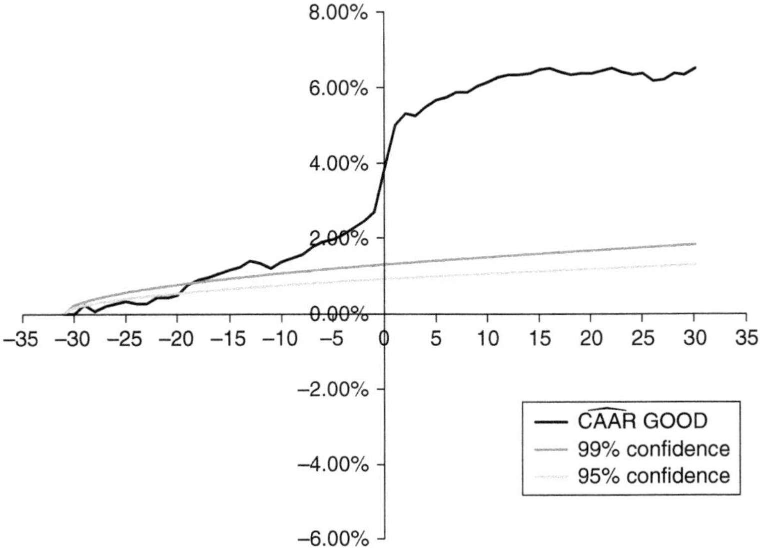

(b)

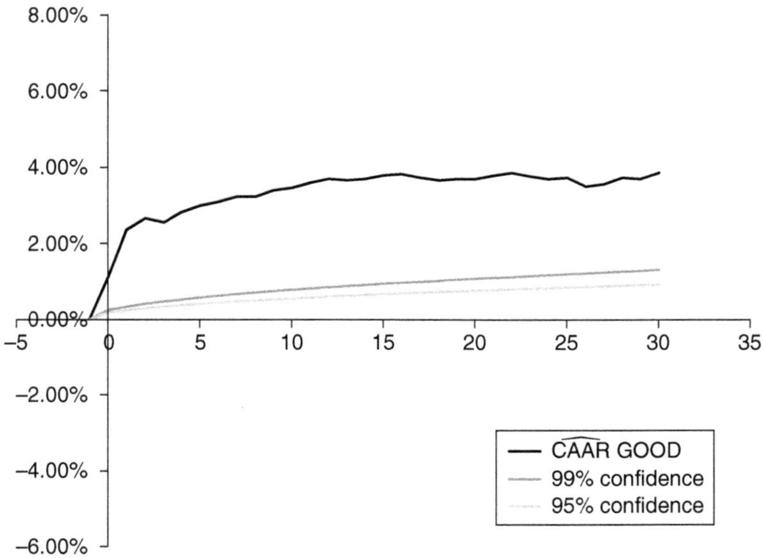

Figure 8.10 Continued on next page.

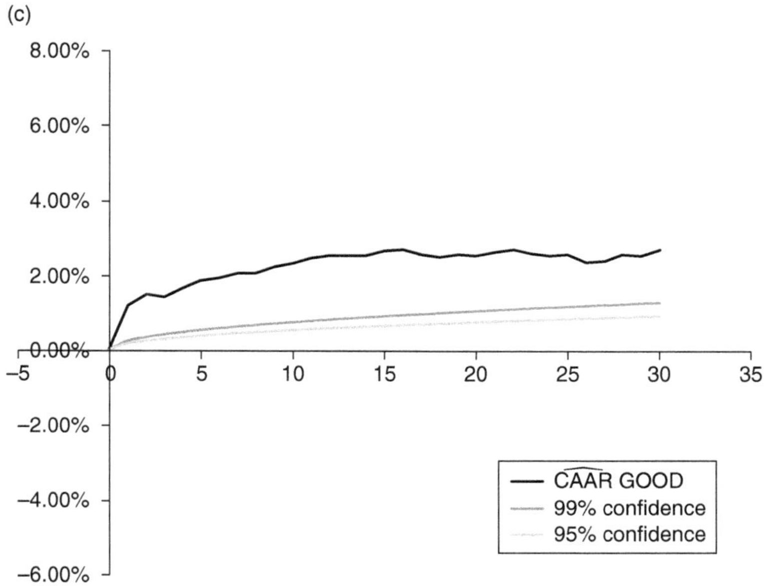

Figure 8.10 Extended exercise, applying the single-factor benchmark of returns: $\widehat{CAAR}_{-30,t}$, $\widehat{CAAR}_{0,t}$, and $\widehat{CAAR}_{1,t}$ for the Upside Surprise category. (a) $\widehat{CAAR}_{-30,t}$ for the Upside Surprise category, (b) $\widehat{CAAR}_{0,t}$ for the Upside Surprise category, and (c) $\widehat{CAAR}_{1,t}$ for the Upside Surprise category.

characteristic line, may be estimated using the respective stock and index data from the estimation window, defined in section 7.3 of chapter 7 (see also Figure 7.1). Note that you may estimate Alpha and Beta with Excel's INTERCEPT and SLOPE functions, respectively.

The results are depicted in Figure 8.9. Overall, there are hardly any differences between the current results and those obtained under the naïve benchmark. In all three Surprise categories, the reactions to the event are similar to those reported in chapter 7.

From the separate analysis of each category, it turns out that the negative reactions in Met Expectations and Downside Surprise categories are somewhat less statistically significant than their naïve benchmark counterparts (See Figures 8.10, 8.11, and 8.12). The graphs of both Surprise categories are crossing their 95 percent confidence threshold, but merely touch their 99 percent thresholds in the graphs depicting the whole event

(a)

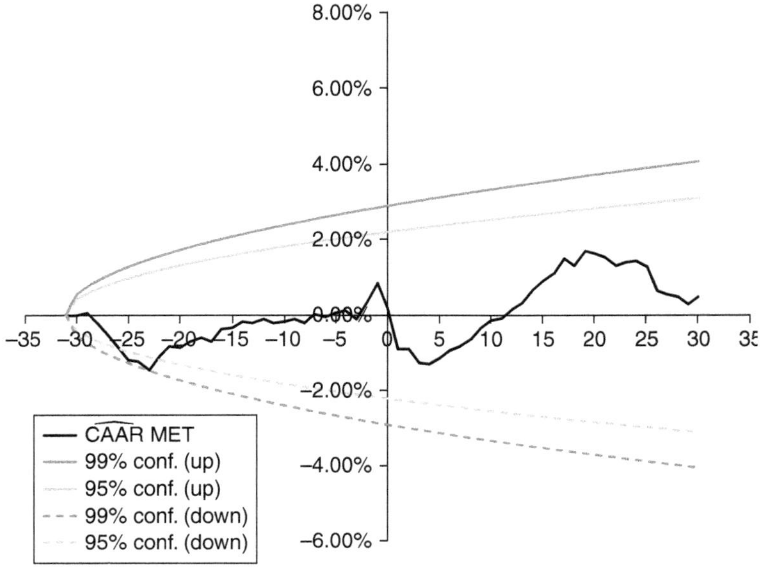

(b)

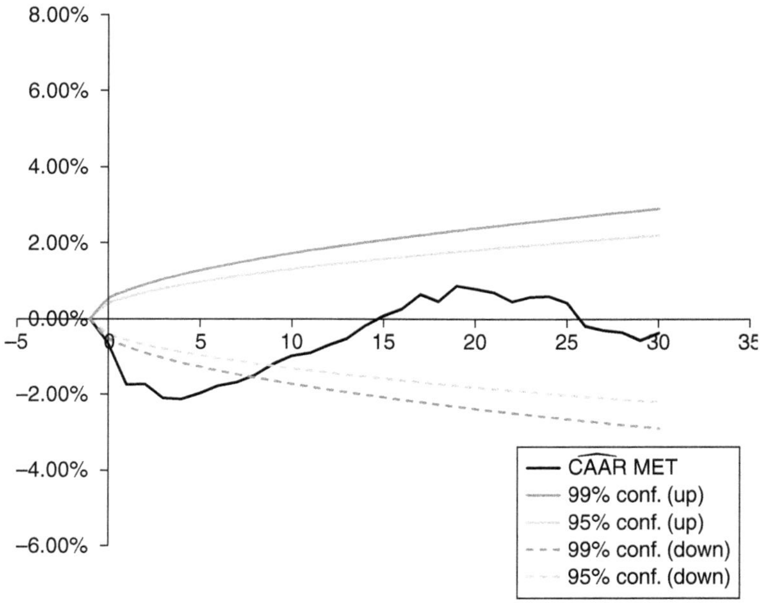

Figure 8.11 Continued on next page.

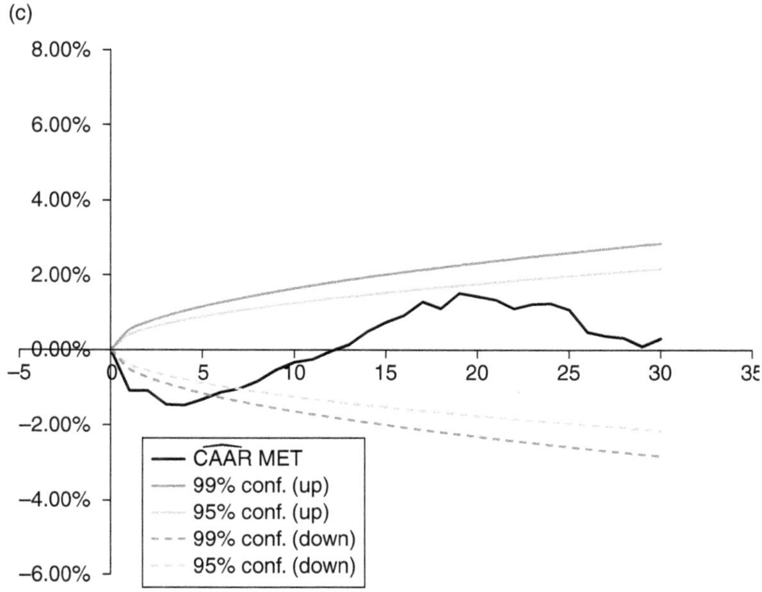

Figure 8.11 Extended exercise, applying the single-factor benchmark of returns: $\widehat{CAAR}_{-30,t}$, $\widehat{CAAR}_{0,t}$, and $\widehat{CAAR}_{1,t}$ for the Met Expectations category. (a) $\widehat{CAAR}_{-30,t}$ for the Met Expectations category, (b) $\widehat{CAAR}_{0,t}$ for the Met Expectations category, and (c) $\widehat{CAAR}_{1,t}$ for the Met Expectations category.

window. Other than that, all the conclusions reached when using the naïve benchmark of returns remain intact.

Thus, we found no evidence suggesting sensitivity of the results to the employed normal-return benchmark. Of course, in actual research projects, one may wish to further check robustness to model specification with yet other normal-return benchmarks, such as those obtained with the three- or four-factor return models.

8.4. Analyzing the Effect of the Magnitude of Surprise

The market reaction to the event may be more deeply examined by employing a finer partition of the data to investigate the effect of the magnitude of the surprise.

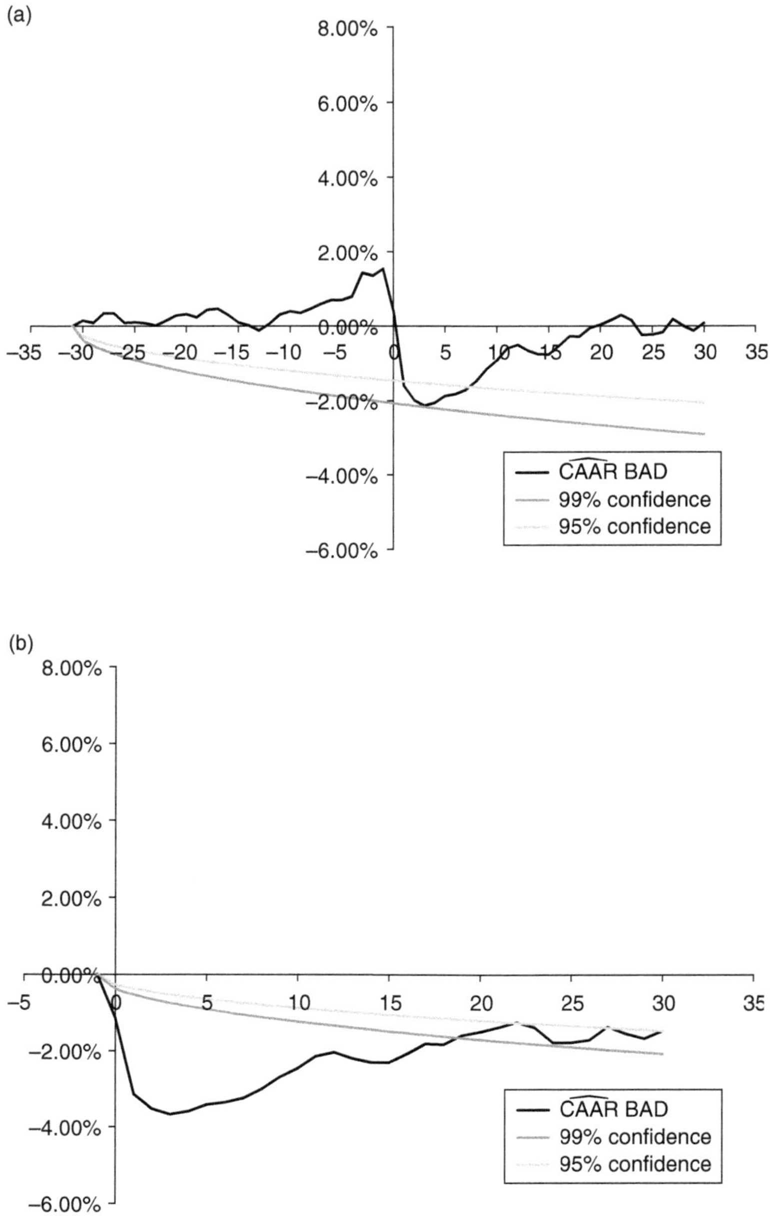

Figure 8.12 Continued on next page.

(c)

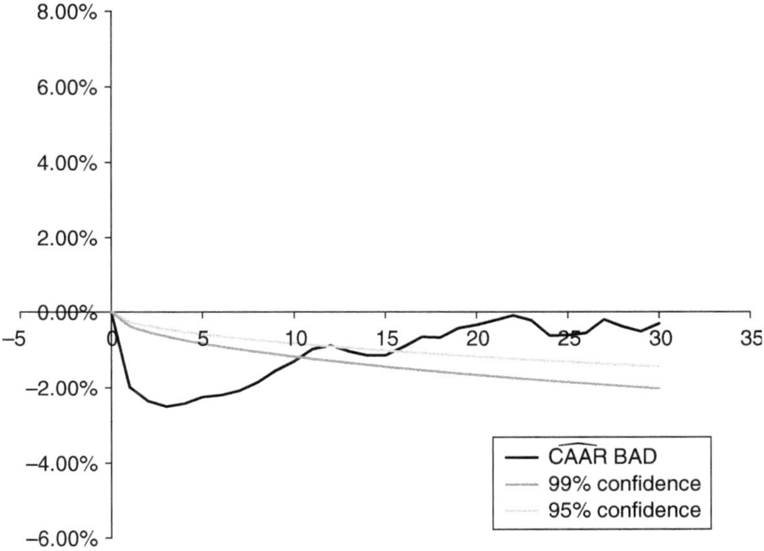

Figure 8.12 Extended exercise, applying the single-factor benchmark of returns: $\widehat{CAAR}_{-30,t}$, $\widehat{CAAR}_{0,t}$, and $\widehat{CAAR}_{1,t}$ for the Downside Surprise category. (a) $\widehat{CAAR}_{-30,t}$ for the Downside Surprise category, (b) $\widehat{CAAR}_{0,t}$ for the Downside Surprise category, and (c) $\widehat{CAAR}_{1,t}$ for the Downside Surprise category.

The exercise template and solution for this section (http://dx.doi.org/10.6084/m9.figshare.1221845 and http://dx.doi.org/10.6084/m9.figshare.1221844, respectively) are downloadable from the book's website. As an alternative to using the predesigned template, you may download a copy of the dataset file (http://dx.doi.org/10.6084/m9.figshare.1221834) and pave your own way to the results.

The stages of the exercise are similar to those of the basic exercise in chapter 7, except for stage 2, where the observations are split into Surprise categories. In the basic exercise, you partitioned the observations into three categories (Upside Surprise/Met Expectations/Downside Surprise), whereas in the current exercise you partition them in a finer manner, into five groups, by splitting the Upside and Downside Surprise categories into two equally sized groups each, according to the intensity of the surprise. The exercise template for this section is prepared to accommodate the further partition.

So, in the current exercise, before proceeding to the next stage, the data have to be sorted by the magnitude of surprise, and all subsequent

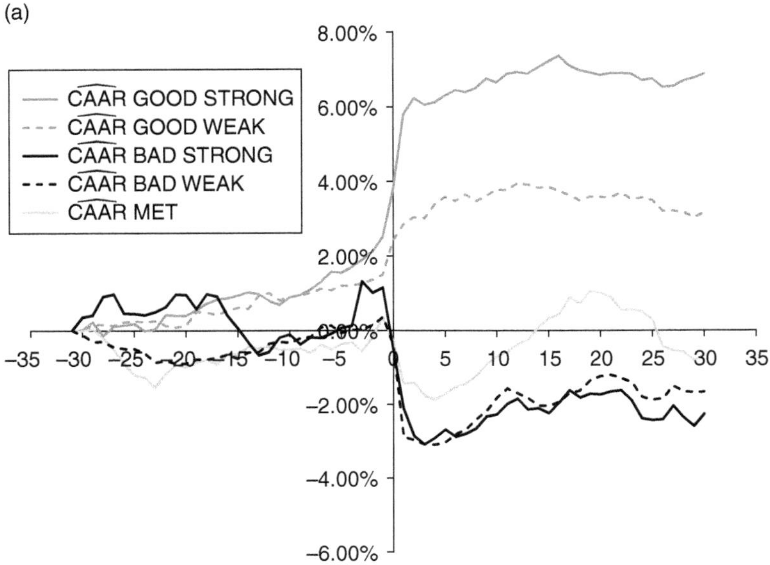

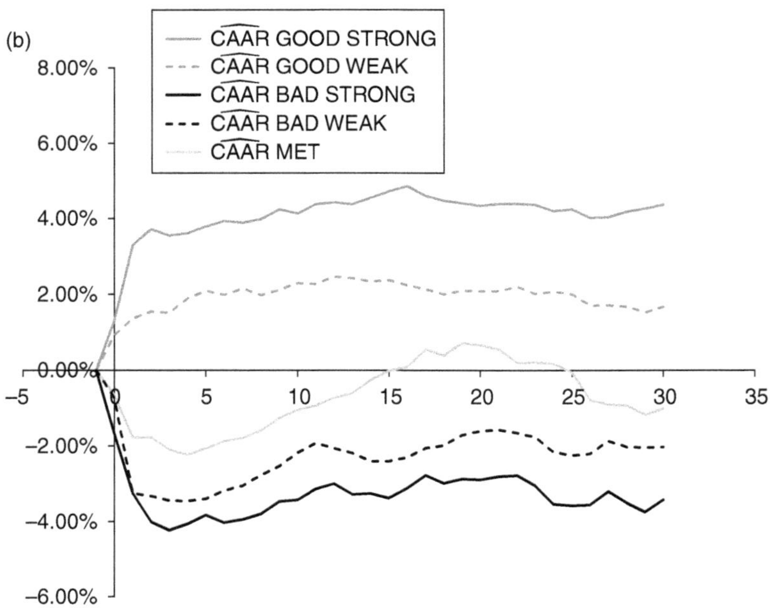

Figure 8.13 Continued on next page.

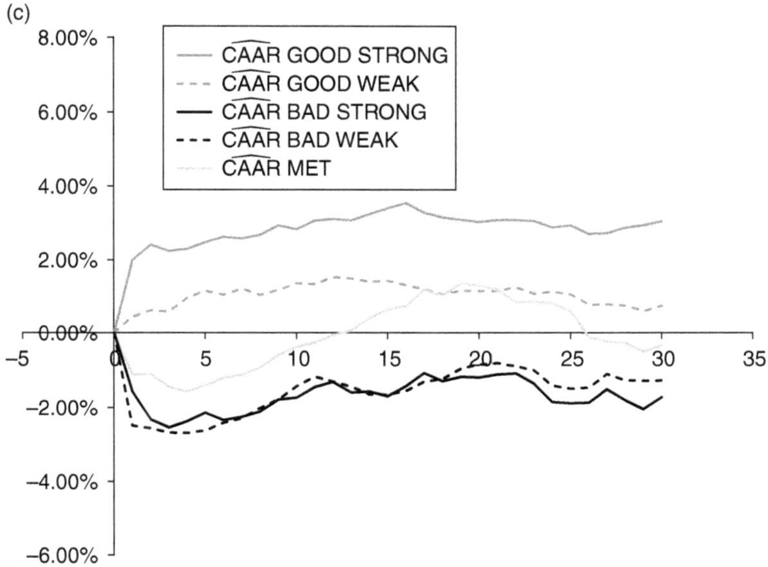

Figure 8.13 Extended exercise, analyzing the effect of the magnitude of surprise: $\widehat{CAAR}_{-30,t}$, $\widehat{CAAR}_{0,t}$, and $\widehat{CAAR}_{1,t}$ for the three Surprise categories. (a) $\widehat{CAAR}_{-30,t}$ for all Surprise categories, (b) $\widehat{CAAR}_{0,t}$ for all Surprise categories, and (c) $\widehat{CAAR}_{1,t}$ for all Surprise categories.

analysis should be separately performed for the strong-positive, weak-positive, strong-negative, weak-negative, and no surprise groups (the latter is identical to the Met Expectations group, as, by construction, it may not be further partitioned by surprise intensity).[6]

The resulting five $\widehat{CAAR}$ series are depicted in Figure 8.13. For an overview of the statistical properties of the resulting $\widehat{CAAR}$ series in one graph, we normalize them by the estimated standard deviations of their $\widehat{AAR}s$. The normalized series, with their 2-tail confidence thresholds, are depicted in Figure 8.14.[7]

The most important conclusion following from partitioning the data by the magnitude of the surprise is the difference between strong- and weak-positive surprise groups. In particular, the market reaction to the strong-positive surprise group was considerably stronger than the reaction to the weak-positive surprise group. No such difference is observed between the strong- and weak-negative surprise groups. Thus, the

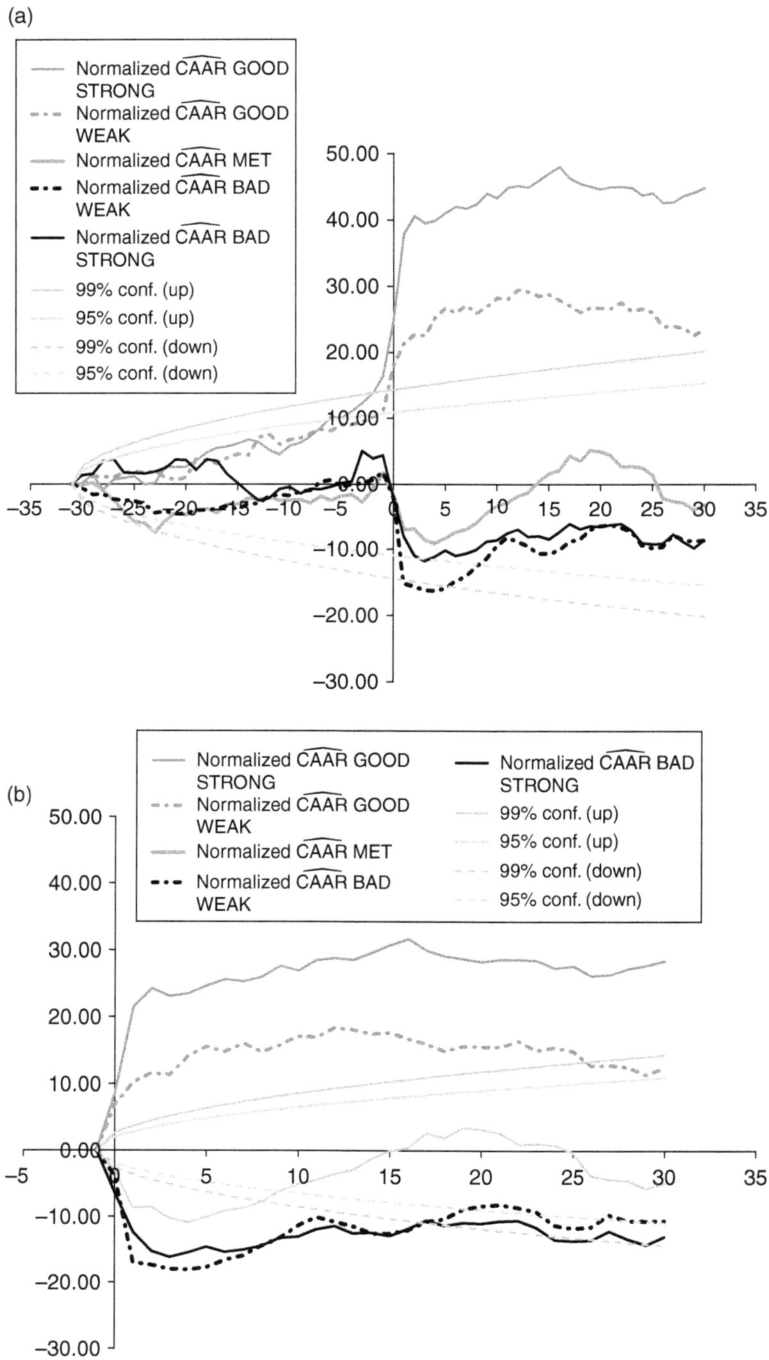

Figure 8.14 Continued on next page.

(c)

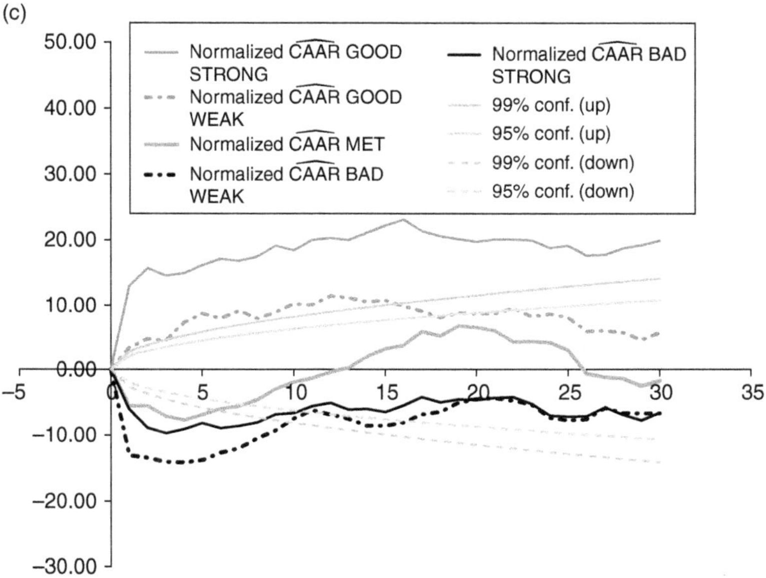

Figure 8.14 Extended exercise, analyzing the effect of the magnitude of surprise: normalized $\widehat{CAAR}_{-30,t}$, $\widehat{CAAR}_{0,t}$, and $\widehat{CAAR}_{1,t}$ for the three Surprise categories. (a) Normalized $\widehat{CAAR}_{-30,t}$ for all Surprise categories, (b) normalized $\widehat{CAAR}_{0,t}$ for all Surprise categories, and (c) normalized $\widehat{CAAR}_{1,t}$ for all Surprise categories.

results surmise, intriguingly, that the magnitude of the surprise in earnings announcements was perceived by the market as more important in the case of positive earnings surprises, than in the case of negative surprises.

For interpretation of the results, one has to keep in mind the following joint hypothesis problem: it could be the case that the magnitude of the earnings surprise matters also in negative surprises, but the technique employed for measuring the surprise was inaccurate. As in the case of joint hypothesis in NR estimation, one may establish a practical remedy to the problem by employing alternative models of earnings surprise assessment and testing the consistency of the results inferred from each.[8] The robustness of the conclusions vis-à-vis the market reaction to the surprise component in earnings announcements would be corroborated if the pictures emerging from the analysis with various models are qualitatively similar.

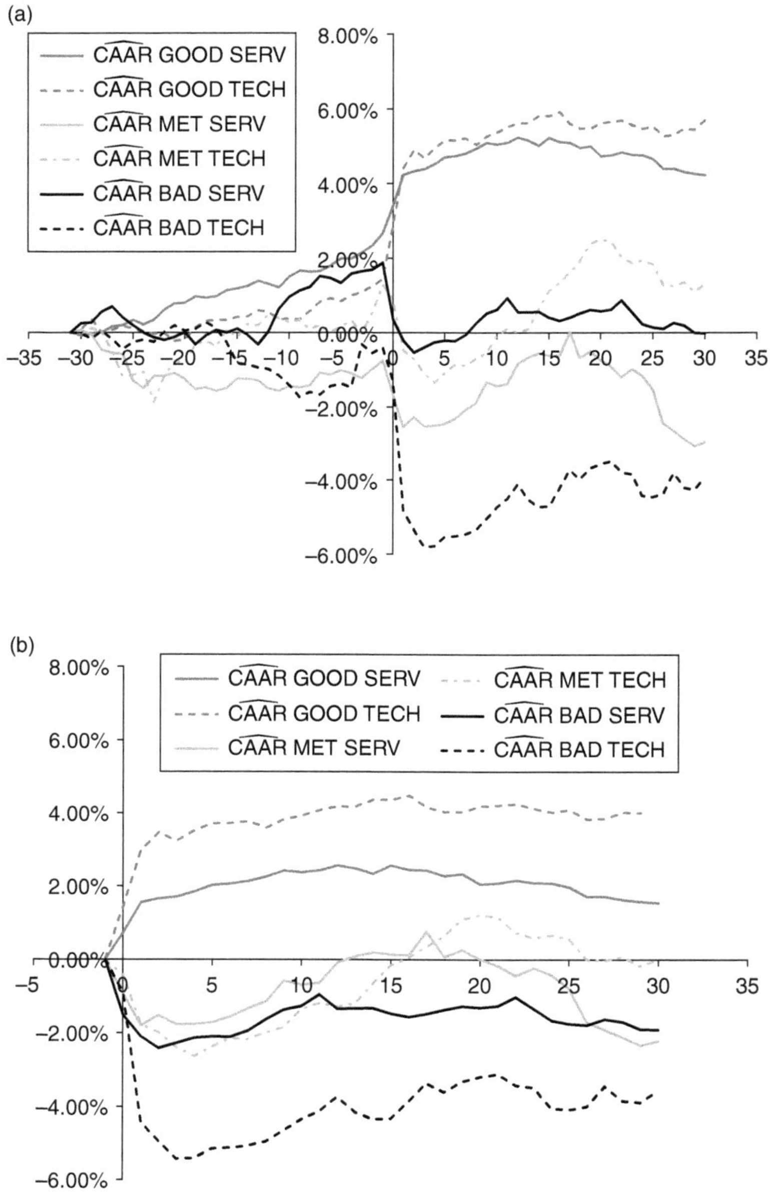

Figure 8.15 Continued on next page.

(c)

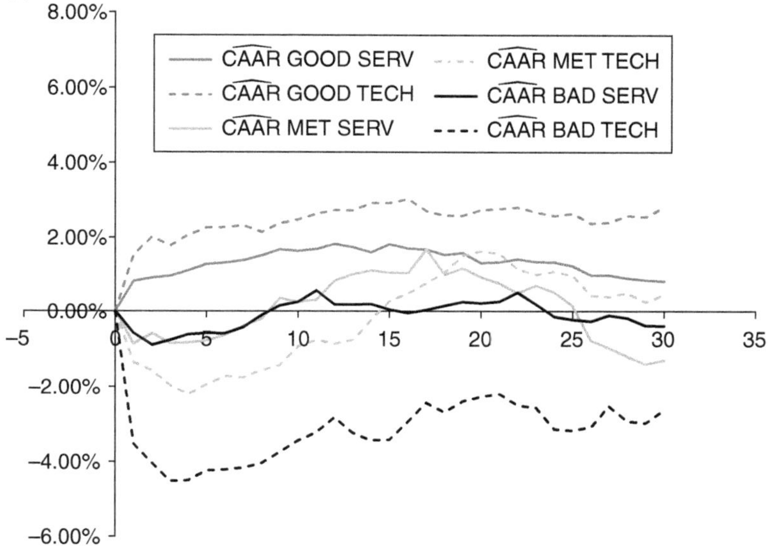

Figure 8.15 Extended exercise, analyzing differential effects by companies' sectors: $\widehat{CAAR}_{-30,t}$, $\widehat{CAAR}_{0,t}$, and $\widehat{CAAR}_{1,t}$ for the three Surprise categories. (a) $\widehat{CAAR}_{-30,t}$ for all Surprise categories, (b) $\widehat{CAAR}_{0,t}$ for all Surprise categories, and (c) $\widehat{CAAR}_{1,t}$ for all Surprise categories.

To conclude, the following caveat should be taken into account. The results of the exercise conduced in this section have to be interpreted with caution. This is because the reaction to the studied event may depend on firm characteristics (such as sector affiliation, discussed in the next section), and observation-specific attributes, which vary over the sample in an uncontrolled manner. More profound, augmented analysis possibilities that are capable of addressing this issue are discussed in section 8.6.[9]

8.5. Analyzing Differential Effects by Companies' Sectors

In section 8.4, the data were sorted by the magnitude of the earnings surprise. Here we follow a similar prescription in order to study possible

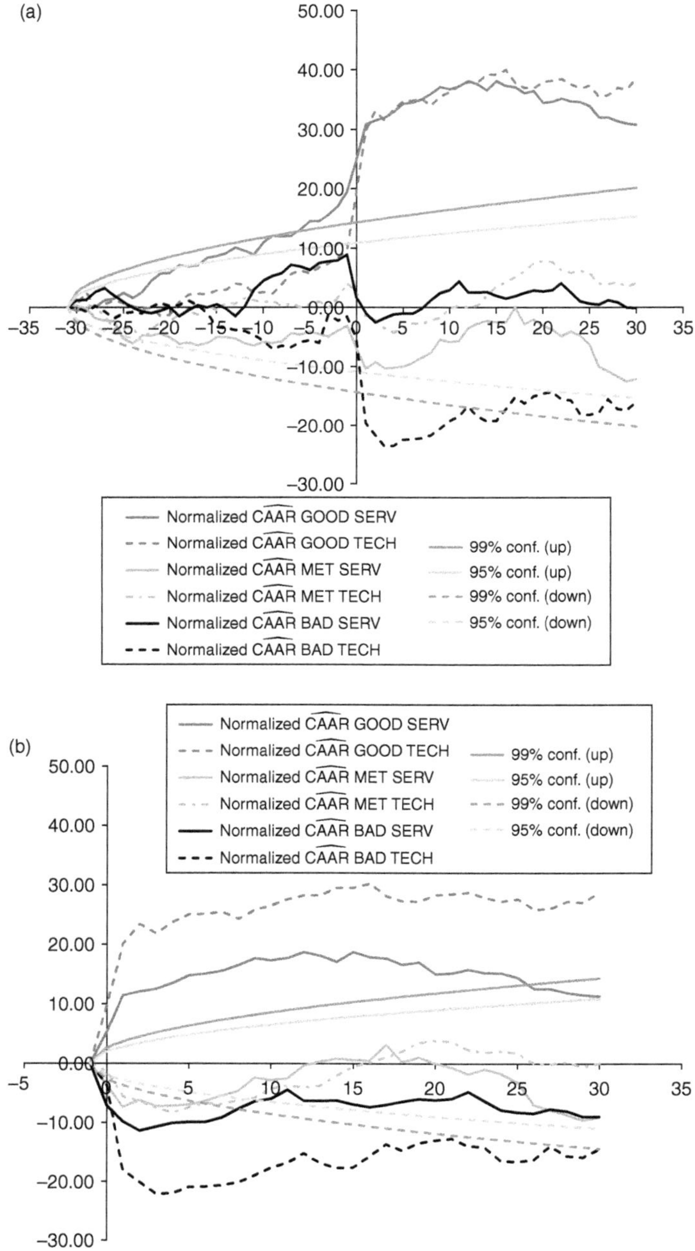

Figure 8.16 Continued on next page.

(c)

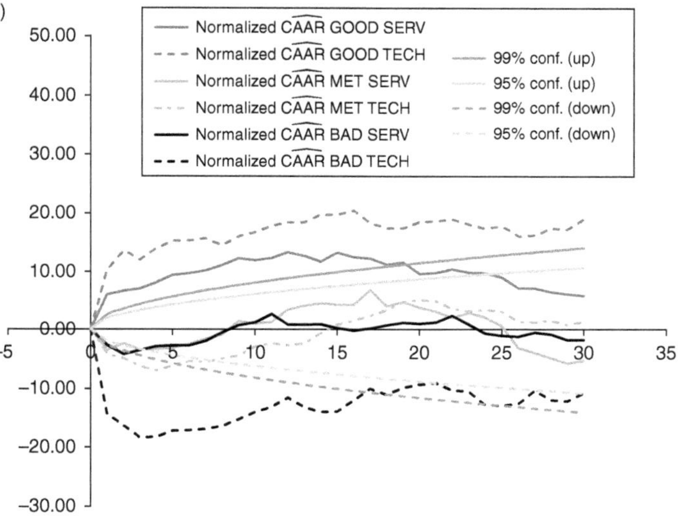

Figure 8.16 Extended exercise, analyzing differential effects by companies' sectors: normalized $\widehat{CAAR}_{-30,t}$, $\widehat{CAAR}_{0,t}$, and $\widehat{CAAR}_{1,t}$ for the three Surprise categories. (a) Normalized $\widehat{CAAR}_{-30,t}$ for all Surprise categories, (b) normalized $\widehat{CAAR}_{0,t}$ for all Surprise categories, and (c) normalized $\widehat{CAAR}_{1,t}$ for all Surprise categories.

differences in market reaction to the earnings announcements between companies' sectors. Recall that the dataset comprises 670 individual earnings announcements of firms from either the services or technology sector. Thus, we may subdivide the data within each of the three Surprise categories (Upside Surprise, Met Expectations, and Downside Surprise) into two sector groups and investigate the differential effect between the sectors.

The template and solution for this exercise (http://dx.doi.org/10.6084/m9.figshare.1221847 and http://dx.doi.org/10.6084/m9.figshare.1221846) are downloadable from the book's website. As before, you may choose to use the predesigned template and guiding instructions or download a copy of the dataset file (http://dx.doi.org/10.6084/m9.figshare.1221834) and work independently.

The exercise stages are once again similar to those provided for the basic exercise in chapter 7, except for data partition (stage 2). While the

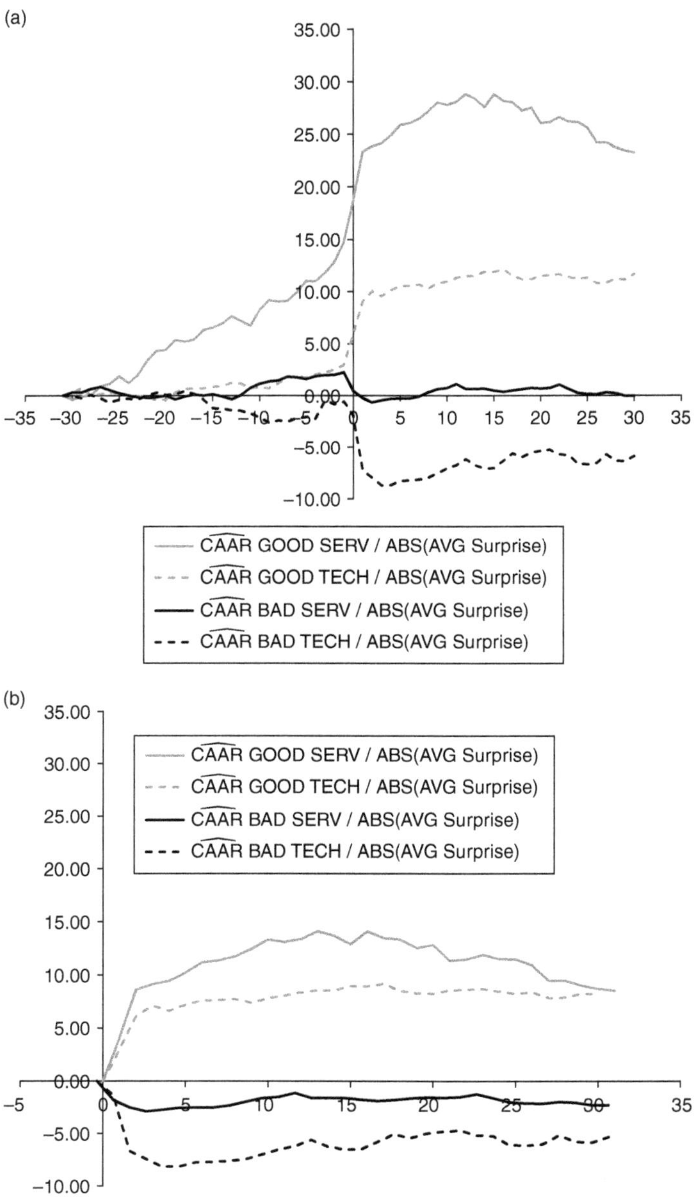

Figure 8.17 Continued on next page.

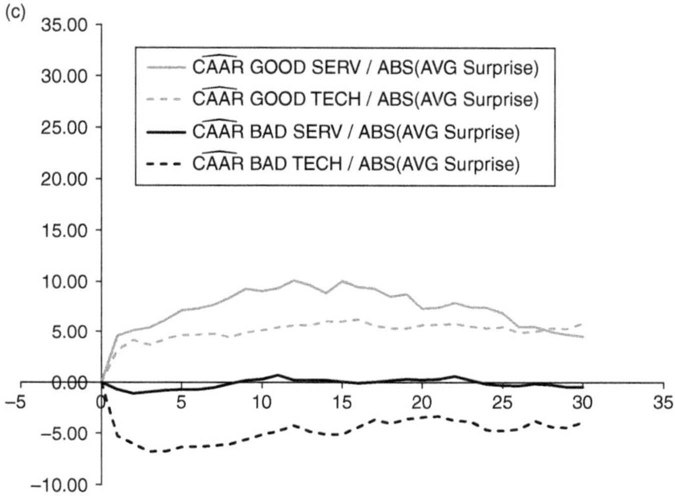

Figure 8.17 Extended exercise, analyzing differential effects by companies' sectors: $\widehat{CAAR}_{-30,t}$, $\widehat{CAAR}_{0,t}$, and $\widehat{CAAR}_{1,t}$ divided by the absolute value of their respective average Surprise figures, for the three Surprise categories. (a) $\widehat{CAAR}_{-30,t}$ divided by absolute value of average Surprise, (b) $\widehat{CAAR}_{0,t}$ divided by absolute value of average Surprise, and (c) $\widehat{CAAR}_{1,t}$ divided by absolute value of average Surprise.

observations in the basic exercise in chapter 7 were partitioned into three categories (Upside Surprise/Met Expectations/Downside Surprise), here you partition them further by the two sectors, within each of the three Surprise categories. As before, the exercise template for this section is prepared to accommodate the further partition.

The resulting six $\widehat{CAAR}$ series (3 Surprise categories×2 sectors) are portrayed in Figure 8.15, and the respective normalized series, along with their 2-tail confidence thresholds, are depicted in Figure 8.16.

According to the results obtained from this data partition, the average market reaction to the earnings announcements in the technology sector seems to be more pronounced, both within the Upside and Downside Surprise.

In order to arrive at conclusions regarding the relative sensitivity of the reaction between the sectors, the result has to be further scrutinized. The reason is that the distribution of the magnitude of the surprise within each Surprise category is different between the two sectors. A first-order sensitivity comparison may be done by comparing the $\widehat{CAAR}$ series after dividing them by the absolute value of their respective average Surprise figures.

Doing so unveils that the effect in the Downside Surprise category is more pronounced in the technology sector than in the services sector. In the domain of Upside Surprise, however, there are signs that the effect may be more pronounced in the services than in the technology sector, especially when measured over the whole event window.

To summarize the exercise conducted in this section, keep in mind that the first-order sensitivity comparison is crude, so the interpretation of its results has to be done with caution. Furthermore, note that the reaction to the studied event may differ across additional firm characteristics, beyond their sector affiliation, and over various observation-specific attributes. In the next section we discuss some more profound, augmented analysis possibilities with which these further issues may be addressed.[10]

8.6. Suggestions for Further Data Analysis Ideas

Further data analysis may include investigation of the extent of reaction to the earnings announcements depending on various firm characteristics (in addition to sector affiliation), as well as on observation-specific attributes (such as the timing of earnings forecasts and earnings announcements, and specific traits of the analysts providing the earnings forecasts).

The dataset of the exercises includes information on one such firm characteristic, namely, market capitalization (MCap). Noteworthy, the average market capitalization (or "size") in our dataset varies across the Surprise categories, with the highest average for the Upside Surprise and the lowest for the Downside Surprise category. Thus, the ceteris paribus assumption, which is required for the empirical investigation, does not hold in that aspect. This may serve as a reminder for an important feature of ESA which has to be taken into account, namely that the analysis is *univariate* in nature.[11]

One way of controlling for the variation in a firms' characteristic is to conduct the event study on groups of observations, partitioned according to that characteristic.[12] An example for this way of action is provided in the exercise introduced in section 8.5, where the sample was partitioned by the firms' sectors, and event study analysis was conducted on the observations within each sector, partitioned by the Surprise categories.

Controlling for variation by finer data partitions, however practical, is limited in the number of characteristics that may be accounted for, as each characteristic entails further partition in an additional dimension. Moreover, this analysis technique is more complicated in case the characteristic is not categorical (such as sector), but numerical (such as size).

Another way of augmenting the analysis to encompass data variability is multivariate regression, the simplest of which may be a cross-sectional regression, where the dependent variable is the individual estimated AR on a selected day t (namely, $\widehat{AR}_t^i$), and the explanatory variables are the news categories (in our case, the Surprise dummies Good/Met/Bad), and desired characteristics as controls.[13]

The regression specification may also be tailored to fit various aspects of the data at hand, for instance, interaction variables between the news categories and control variables. Further possible generalization of the regression analysis is using the individual estimated CAR from a specific starting point s up to a subsequent date t within the event window ($\widehat{CAR}_{s,t}^i$) as dependent variable.

Chapter 9

Conclusion

Event studies are a primary tool for financial research. They provide means for assessing the effect of corporate and environmental occurrences on the market values of securities. Numerous events such as earnings announcements, releases of quarterly and annual financial reports, dividend announcements, stock splits and reverse splits, and initial and seasoned public offerings are amenable to the event study research analysis technique. In addition to addressing the impact of various events on security prices, the ESA helps to shed light on the efficiency of capital markets.

Our main goal in this book was to help our readers become familiar with the ESA and place it in their toolbox of empirical financial research. A critical part of the book was concerned with hands-on experience provided in the form of practical exercises based on real market data. These exercises were devised to help readers master the technical skills necessary for conducting their own comprehensive event studies. To that end, complete solutions are provided to all the exercises, and detailed instructions are presented to the fundamental ones.

The chapters concentrated on the main ESA features, while keeping track of potentially complicating caveats and relevant application details. Throughout the book, references and directions for further reading are weaved into the text, enabling the readers to find a thread to many additional ESA aspects.

On a closing note, we hope the book readers have benefited from our comprehensive guide to event studies. Our main objective was to present an accessible, yet not oversimplified, path to event study research, starting from the theoretical foundations of ESA, through its basic definitions and technical details, and up to hands-on real data application. Whether you are a student, researcher, or practitioner, we hope we have provided you with the right balance between rigor of formulation and accessibility of presentation, for a headstart in navigating through the world of financial research with the fascinating approach of event studies.

Notes

2 Infrastructure: The Efficient Market Hypothesis

1. To read about the infamous story of an investor with seemingly extraordinary performance, see Apropos Box "Beating the Market?—The Case of Bernard L. Madoff."
2. Also see surveys by Beechey, Gruen, and Vickery (2000) and LeRoy (2000) for a comprehensive exposition of EMH and related issues.
3. To learn more about Fama and his research, read Apropos Box "Father of Modern Finance—Eugene F. Fama."
4. According to Fama (1970), the distinction between strong and weak efficiency tests was originally suggested by Harry Roberts (1967).
5. Note that finding traces of private information in market prices is insufficient to lead to the conclusion that the strong form of EMH holds, because such a conclusion requires that *all* confidential information would be reflected in the market prices, at any point in time.
6. Cowles presented his work in front of the distinguished Econometric Society and American Statistical Association (see Cowles 1933). Timmermann and Granger (2004) reviewed EMH versus price forecasting frameworks and discussed corresponding theoretical considerations and empirical evidence.
7. So, can the market be predicted? Perhaps, some hints for an answer could be found in the amazing story of Livermore, abridged in Apropos Box "'Plunger Boy' Jesse Lauriston Livermore."
8. To learn more about Malkiel and his insights about market efficiency, read Apropos Box "A Random Walk down Wall Street—Burton G. Malkiel."
9. See Royal Swedish Academy of Sciences (2013) and Nobel Media AB (2013).
10. According to MacKinlay (1997), the general idea of event studies may be traced back to 1933 when James Dolley published a work on stock splits, which is incidentally also the topic of Fama et al. (1969); however, the approach endorsed by the latter is one that has become a standard for the event studies we know today.

11. For instance, Ball and Brown (1968) employed essentially the same approach to analyze the information content of accounting income numbers; see MacKinlay (1997) for a survey of the historical development of ESA.

3 The Event Study Approach

1. The spread of the event window around the event date varies from one study to another. While there is no universal rule for determining the "right" period, the general idea is to identify, possibly based on preliminary analysis or previous studies, the earliest and the latest time points around the event date where an abnormal security price behavior may be detected; to wit, the idea is that it is always better to investigate too broad, rather than too narrow, windows. One may draw an analogy to bird watching: it is easier to detect a flock of birds by starting with the smallest magnification and then, after spotting some activity, zooming in to see details.
2. The issue of bidirectional reaction to events is elaborated further in section 6.3 of chapter 6.
3. Some adjustments may be necessary in order to apply the analysis to securities other than stocks. We address this issue in section 6.4 of chapter 6, in particular in reference to the analysis of bond prices.
4. This calculation of the stock return is valid under the assumption that neither dividends nor stock splits took place between $t-1$ and t. A conceivable way of adjusting the return to take into account a *$D* per share dividend distribution within that time period is by the formula $R_t^i = (P_t^i + D - P_{t-1}^i)/P_{t-1}^i$. Another way to take dividend distribution into account is by transforming the prices to "adjusted prices" by subtracting the dividend per share amounts from prices on dates preceding the ex-dividend day. Similarly, split-adjusted prices eliminate spurious impact of stock splits on returns. In the sequel, unless explicitly stated otherwise, we assume that dividend- and split-adjusted prices are employed in all calculations.
5. We adopt this notation throughout, referring to the period from time t–1 to t as period t.
6. The ESA procedures and calculations presented in this book are applicable to both arithmetic and logarithmic returns. Thus, for the rest of the book, we suppress the notation differentiating them.
7. For a demonstration of possible effects of benchmark model specification on ESA results, see Brown and Warner (1980).
8. The Center for Research in Security Prices (CRSP) is one of the leading financial research and learning centers. CRSP, administered by the University of Chicago's Booth School of Business, has been operative since the 1960s, providing economic, financial, and related data to scholars and investors around the world. Among other things, CRSP maintains market indices that are

used as investment benchmarks by academic researchers and capital market professionals.

9. Broby (2007) provides a comprehensive exposition of various equity indices and the basics of their theoretical construction, technical calculation, and practical applications.
10. Note that, unlike other customary benchmarks, no parameter estimation is required for applying the naïve benchmark. Thus, this benchmark should be considered as a means appropriate only for simplified ESA applications. Note also that the asymptotical considerations that are mentioned in the sequel of the book might not apply in this case.
11. This line of work was further developed by Sharpe (1964), Lintner (1965), and Mossin (1966); see Appendix of this chapter for more details.
12. We delve into this point in chapter 5 and provide more detail within the discussion of the basic event study design.
13. For example, Sharpe, Alexander, and Bailey (1995) enumerate the growth rate of gross domestic product, the interest and inflation rates, and the level of oil prices, among possible sources of pervasive influence on stock returns. They also discuss the so-called sector-factor models, which account for the stock's industry classification in modeling the return-generating process.
14. Fama and French also offer two bond market factors related to maturity and default risks. We discuss ESA in a bond-related context in section 6.4 of chapter 6. Details on the five factors may be found in Fama and French (1993).
15. We provide here only a general description; for a more detailed definition of the model, see Fama and French (1993, 1995).
16. For a detailed definition of the model, see Carhart (1997).
17. See Jegadeesh and Titman (1993, 2001).
18. To arrive at the estimated CAARs, one can first generate a separate cumulative series of each stock's estimated CARs and then average the CARs within subsamples. This path is described in the subsequent section.
19. In the United States, insiders are subject to Securities and Exchange Commission (SEC) rules 10b5 and 10b5–1, which are enactments designed to prevent securities fraud and, specifically, insider trading. See Keown and Pinkerton (1981) for a classical study of merger announcements and related insider trading; moreover, Mitchell and Netter (1994) survey a number of prominent SEC enforcement cases where event study analysis was employed to detect securities fraud.
20. Sometimes the timing of the news release does not permit immediate market reaction, as, for example, when the information arrives after trading hours. In such cases, the reaction may occur on the next trading day; see Peterson (1989) for a brief discussion on this topic and some examples of studies dealing with the issue.
21. However, as noted above, it is important to keep in mind that in such a case there is also a possibility that the event *is* pricing-relevant, but the information *was not new* anymore at the time it was officially announced.

22. In 1990, Harry M. Markowitz and William F. Sharpe were awarded the Sveriges Riksbank Prize in Economic Sciences in Memory of Alfred Nobel for their respective contributions to financial economics, namely, the theory of portfolio management (MPT) and the theory of financial assets pricing (CAPM). French (2003) explains that Treynor (1961, 1962) also deserves the credit for developing CAPM, but this fact is not consistently recognized by many sources. According to the author, the reason for this is that the original contributions of Treynor have not been published in time, despite the significant impact and the wide recognition his work had received in the 1960s, when his manuscripts were circulated among financial economists. Noteworthy as well in this context are the late John V. Lintner Jr. and Jan Mossin, who would possibly have shared the prize had they lived, for having devised significant relevant contributions.
23. For a review of main theoretical problems and empirical issues associated with the application of CAPM, see Fama and French (2004). Stapleton and Subrahmanyam (1983) clarify the connection between CAPM and the single-factor model and show that CAPM's linear relationship between expected returns and asset Betas, one of the central results of the theory, can be derived from the single-factor model under certain conditions; however, the authors also note that the required conditions may not be satisfied in practice. Roll (1977) offers a critique of empirical tests of CAPM, pointing out that essential components of the CAPM framework—the market portfolio, for instance—cannot be constructed in practice, while substituting a proxy, such as a market index, may lead to invalid conclusions.

4 A Simplified Example: The Effect of Air Crashes on Stock Prices

1. The details of crashes were chosen such that the operator had to be a US-based stock exchange traded company. A more comprehensive and meticulous study would use a representative, larger sample and control for a range of potentially important factors, such as the severity of the accident. Our aim here is not to assess the magnitude of the effect of air crashes on stock prices. Our purpose is to demonstrate the application of ESA in a concise setup. Therefore, the specimen we exploit is not representative of the phenomenon, and the results should not be considered as evidence of the existence, or magnitude, of any effect.
2. The prices are adjusted for stock splits and dividend distributions.
3. You may view the Excel implementation of all the equations used in the example in the chapter's Excel file (http://dx.doi.org/10.6084/m9.figshare.1221810).
4. Alternative benchmark models of returns may be employed for the estimation of ARs, for instance, the factor models introduced in the subsections 3.1.2 to

3.1.4. Note that employing these models is a bit more complicated, as it entails a prerequisite stage of estimating the model's parameters. As explained earlier, employing several alternative benchmarks would help in assessing the robustness of the results to the models' specification. We shall get back to this issue in the sequel and walk through an example with the single-factor benchmark in chapter 8.

5. As noticed in section 3.3, statistical tests are required to determine whether the apparent estimated CAAR irregularity is too strong to be attributable to chance. These tests will be introduced and exercised in the sequel.

5 The Basic ESA Design

1. The case of clustering is discussed further in chapter 6.
2. Recall that employing the naïve benchmark does not entail any parameter estimation and, thus, does not require defining and using an estimation window. This makes the naïve benchmark easy to use and appropriate for simplified ESA applications. Note that the asymptotical considerations mentioned in the sequel might not apply in this case.
3. As elaborated earlier, employing different benchmark models within the same study would help in evaluating the final results and conclusions, which are said to be robust in the aspect of benchmark model specification if they are not qualitatively different among the employed models. That said, we should also note that in short-run event studies the test statistics employed for hypothesis testing (such as that presented below) usually are not strongly affected by the benchmark model of returns.
4. For more details on measuring and analyzing ARs, see MacKinlay (1997).
5. Formulas taking into account intertemporal correlations may be found in Salinger (1992).
6. Noteworthy, while employing a longer estimation window may enhance the precision of estimates and thus mitigate the problem, there are circumstances in which it might introduce other difficulties. For example, in the case of a nonstationary return process, it might adversely affect the obtained estimates.
7. For a thorough discussion on statistical issues and technical details of the procedure, see Brown and Warner (1985); for extended discussions on the method, see MacKinlay (1997) and Campbell, Lo, and MacKinlay (1997).
8. This large sample property of the variance may be employed for "long enough" estimation windows. For short estimation windows, the variance of $\widehat{CAR}^i_{s,t}$ should be adjusted for estimation-error effects.
9. This basic approach may be modified toward increasing the power of test, for example, by standardizing the ARs of each stock using an estimator of its own standard deviation. To that end, see Patell (1976) and Brown and Warner (1980, 1985).

10. Kothari and Warner (2007) point out that if the event under study affects the *variability* of returns, it might lead to incorrect conclusions regarding ARs, as rejecting the null hypothesis could be due to increased returns volatility. They also suggest a way of correcting for the possible bias. This is beyond the scope here, but note that the null hypothesis assumes the absence of any market reaction, including increased event-time returns variability.

6 Issues in ESA Design

1. Many authors refer to the issue of clustering and offer possible solutions. For instance, Bernard (1987) approaches the issue in a systematical manner, examines its implications, and indicates a number of methods that can be employed to handle the problem. It is beyond the scope of this book to thoroughly review all existing methods and related caveats, so we hereby outline the most straightforward approach. Detailed expositions and discussions of other methods may be found in Brown and Warner (1980), Bernard (1987), Kothari and Warner (2007), and a range of relevant sources cited therein.
2. The approach we present here may be viewed as a simplified version of "crude dependence adjustment" (Brown and Warner 1980), "cross-sectional aggregation" (Bernard 1987), and "portfolio approach" (MacKinlay 1997). For an exposition of the approach in a broader context, see Kothari and Warner (2007).
3. Often, the calculation may be simplified, as under standard estimation in balanced panel, this term may equal zero.
4. As in the basic case described in the previous chapter, this estimation approach has an implicit assumption of intertemporal independence of ARs. See chapter 5 for explanations related to this assumption.
5. The sign test may be conducted more generally on the signs of estimated CARs. To that end, replace $\widehat{AR}_t^i$ by $\widehat{CAR}_t^i$. Note that the sign test is specified under the assumption that the ARs (and, more generally, CARs) are independent across the securities. Note also that the test statistic discussed here assumes the sample size is large enough, such that a continuity correction of the normal approximation to the binomial distribution is inconsequential. Lastly, note that the test statistic may require further attention in case there are ties (in the shape of zeroes) in the measured variables.
6. Throughout, for tractability, we assume that the number of observations within each subgroup is constant over time.
7. The number of estimated ARs in the event window is $\left(t_{End}^{EventWin} - t_{Start}^{EventWin}\right)$.
8. Ranking the $\widehat{ARs}$ in ascending order aligns the hypothesized sign of TS_0^{rank} and its parametric counterpart under the alternative hypothesis.

9. Similarly to the sign test, the rank test may also be conducted more generally on the ranks of estimated CARs. Note that, similarly to the sign test, attention may be required to issues regarding the normal approximation and ties in the measured variables.
10. Note that two-tailed, rather than one-tailed, statistical tests may be more appropriate in this situation.
11. For more details on the application of other aspects, see, for example, Bailey, Karolyi, and Salva (2006), who employ return volatility in conjunction with trading volume for assessing the impact of increased disclosure faced by firms whose stocks became internationally cross-listed. An example of a joint application of all mentioned aspects may be found in Bhattacharya, Daouk, Jorgenson, and Kehr (2000), who studied market reactions to Mexican corporate news announcements.
12. Note the similarity to the single-factor benchmark of returns explained in chapter 3.
13. Often, the calculation may be simplified, as under standard estimation in balanced panel, the term $\overline{AAV}$ may equal zero.
14. For more details on the construction of benchmark portfolios, see the original paper by Weinstein (1977).
15. As in chapter 3, here also only a general description is provided; for a more detailed definition of the model, see Fama and French (1993).
16. Comprehensive research summaries in this area are offered by Kothari and Warner (1997) and Hirshleifer (2001).
17. Note that the Jensen's Alpha portfolio approach accounts for clustering, as it involves forming a portfolio whose returns account for cross-sectional correlation of its constituents.
18. The issues discussed here do not encompass the whole range of issues dealt with by Brown and Warner. For instance, the authors also address the question of costs and benefits of adjusting daily data for clustering, as well as the question of stationarity of daily variances. The interested reader may find more details in the original paper.

7 Hands-on Exercise

1. As explained earlier, employing alternative benchmarks may help in coping with the joint hypothesis issue, as consistent results in this case enhance the general conclusions' credibility. For simplicity, we employ only the naïve benchmark in the current chapter, reminding that the random variables' asymptotical properties described earlier might not apply in this case. We refine the analysis to include the single-factor benchmark (see subsection 3.1.2 of chapter 3) in the exercise extensions presented in the next chapter.

2. The normalization provides per-dollar values, which are comparable across firms with different stock prices. One may also wish to consider normalization by pre-event stock prices (to eliminate interference by price reaction to the event), as well as by nonmarket values, such as per-share equity book values.
3. Recall that the basic process described in chapter 5 assumes the absence of data clustering. The fact that this assumption does not completely hold in the dataset is inconsequential for instructional purposes, which are the goal of the exercise.
4. Note that $\widehat{CAAR}_{1,t}$ along with its relevant statistics is being generated automatically from your work.

8 Further Hands-on Exercises

1. If you wish to review specific details, please review sections 7.1 to 7.3 in chapter 7.
2. Throughout this chapter, we use the terms *DataSheets*, *WorkingSheets*, and *GraphSheets*, which were introduced in chapter 7. Recall that the tabs of *DataSheets* and *GraphSheets* are red, and those of *WorkingSheets* are green, to remind you in which sheets you are allowed (green) or not allowed (red) to modify cell contents.
3. Note that the proximity of event dates within the studied sample might cause also intertemporal dependencies in the AARs. Dealing with this issue is beyond the scope of the current discussion.
4. Recall that $\widehat{CAAR}_{1,t}$ along with its relevant statistics is being generated automatically from your work.
5. The tests used in this section are correctly specified given the assumption that the ARs (and, more generally, CARs) are independent across the securities. This assumption might not hold for the specific dataset used in the example, so the analysis here should be credited for the purpose of demonstration only.
6. Surprise was calculated as the difference between reported and consensus EPS, normalized by day 0 stock price. Recall it may be worthwhile to consider normalization by pre-event stock prices (to eliminate interference by price reaction to the event), as well as by non-market values, such as per-share equity book-values. In addition, for in-depth analysis, one may wish also to take into account the levels of cEPS and rEPS, rather than merely their difference.
7. Normalizing in this way generates series which are expressed in units of estimated standard deviation, allowing thereby plotting all the series on one set of confidence thresholds.
8. Such models, for instance, may weigh differently the earnings forecasts of different analysts according to their past success rate; put a heavier weight on forecasts that were published immediately before the firms' earnings

announcements (i.e., disregarding "stale" forecasts); or introduce multivariate considerations into the surprise model, controlling for firm-specific attributes, such as size and industry affiliation.

9. For simplicity, the results are discussed here on the basis of graph comparison, without statistical testing of their significance.
10. For simplicity, we base the discussion of the results on the graphs, without statistical testing of their significance.
11. For rigorous analysis, one may wish to consider using pre-event market capitalization values (to avoid interference by price reaction to the event), as well as non-market "size" measures, such as equity book-values.
12. An observation-specific attribute may be controlled in a similar manner.
13. The bond rating event study by Kliger and Sarig (2000), discussed in section 6.4 of chapter 6, is an example of research making use of controlled multivariate regression analysis.

Bibliography

Aharony, J., Swary, I. 1980. Quarterly dividend and earnings announcements and stockholders' returns: an empirical analysis. *The Journal of Finance*, 35:1, 1–12.

Arnott, R. D., Hsu, J., Moore, P. 2005. Fundamental indexation. *Financial Analysts Journal*, 61:2, 83–99.

Arvedlund, E. E. 2009. *Too Good to Be True: The Rise and Fall of Bernie Madoff.* Portfolio: Penguin Group.

Bachelier, L. 1964. Theory of speculation. In Cootner, P. (ed.), *The Random Character of Stock Market Prices.* Cambridge: Massachusetts Institute of Technology Press.

Bailey, W., Karolyi, G. A., Salva, C. 2006. The economic consequences of increased disclosure: evidence from international cross-listings. *Journal of Financial Economics*, 81:1, 175–213.

Ball, R., Brown, P. 1968. An empirical evaluation of accounting income numbers. *Journal of Accounting Research*, 6:2, 159–178.

Bartov, E., Radhakrishnan, S., Krinsky, I. 2000. Investor sophistication and patterns in stock returns after earnings announcements. *The Accounting Review*, 75:1, 43–63.

Beechey, M., Gruen, D., Vickery, J. 2000. The efficient market hypothesis: a survey. Research discussion paper 2000–01. Economic Research Department, Reserve Bank of Australia.

Bernard, V. L. 1987. Cross-sectional dependence and problems in inference in market-based accounting research. *Journal of Accounting Research*, 25:1, 1–48.

Berry, M. A., Gallinger, G. W., Henderson, G. V. 1990. Using daily stock returns in event studies and the choice of parametric versus nonparametric test statistics. *Quarterly Journal of Business and Economics*, 29:1, 70–85.

Bhattacharya, U., Daouk, H., Jorgenson, B., Kehr, C. -H. 2000. When an event is not an event: the curious case of an emerging market. *Journal of Financial Economics*, 55:1, 69–101.

Broby, D. 2007. *A Guide to Equity Index Construction*. London: Risk Books.

Brown, R. 1828. A brief account of microscopical observations made in the months of June, July, and August, 1827, on the particles contained in the pollen of plants; and on the general existence of active molecules in organic and inorganic bodies. *Edinburgh New Philosophical Journal*, July–September, 358–371.

Brown, S. J., Warner, J. B. 1980. Measuring security price performance. *Journal of Financial Economics*, 8, 205–258.

———. 1985. Using daily stock returns: the case of event studies. *Journal of Financial Economics*, 14, 3–31.

Campbell, C. J., Wasley, C. E. 1993. Measuring security price performance using daily NASDAQ returns. *Journal of Financial Economics*, 33:1, 73–92.

———. 1996. Measuring abnormal trading volume for samples of NYSE/ASE and NASDAQ securities using parametric and nonparametric test statistics. *Review of Quantitative Finance and Accounting*, 6:3, 309–326.

Campbell, J. Y., Lo, A. W., MacKinlay, A. C. 1997. *The Econometrics of Financial Markets*. Princeton, NJ: Princeton University Press.

Cardano, G. (c. 1564). Liber de Ludo Aleae. First published in Latin in Vol. 1, *Opera Omnia*, edited by Charles Spon (Lyons, 1663). Translated into English in Oystein Ore, *Cardano: The Gambling Scholar* by Sydney Henry Gould (Princeton University Press, 1953). Reprinted in *The Book on Games of Chance* (Holt, Rinehart and Winston, 1961).

Carhart, M. M. 1997. On persistence in mutual fund performance. *The Journal of Finance*, 52:1, 57–82.

Chen, Y., Nguyen, N. H. 2013. Stock price and analyst earnings forecast around product recall announcements. *International Journal of Economics and Finance*, 5:6, 1–10.

Clatworthy, M. 2005. *Transnational Equity Analysis*. Chichester, England: John Wiley & Sons.

Corrado, C. J. 1989. A nonparametric test for abnormal security-price performance in event studies. *Journal of Financial Economics*, 23, 385–395.

Cowan, A. R. 1992. Nonparametric event study tests. *Review of Quantitative Finance and Accounting*, 2, 343–358.

Cowles, A. 1933. Can stock market forecasters forecast? *Econometrica*, 1:3, 309–324.

Davidson, L. 2012. The history of exchange-traded funds (ETFs). *Morningstar*, March 12 http://www.morningstarthailand.com/th/news/articles/104958/The-History-of-Exchange-Traded-Funds-%28ETFs%29.aspx.

De la Merced, M. J. 2008. Effort under way to sell out Madoff unit. *NYTimes.com*, December 25, p. B1.

Dodd, P. 1980. Merger proposals, management discretion, and stockholder wealth. *Journal of Financial Economics*, 8:2, 105–137.

Dolley, J.C. 1933. Characteristics and procedure of common stock split-ups. *Harvard Business Review*, 11, 316–326.

Einstein, A. 1905. Über die von der molekularkinetischen Theorie der Wärme geforderte Bewegung von in ruhenden Flüssigkeiten suspendierten Teilchen. *Annalen der Physik*, 322:8, 549–560.

Elton, E. J., Gruber, M. J., Brown, S. J., Goetzmann, W. N. 2003. *Modern Portfolio Theory and Investment Analysis*. 6th ed. New York: John Wiley & Sons.

Fama, E. F. 1965. The behavior of stock-market prices. *The Journal of Business*, 38:1, 34–105.

———. 1970. Efficient capital markets: a review of theory and empirical work. *The Journal of Finance*, 25:2, 383–417.

———. 1991. Efficient capital markets: II. *The Journal of Finance*, 46:5, 1575–1617.

Fama, E. F., Fisher, L., Jensen, M., Roll, R. 1969. The adjustment of stock prices to new information. *International Economic Review*, 10:1, 1–21.

Fama, E. F., French, K. R. 1993. Common risk factors in the returns on stocks and bonds. *Journal of Financial Economics*, 33, 3–56.

———. 1995. Size and book-to-market factors in earnings and returns. *The Journal of Finance*, 50:1, 131–155.

———. 2004. The capital asset pricing model: theory and evidence. *Journal of Economic Perspectives*, 18:3, 25–46.

———. 2010. Luck versus skill in the cross-section of mutual fund returns. *The Journal of Finance*, 65:5, 1915–1947.

Foerster, S. R., Karolyi, G. A. 2000. The long-run performance of global equity offerings. *Journal of Financial and Quantitative Analysis*, 35:4, 499–528.

French, C. W. 2003. The Treynor capital asset pricing model. *Journal of Investment Management*, 1, 60–72.

Friedman, M. 1953. The case for flexible exchange rates. In Friedman, M. (ed.), *Essays in Positive Economics*. Chicago: University of Chicago Press, 157–203.

Gibson, G. R. 1889. *The Stock Exchanges of London, Paris, and New York: A Comparison*. New York: G. P. Putnam's Sons.

Grossman, S. J., Stiglitz, J. E. 1980. On the impossibility of informationally efficient markets. *American Economic Review*, 70:3, 393–408.

Handjinicolaou, G., Kalay, A. 1984. Wealth redistributions or changes in firm value: an analysis of returns to bondholders and stockholders around dividend announcements. *Journal of Financial Economics*, 13:1, 35–63.

Haugen, R. A. 1997. *Modern Investment Theory*. Upper Saddle River, NJ: Prentice Hall.

Henriques, D. B. 2008. Madoff scheme kept rippling outward, across borders. *NYTimes.com*, December 20, p. A1.

Hirshleifer, D. 2001. Investor psychology and asset pricing. *The Journal of Finance*, 56:4, 1533–1597.

Hite, G. L., Owers, J. E. 1983. Security price reactions around corporate spin-off announcements. *Journal of Financial Economics*, 12:4, 409–436.

Jegadeesh, N., Titman, S. 1993. Returns to buying winners and selling losers: implications for stock market efficiency. *The Journal of Finance*, 48:1, 65–91.

Jegadeesh, N., Titman, S. 2001. Profitability of momentum strategies: an evaluation of alternative explanations. *The Journal of Finance*, 56:2, 699–720.

Jensen, M. 1978. Some anomalous evidence regarding market efficiency. *Journal of Financial Economics*, 6:2/3, 95–101.

Kliger, D., Gurevich, G., Haim, A. 2012. When chronobiology met economics – seasonal affective disorder and the demand for initial public offerings. *Journal of Neuroscience, Psychology, and Economics*, 5:3, 131–151.

Kliger, D., Sarig, O. 2000. The information value of bond ratings. *The Journal of Finance*, 55:6, 2879–2902.

Kothari, S. P., Warner, J. B. 1997. Measuring long-horizon security price performance. *Journal of Financial Economics*, 43:3, 301–339.

———. 2007. Econometrics of event studies. In Espen Eckbo, B. (ed.), *Handbook of Corporate Finance: Empirical Corporate Finance*, Vol. 1. North Holland: Elsevier.

Keown, A. J., Pinkerton, J. M. 1981. Merger announcements and insider trading activity: an empirical investigation. *The Journal of Finance*, 36:4, 855–869.

Lakonishok, J., Vermaelen, T. 1990. Anomalous price behavior around repurchase tender offers. *The Journal of Finance*, 45:2, 455–477.

Langetieg, T. C. 1978. An application of a three-factor performance index to measure stockholder gains from merger. *Journal of Financial Economics*, 6:4, 365–383.

Lefévre, E. 1923. *Reminiscences of a Stock Operator*. New York: G. H. Doran. Latest edition: *Reminiscences of a Stock Operator: With New Commentary and Insights on the Life and Times of Jesse Livermore*. Hoboken, NJ: John Wiley & Sons, 2010.

LeRoy, S. F. 2000. Efficient market hypothesis. *Encyclopedia of Quantitative Finance*. Chichester, England: John Wiley & Sons.

Lintner, J. 1965. The valuation of risk assets and the selection of risky investments in stock portfolios and capital budgets. *Review of Economics and Statistics*, 47, 13–37.

Livermore, J. L. 1940. *How to Trade in Stocks: The Livermore Formula for Combining Time Element and Price*. New York: Duell, Sloan & Pierce.

Loughran, T., Ritter, J. 1995. The new issues puzzle. *The Journal of Finance*, 50:1, 23–52.

MacKinlay, A. C. 1997. Event studies in economics and finance. *Journal of Economic Literature*, XXXV, 13–39.

Malkiel, B. G. 1973. *A Random Walk Down Wall Street: The Time-tested Strategy for Successful Investing*. New York: W.W. Norton (Latest revised and updated edition, 2012).

Malkiel, B. G. 2003. The efficient market hypothesis and its critics. *The Journal of Economic Perspectives*, 17:1, 59–82.

———. 2005. Reflections on the efficient market hypothesis: 30 years later. *The Financial Review*, 40, 1–9.

Mandelbrot, B. 1966. Forecasts of future prices, unbiased markets, and "martingale" models. *Journal of Business*, 39:1/2, 242–255.

Mandelker, G. 1974. Risk and return: the case of merging firms. *Journal of Financial Economics*, 1, 303–335.
Markopolos, H., Casey, F., Chelo, N., Kachroo, G., Ocrant, M. 2010. *No One Would Listen: A True Financial Thriller*. Hoboken, NJ: John Wiley & Sons.
Mason, T. 2005. Malkiel ends Vanguard run. *The Inquirer Daily News*, August 13. http://articles.philly.com/2005–08–13/business/25425084_1_index-funds-vanguard-group-john-c-bogle.
Mitchell, M. L., Netter, J. M. 1994. The role of financial economics in securities fraud cases: applications at the Securities and Exchange Commission. *The Business Lawyer*, 49:2, 545–590.
Mossin, J. 1966. Equilibrium in a capital asset market. *Econometrica*, 34, 768–783.
Nobel Media AB. 2013. The Prize in Economic Sciences 2013–popular information. *Nobelprize.org*, May 26. http://www.nobelprize.org/nobel_prizes/economic-sciences/laureates/2013/popular.html.
Patell, J. M. 1976. Corporate forecasts of earnings per share and stock price behavior: empirical test. *Journal of Accounting Research*, 14:2, 246–276.
Peterson, P. P. 1989. Event studies: a review of issues and methodology. *Quarterly Journal of Business and Economics*, 28:3, 36–66.
Rendleman, R. J., Jones, C. P., Latané, H. A. 1982. Empirical anomalies based on unexpected earnings and the importance of risk adjustments. *Journal of Financial Economics*, 10, 269–287.
Roberts, H. V. 1967. Statistical versus clinical prediction of the stock market. Paper presented at the Seminar on the Analysis of Security Prices, University of Chicago.
Roll, R. 1977. A critique of the asset pricing theory's tests Part I: On past and potential testability of the theory. *Journal of Financial Economics*, 4:2, 129–176.
Royal Swedish Academy of Sciences. 2013. Scientific background on the Sveriges Riksbank Prize in Economic Sciences in memory of Alfred Nobel 2013.
Salinger, M. 1992. Standard errors in event studies. *The Journal of Financial and Quantitative Analysis*, 27:1, 39–53.
Samuelson, P. A. 1965. Proof that properly anticipated prices fluctuate randomly. *Industrial Management Review*, 6:2, 41–49.
Scholes, M., Williams, J. 1977. Estimating betas from nonsynchronous data. *Journal of Financial Economics*, 5:3, 309–327.
Sewell, M. 2011. History of the efficient market hypothesis. Research note 11/04. UCL Department of Computer Science.
Sharpe, W. F. 1963. A simplified model for portfolio analysis. *Management Science*, 9:2, 277–293.
———. 1964. Capital asset prices: a theory of market equilibrium under conditions of risk. *The Journal of Finance*, 19, 425–442.
Sharpe, W. F., Alexander, G. J., Bailey, J. V. 1995. *Investments*, 5th edn. Englewood Cliffs, NJ: Prentice-Hall.
Shiller, R. J. 1992. *Market Volatility*. Cambridge, MA.: MIT Press.

Smitten, R. 2001. *Jesse Livermore: World's Greatest Stock Trader*. New York: John Wiley & Sons.

Time Magazine. 1940. Business: Boy Plunger. December 9.

Stapleton, R. C., Subrahmanyam, M. G. 1983. The market model and capital asset pricing theory: a note. *The Journal of Finance*, 38:5, 1637–1642.

Timmermann, A., Granger, C. W. J. 2004. Efficient market hypothesis and forecasting. *International Journal of Forecasting*, 20, 15–27.

Treynor, J. L. 1961. *Market Value, Time, and Risk*. Unpublished manuscript.

———. 1962. *Toward a Theory of Market Value of Risky Assets*. Unpublished manuscript. A final version published in in *Asset Pricing and Portfolio Performance: Models, Strategy and Performance Metrics*, edited by Robert A. Korajczyk. London: Risk Books, 1999, 15–22.

Vanguard's official website, www.vanguard.com.

Weinstein, M. I. 1977. The effect of a rating change announcement on bond price. *Journal of Financial Economics*, 5:3, 329–350.

Index

www.ingramcontent.com/pod-product-compliance
Ingram Content Group UK Ltd.
Pitfield, Milton Keynes, MK11 3LW, UK
UKHW020155290926
15471UKWH00005B/877
* 9 7 8 1 3 4 9 4 9 3 1 8 0 *